KIDS IN
CONTEXT

KIDS IN CONTEXT

The Sociological Study of Children and Childhoods

Sarane Spence Boocock and Kimberly Ann Scott

ROWMAN & LITTLEFILED PUBLISHERS, INC.
Lanham • Boulder • New York • Toronto • Oxford

ROWMAN & LITTLEFIELD PUBLISHERS, INC.

Published in the United States of America
by Rowman & Littlefield Publishers, Inc.
A wholly owned subsidary of The Rowman & Littlefield Publishing Group, Inc.
4501 Forbes Boulevard, Suite 200, Lanham, Maryland 20706
www.rowmanlittlefield.com

PO Box 317
Oxford
OX2 9RU, UK

British Library Cataloguing in Publication Information Available

Library of Congress Cataloging-in-Publication Data
Boocock, Sarane Spence.
    Kids in context : the sociological study of children and childhoods / Sarane Spence Boocock and Kimberly Ann Scott.
        p. cm.
    Includes bibliographical references and index.
    ISBN 0-7425-2024-2 (cloth : alk. paper)—ISBN 0-7425-2025-0 (pbk. : alk. paper)
    1. Children—Social conditions. I. Scott, Kimberly Ann, 1969– II. Title.
    HQ767.9.B67 2005
    305.23—dc22   2005011548

Printed in the United States of America

♾™ The paper used in this publication meets the minimum requirements of American National Standard for Information Sciences—Permanence of Paper for Printed Library Materials, ANSI/NISO Z39.48-1992.

To Wally and Steve,
beloved partners

and

To all the kids who marched for human rights and social justice in
Afghanistan, in Soweto, South Africa, and in Birmingham, Alabama,
U.S., whose courage, tenacity, and adherence to the principles of non-
violence showed us the way toward a world fit for everyone

Childhood has changed since many of us were children.

—Anne Quinlen

Children are the best sources for understanding childhood.

—William Corsaro

We want a world fit for children, because a world fit for us is a world fit for everyone.

—Gabriela Azurdy Arrieta

CONTENTS

PREFACE

When Sarane Boocock, a European American woman, submitted a proposal to the Russell Sage Foundation in 1974 for a study of the ways in which social change was affecting the status of children and the patterns of their daily lives, the initial response of most of the foundation's researchers and trustees was far from enthusiastic. Was such an investigation really needed? asked one trustee, who claimed to see no unattended children in the streets during the daily drive from his midtown New York City apartment to his Wall Street office. What was the problem? Didn't we already know all we needed to know about children in order to promote their welfare? The strongest resistance was to Boocock's plan to seek information directly from children and to employ—and pay—children as data gatherers as well as informants. What could children tell us? she was asked. How would she know whether they were telling the truth? Wouldn't she get more "accurate" information by talking to their parents or teachers instead? Anyway, aren't kids supposed to be playing, not working, especially not for money?

The project was eventually approved, and the fieldwork demonstrated that children's social worlds were rich and varied, that children as young as four were capable of reporting on many aspects of their daily lives, and that children as young as ten could, if adequately trained, be as competent data gatherers as their adult counterparts. During the following decade, intriguing findings about the ways in which children experienced their own lives, based on data collected from and occasionally by children, were reported by other social scientists, but they were few and far between. As late as the mid-1980s, a survey of textbooks, scholarly journals, and theoretical works documented the "negligible place children occupy in sociological writings" (Ambert 1986, 17). Financial support for such research was virtually nonexistent, and one researcher (Mayall 2001, 8) maintains that consulting *children* about the design of a research study *about children* is still likely to reduce its chances of getting funding.

By the early 1990s, a new wave of scholarly activity based on new perspectives on children and childhood and new ways of studying them had begun to move the study of children from the margins of sociological research. A five-year project, Childhood as a Social Phenomenon, begun in 1987 under the auspices of the European Centre for Social Welfare Policy and Research, based in Vienna, organized international meetings and seminars, gathered statistical data on the status of children in the sixteen participating countries,[1] assembled a bibliography of sociologically relevant literature on childhood, and published a number of influential reports and books.[2] Another major turning point was the publication in 1990 of *Constructing and Reconstructing Childhood*, a collection of studies, most by European sociologists. The introduction to the volume by its editors, Alan Prout and Allison James, contained a paradigm for the study of children and childhood that has shaped much of the subsequent research and stimulated theoretical debates (a second edition was published in 1997). Among North Americans, Anne-Marie Ambert, William Corsaro, and Barrie Thorne identified crucial areas of children's lives and experiences that had been ignored and developed data-gathering techniques that were more "child friendly" and that encouraged greater reflexivity on the part of the researcher. Somewhat to the surprise of its publisher, Thorne's *Gender Play* was for several years one of its best-selling books. In 1992, the American Sociological Association officially acknowledged the new subdiscipline by approving the formation of a section on the sociology of children.

Given the rapid growth of the field and the ever-greater diversity of sociologists studying children and childhood, an unevenness of development is to be expected. If Boocock's research illustrated the difficulties of gaining support (intellectual as well as financial) for research incorporating new ways of perceiving children and childhood, the difficulties encountered by Kimberly Scott, an African American woman, in the late 1990s, when she began her study of African American girls' playground behavior, illustrate some of the problems associated with its current stage of development. First, in developing her theoretical framework, Scott found that the dominant social science theories did not explain much of what she was observing and hearing in her fieldwork. Socialization models were still based on males and Caucasian children, with the implicit assumption that such models would apply to all children; children who did not fit these models were ignored or defined as deviant. Empirical studies of children's informal activities, few in number, tended also to focus on the behavior of White, middle-class boys. Girls of color were still largely absent from the theoretical and empirical research literature.[3] Second, because of the recent proliferation of government and university regulations regarding protection of human subjects in general and children in particular, obtaining approval for Scott's fieldwork was a long and arduous process. Ironically, just as the importance of allowing children to speak for themselves is becoming more widely accepted, growing concern with their protection is making it more difficult to enable them to do so. Moreover, as one frustrated researcher complained, "Universities in North America have in recent years become stringent about obtaining permission from both parent and child, but this is usually a strategy of obtaining a legal safeguard rather than truly empowering the child in the decision" (Hart 1992, 18). Third, reactions to Scott's presentations of her work revealed a depressing resilience of stereotypical beliefs about race and gender among researchers and educators. Some expressed concern that White children might feel hurt by their "exclusion" from the study; others did not believe (or want to believe) some of her findings, in particular, evidence of the extent of stigmatizing of, and discriminatory behavior toward, minority girls by school staff; a few even questioned her credentials as a researcher—mightn't Scott have gotten "better" data had she worked with a White male partner?

Thus, we view ourselves as participants in an exciting new enterprise. The work of a small but highly creative and productive group of scholars has helped relocate the study of children and childhoods to a more central position in the discipline of sociology, although asking children their opinions and treating them as research partners as well as research subjects, ideas that were revolutionary in the 1970s, remain controversial today. We are deeply indebted to these pioneers in the field and will try in this book to do justice to their contributions. We'll also introduce important research by scholars outside the western European and North American countries that have dominated the field until recently. By widening the range of national and cultural contexts studied and by reminding us that most of the world's children live in the developing nations of the world's Southern Hemisphere, this research has further challenged conventional views of what constitutes a "normal" child and a "good" childhood. In the papers presented and in her informal conversations with the scholars and practitioners attending the 2004 World Congress of Comparative Education hosted in Havana, Cuba, Scott also sensed an emerging consensus in favor of greater cross-national collaboration and cooperation in addressing the needs of the world's children—a perspective that was reflected in the words of Cuba's minister of education, Luis Gomex Gutierrez, who urged the members of this international assembly to "learn from one another by sharing our diverse experiences and adapting them to our own situations."

Though the core discipline underpinning this book is sociology, our approach is multidisciplinary as well as comparative. We have drawn from other social sciences, anthropology, history, and psychology in particular; from recent biological research on human development in infancy and childhood; from the multidisciplinary fields of gender studies, Africana studies, Hispanic studies, and Asian studies; and from research in education and policy studies. In keeping with the new paradigm that views children as social actors who both shape and are shaped by their social circumstances, we have made special effort to include research that incorporates children's perspectives and allows them to speak for themselves. While we have tried to identify the central important theoretical and methodological concerns of the field and to provide a generous sample of findings from empirical research that meets rigorous criteria of substantive significance and good research design, we do not claim to have covered the field comprehensively. Heeding the advice of one of our reviewers, we have tried to provide a coherent synthesis of some of the best work without reducing the text to a series of lists or inventories. We regret having to omit so many good studies.

We wholeheartedly endorse Myra Bluebond-Langner's prediction, made during her remarks at the opening of the Rutgers Center for Children and Childhood Studies in 2000, that childhood studies will be to the twenty-first century what women's studies was to the twentieth century. We also believe that the issues raised by sociologists of children and childhoods and the knowledge being generated by this new field are of more than scholarly interest. Thus, we have tried to present material so that it is accessible and useful not only to our colleagues and students but also to all those who interact with children either professionally or personally. Understanding the complex and rapidly changing world in which children are growing up will, we hope, contribute not only to the social sciences but also to the development of policies and practices that will enhance the well-being of children—and of nonchildren as well. To paraphrase from the address delivered by thirteen-year-old Gabriela Azurdy Arrieta, a delegate from Bolivia to the May 2002 United Nations Special Session on Children and the first child invited to speak at a session of the UN General Assembly, everyone should be concerned with creating a world fit for children because a world fit for children is a world fit for everyone.

NOTES

1. Canada, Czechoslovakia, Denmark, England and Wales, Finland, Germany, Greece, Ireland, Israel, Italy, Norway, Scotland, Sweden, Switzerland, the United States, and Yugoslavia.

2. The volume edited by Qvortrup et al., *Childhood Matters: Social Theory, Practice and Politics* (1994), might be viewed as the culminating work of this project.

3. Scott's experience mirrored that of Finnish sociologist Leena Alanen (1994), who also found that the social sciences by and large continue to accept the White, middle-class male experience as the universal or "essential" childhood (28–29).

I

INTRODUCTION TO THE SOCIOLOGY OF CHILDREN AND CHILDHOODS: CONCEPTS, THEORIES, AND METHODS

INTRODUCTION

When we think about children, many of us envision kids going to school, playing games or playing with toys, hanging out with other kids, watching TV, going to birthday parties, dressing up for Halloween, or going shopping with their parents or friends. We imagine childhood as a happy interlude of free time, fun, and freedom from adult responsibilities. For others, childhood is viewed as a period of preparation for adult life when, lacking knowledge, skills, and experience, kids need the protection and guidance of responsible and caring adults. Still others of us dismiss these visions of children and childhood as myths created by adults to serve their own purposes. To be sure, some kids enjoy safe, comfortable, and enjoyable lives, but many others suffer from poverty, overwork, and violent and chaotic surroundings. Finally, an English scholar specializing in children's rights reminds us that whether they live in comfort and safety or in poverty and danger, for most children "the dominating feature of childhood is that of powerlessness and lack of control over what happens to them" (Lansdown 1994, 34).

Is there evidence that any of these views is an accurate portrayal of contemporary children and childhood? The box on pages 4 and 5 contains a sampling of data, or empirical evidence, about children's experiences during the late twentieth and early twenty-first centuries. It shows that some kids exercised considerable clout as consumers, while others died or were disabled by lack of food or medical care. Many were involved in wars, some as victims and others as soldiers, a few as both. Some took part in major political movements; others followed world events on television or not at all. Some were inventors, and others engaged in criminal activities. In sum, the "facts" about children and childhood seem as varied and contradictory as people's opinions. How can we know what children and the experience of childhood are really like? Do we know what a good childhood is like and how it might be attained for all, or at least more, children?

A FEW FACTS ABOUT KIDS*

- At the end of the twentieth century, American children's annual income, from allowances, gifts, and their own earnings, totaled more than $27 billion, of which they spent about $7 billion for snacks and another $7 billion for toys, games, and sports equipment. Purchases by kids between the ages of four and twelve tripled during the 1990s.
- In the United States and most western European countries, the majority of teenagers have their own bedrooms, where they spend at least half of their at-home waking hours. Of those who have their own rooms, more than half have their own TV, and more than a third have their own phone or phone extension, stereo system, and/or video game system.
- Almost 20 percent of all American children under age five live in poverty.
- Worldwide, nearly 40,000 children die each day of hunger and hunger-related diseases.
- In the last decade of the twentieth century, about 2 million children were killed, 6 million were seriously injured or permanently disabled, and 12 million were made homeless by wars fought in their countries. According to United Nations estimates, nearly half of all people killed in wars since 1990 were children. Child soldiers are engaged in military combat in more than forty countries.
- Between 1990 and 2005, the United States sentenced more children to death or to life imprisonment than any other nation, and it may be the only nation to have executed juveniles since 2001. In March 2005, the United States joined the rest of the world when the Supreme Court ruled that the death penalty for persons under age eighteen was inconsistent with evolving world standards as well as with the U.S. Constitution.

- In 1999, more American children and teens died in gun-related violence than from HIV/AIDS, cancer, pneumonia, asthma, and influenza combined. A study of high schools in four states found that nearly a third of all male students owned at least one gun, 15 percent owned three or more guns, and 12 percent reported carrying a gun all or most of the time.
- Every year, approximately 1 million persons younger than eighteen enter the sex business, many of them involuntarily. In the United States, the average age of entry into prostitution is fourteen.
- During the Russian, Northern Alliance, and Taliban occupations of Afghanistan (1978–2002), thousands of schoolgirls participated in public demonstrations and underground resistance activities. The number of girls killed, tortured, or imprisoned for their political activities is unknown.
- The Soweto Uprising of 1976, which signaled the beginning of the end of the apartheid system in South Africa, began with a school boycott initiated by Black elementary and middle school students. In one peaceful demonstration in June 1976, more than 500 students were killed by South African police.
- African American children as young as six marched in the 1963 civil rights demonstrations that brought about the end of racial segregation in Birmingham, Alabama. Nearly a thousand schoolchildren were jailed after the first day's march. In some marches, kids outnumbered adults.
- In a campaign to end illiteracy in Cuba, begun in 1961, almost all of the approximately 100,000 teachers were schoolchildren; the youngest teachers were eight-year-olds. An evaluation of large-scale literacy programs in twelve developing nations found the Cuban program the most effective at raising the national literacy rate.
- An organization founded by a Canadian boy when he was twelve years old is now an international movement devoted to exposing abuses and exploitation of children, improving the conditions of child workers, and extending children's legal rights.
- In Hawaii and Nicaragua, new languages created entirely by children, independent of any languages spoken by their parents or other adults and taught by older to younger children, have now been passed on to several generations of children.

* Documentation for each of these facts will be provided when it is discussed in the main text of the book.

WHY A SOCIOLOGY OF CHILDREN AND CHILDHOODS?

This book is about a relatively new but rapidly developing field of sociology. Unified by a view of children as active and constructive members of society and childhood as an integral part of the social fabric, the scholars who are creating the sociology of children and childhoods call on their colleagues to focus on the "empirical circumstances of children's real, ordinary, everyday lives" and to invite children themselves to tell us how they are experiencing their lives. The outcome of these endeavors will, they believe, be as important to twenty-first-century scholarship as women's studies and the study of racial and ethnic minorities were to twentieth-century scholarship (Bluebond-Langner 2000; Corsaro 1997; Hutchby and Moran-Ellis 1998; James, Jenks, and Prout 1998; Qvortrup 1990).

Is a new field called "sociology of children and childhoods" really needed? What can it tell us that we wouldn't learn from a course or text on the family, education, age and the life course, gender, or race and ethnicity? What does a sociological approach contribute to our knowledge that has not already been addressed by other scholarly disciplines, such as psychology, biology, or history, or by interdisciplinary programs in women's studies, Africana studies, Latino studies, or Asian studies? For that matter, what can it tell us that sensible people don't already know?

We maintain that the contents of this book cannot be subsumed under some other topic or discipline. The sociology of children and childhoods is a field in its own right because 1) it examines a wider range of children's experiences than other fields of sociology and 2) it challenges the conventional role of children in society and in social science research. It is also distinguished by the questions it asks and how it goes about answering these questions.

A FEW WORDS ABOUT TERMINOLOGY

We have titled this book *Kids in Context* because sociologists who have incorporated children's perspectives into their research have learned that their subjects refer to themselves more often as "kids" than as "children." We'll use the two words interchangeably throughout this book. Similarly, the words "friends" and "peers" will be used interchangeably.[1]

As indicated in the book's subtitle, we call what we are studying the sociology of children *and* childhoods—not just sociology of children or sociology of childhood—to distinguish between 1) those human beings who are in the category of nonadults and 2) the period in the life course in which children live their lives and through which all pass on their way to becoming adults.[2] Although the following chapters will include data about individual cases and statements made by individual children, we will usually talk about "children" or "kids" in the plural rather than "child" or "kid" in the singular because our focus is on children as *social beings*. In contrast to other ways of studying children, our focus is on their social positions in their communities and societies, their membership in social groups, their interactive relationships with other children and with adults, and their contributions to their society and its culture. For the same reason, we'll usually talk about "childhoods" in the plural rather than "childhood" in the singular, underscoring the various forms that childhood has taken in various times and places.

THE THREE C's OF SOCIOLOGICAL ANALYSIS: CONTEXT, COMPARISON, AND CHANGE

The way in which sociologists attempt to identify patterns in children's social lives is by systematic analysis of the following:

- *Context*, or the social environments in which children live
- *Comparisons*, between children and childhoods in various groups across diverse societies
- *Change*, both the transitions in children's lives and historical changes over time

That is, in order to understand children and childhood as social phenomena, sociologists make *comparisons* between children or groups of children in various *contexts* and over *time*. We do not claim that these are the only variables or factors that explain children's lives and development but rather that they are distinctive to the sociological approach.

Context

Figure 1.1 is a rough map of the social context of childhood, represented as a series of social environments, some overlapping, some nested
within others. In the center is the neighborhood or community (area 4 in
figure 1.1) containing children's families, peer groups, and schools (areas

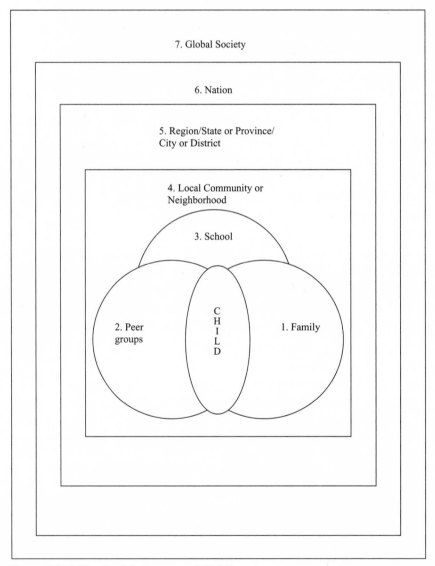

Figure 1.1.   The Social Context of Childhood

1, 2, and 3, respectively). These are the places where children have close interpersonal relationships, involving face-to-face interaction on a regular basis, and where they learn the routines of everyday life.

The overlap of children's home, school, and peer environments in figure 1.1 indicates their close connections in most communities. For example, in a study comparing suburban and inner-city neighborhoods (Bould 2003, to be discussed further in chapter 5), it was found that middle-class White families could generally choose to live in suburban neighborhoods that provided good schools, a safe environment, neighbors who could be counted on to keep an eye on each others' kids, and ready access to prompt medical and police assistance in emergencies, while low-income families, especially if they were Black, were limited to inner-city neighborhoods that were more dangerous, had poorer schools, and had limited or no access to public services of all kinds. In other words, families, neighbors, schools, and community services with ample resources were clustered in affluent suburban communities, and those with scant resources were clustered in poor inner-city communities; the result was a huge gap between inner-city and suburban communities in the *social capital* available to kids.

The areas outside the neighborhood or community and extending to the edges of figure 1.1 refer to those aspects of social context beyond a child's immediate environment. They include the dominant political, social, economic, legal, educational, and cultural systems at the state, regional, national, and international levels. Because these *external* environments often seem far removed from children's immediate surroundings and everyday lives, their effects are less evident than, say, the effects of family life, but as we'll see in chapter 10, where in the world a child is born is highly predictive of the kind of childhood she will experience, from her chances of surviving infancy to her likelihood of attending high school.[3]

Comparison

As we'll see in the substantive chapters of this book, the concepts of children and childhood may differ widely from one society or social group to another and *within* societies and social groups as well. There is no single or universal experience of childhood; rather, there are various childhoods. A major objective of the sociology of children and childhood is to "develop a comparative understanding of children and childhood across diverse societies" (James et al. 1998, 125).

Thanks to the increasing internationalization of the field, sociologists have access to data from a broader range of the world's societies. Through historical, cross-cultural, and within-cultural comparisons, they can begin to identify major commonalities and differences in children's social status and experience in different societies and in different groups within societies. By comparing multiple studies on a given topic, it is possible to distinguish between findings that can be generalized across societies or cultures—that is, that are true of all or most children—from those that characterize a particular society or culture. A comparative perspective also enables researchers to avoid or correct *ethnocentric bias*, that is, the assumption, conscious or unconscious, that the way things are done in one's own society or community is universal or "normal" and that behavior that deviates from the norm is inferior or at least problematic. As the American anthropologist Meredith Small (2001) has put it,

> The cross-cultural view shows that we in the West are rather insulated from what the majority of the world's population is doing during their early years of childhood. Our view of childhood is critically warped by a very recent economic affluence that allows most of our kids the luxury of play, school, and little responsibility. Other cultures teach us that there are other ways to socialize, other ways to play, and other ways for kids to become moral citizens. (5–6)

Change

Just as children and childhoods may or may not differ in various places, so they may or may not differ at various points in time. A noted scholar of aging, John Riley, once observed that people grow up and grow old not in research laboratories but rather in constantly changing societies. Riley's observation alludes to the twofold quality of change in human lives. That is, children move simultaneously through the life course and through historical time. On the one hand, every child "is first and foremost a transitory being that is constantly changing, growing, developing" (Gittins 1998, 21). On the other hand,

> features of the person's historical setting often shape personality, and social and intellectual functioning, to an extent often much greater than

maturational or age-associated changes. General historical events, such as wars, economic privations, or political upheavals—as well as personal events, such as marriage, divorce, illness, death, or career change—are often seen to provide potent shapers of the quantity of life changes and of the quality of the life course. These studies also indicate that there are multiple paths through life. (Lerner and Spanier 1978, 2–3)

One of the themes connecting the substantive chapters of this book is that changing *perceptions* of children and childhood over time and space affect children's social status and the way they are treated.

OVERVIEW OF CHAPTERS

Having introduced the subject of this book and basic concepts that we'll use in our analysis, we'll devote the two remaining chapters in part I to the design of sociological research on children and childhoods. (Readers who wish to begin with substantive findings can postpone the next two chapters and go directly to part II.) In chapter 2, we'll present an overview of sociological perspectives, classical and contemporary, that seem most applicable to the study of children and childhoods, followed by an introduction to theoretical perspectives from other disciplines and fields that offer additional insights. In chapter 3, we'll review alternative ways of gathering and analyzing empirical evidence about children and childhoods. In keeping with our conception of children as active and constructive members of society, we'll give special attention to research designs that enable kids to speak for themselves.

Parts II to V, each containing a pair of chapters, will be devoted to substantive findings about children's experiences in one or more of the contextual environments charted in figure 1.1. Children's family lives will be the subject of part II. In chapter 4, we'll examine the demographic trends that have produced profound changes in family structure and functioning and consider the impact of these changes on children's experience of childhood. In chapter 5, we'll trace the ways in which children and their parents shape each others' attitudes and behavior in the process known as socialization. We'll also consider the costs and benefits of family life to kids and their mothers and fathers and how resources like money, space, and time are distributed among family members.

In part III, we'll explore children's experiences in social groups outside their homes. Chapter 6 contains research findings on how, from earliest childhood, kids learn from each other, become best friends or worst enemies, and create distinctive peer cultures. We'll also revisit the continuing debate over the relative strength of peer influences versus parental influences. In chapter 7, we'll enter the two worlds of school experienced by most kids: one the formal educational system designed and controlled by adults with little input from children, the second the friendship groups, clubs, and cliques created and controlled by their peers where kids learn, among other things, how to survive the "daily grind" of classroom life. We'll look for clues to understanding variations in peer group behavior and outcomes—why, for example, some groups appear to nurture creativity, loyalty, and generosity among their members while others precipitate abusive and disorderly, even violent, behavior.

Though childhood occurs in all societies, children are differentiated on a number of social characteristics that shape their childhood experiences and opportunities (thus the importance of the comparative approach). The various childhoods resulting from differences in social background are the subject of part IV. In chapter 8, we'll see how inequalities of race, ethnicity, and social status that have little or no basis in biological differences nevertheless reproduce social stereotypes and hierarchies that determine how children are perceived and treated by other kids and by adults. Special attention will be paid to those children, often described as "marginalized" or "invisible," who have generally been excluded from mainstream research or studied mainly as social problems. In chapter 9, we'll look for comparable patterns with regard to gender, drawing from a large and growing body of research showing how socially constructed assumptions about female–male differences prevent us from seeing equally important similarities and how exaggeration of gender differences leads to differential treatment of girls and boys that not only divides them but often sets them in opposition to each other as well. In both chapters, we'll present research evidence that explodes the myth that young children are innocent of sexism, racism, ethnocentrism, and classism. We'll end part IV with an examination of the relationships between background variables and the combined interactive effects of race, ethnicity, gender, and socioeconomic status.

In part V, the last pair of substantive chapters, we'll turn to contextual effects at the societal and global levels. In chapter 10, we'll examine how enormous differences in children's status and well-being are explained by where in the world they live and how their childhoods may be transformed by political events and social and economic trends that originate far from their homes and local communities. We'll be especially concerned with the impact of the massive changes in economic, political, and social institutions accompanied by mass movements of people, money, and goods across national boundaries, commonly subsumed under the term *globalization*, that have coincided with increased numbers of poor, ill, and mistreated children even in affluent societies. In chapter 11, we'll examine the technologies, mass media, consumer goods, and popular culture that are connecting kids to a global culture, asking, among other things, whether the commonalities induced by familiarity with the same music, video games, fast foods, and clothing styles are as significant as the vast socioeconomic inequalities that divide kids and how the so-called *international children's culture* is affecting relations between kids and adults.

In the final chapter, we'll apply what we have learned from social science research to the task of bettering children's lives. How can research help us design policies and practices capable of withstanding the pressures of global change? At what contextual level—family, community, regional, national, or international—should they be implemented? What role, if any, should kids play in social reform? Using the preceding chapters as a framework, we'll assess a few of the noteworthy strategies that have been proposed (and to varying degrees tested) for strengthening families, improving schools, extending children rights, and enhancing kids' participation in society. We'll conclude by describing a few thought-provoking efforts to offer children better childhoods by creating alternative societies or communities.

NOTES

1. When she began her pioneering work on gender and play patterns, Barrie Thorne resisted using "kids" because she thought it sounded "diminishing." She soon learned that many of her subjects felt otherwise, insisting "that 'children'

was more of a put-down than 'kids.' As one sixth-grader said, 'Kids is better than children; children sounds so young.' Indeed, 'kids' moves across the finer age divisions—'infant,' 'toddler,' 'child,' 'teen'—carved into the contemporary life course; some college undergraduates still call themselves 'kids.' The term also evokes generational solidarity, a kind of bonding in opposition to adults." Thorne also "avoided the term 'peer group,' which also sets kids apart and diminishes the full luster of their experiences. As adults, we claim 'friends' and 'colleagues'; why do we so often compress kids' relations into the flattening notion of 'peers'?'" (Thorne 1993, 9).

2. Corsaro (1997) and Qvortrup (1994) make the further distinction between childhood as a period in the life course and childhood as a category or component of social structure, like social class. As Corsaro puts it, while childhood is "a temporary period for children, it is a permanent structural category in society" (30).

3. The different levels of context mapped in figure 1.1 are often referred to in the sociological literature as distinctions between *micro*-environments or context and *macro*-environments or context. The former, corresponding to areas 1 to 4 in figure 1.1, have been defined by one sociologist of childhood (Waksler 1991) as "that part of the social world within an individual's immediate grasp," in contrast to the latter (areas 5 to 7), which refer to "that part of the social world that seems to lie outside of the individual and may be perceived as existing 'out there', [including] laws, governments, religion, and other aspects of the social world that appear massive and beyond one's grasp" (11). Some identify a third level, or *meso*-context, which refers to the interrelations of multiple micro-environments (e.g., between the family, school, and peer environments). These terms are defined differently by different authors, and the different contextual levels are interrelated in complicated ways. For example, the family can be viewed from a macro- or meso-perspective as well as from a micro-perspective. On the other hand, "the macro-world is itself composed of micro-worlds—laws are hammered out through social interactions among individuals, government officials meet face to face, and religious experiences take place on the individual level" (Waksler 1991, 11). To avoid these complexities, we decided not to introduce the terms *micro*-, *macro*-, and *meso*- into the main text. Excellent discussions of the application of these concepts to sociological research on children and childhoods can be found in Qvortrup (2000b) on macro-analysis and in Tesson and Youniss (1995) on micro-analysis.

For our conceptualization of social context, including figure 1.1, we are also indebted to Urie Bronfenbrenner, whose ecological theory of human development will be discussed in chapter 2. His definitions of the various contextual levels can be found in Bronfenbrenner (1977).

2

THINKING ABOUT CHILDREN
AND CHILDHOODS:
THEORETICAL PERSPECTIVES

Whatever their particular substantive interests, researchers in the developing field of sociology of children and childhoods are unified by the conviction that "children are theoretically central to understanding how social life is reproduced and how it changes over time" (Johnson 2001, 73).

In the first half of this chapter, we'll provide a brief overview of sociological perspectives that have been applied to the study of children and childhoods, with examples of empirical studies based on these perspectives. In the second half, we'll turn to some other disciplines or fields that, by viewing the same phenomena from nonsociological vantage points, reveal additional facets of children's social lives and their experience of childhood. We take the position of British sociologists Allison James, Chris Jenks, and Alan Prout (1998) that different ways of thinking about children and childhood may be complementary rather than competing, and we will not attempt to identify a "best" perspective.

SOCIOLOGICAL PERSPECTIVES

Functionalist Perspective

Functionalism was widely recognized as the dominant theoretical perspective in sociology during much of the twentieth century—indeed, one prominent sociologist (Davis, 1959) announced that all sociologists are functionalists. Sociologists using this perspective conceive of societies and social groups as systems of interrelated parts that are assumed to "work together with a sufficient degree of harmony or internal consistency, *i.e.*, without producing persistent conflicts which can neither be resolved nor regulated" (Radcliffe-Brown, quoted in Merton 1957, 26). Such sociologists attempt to identify the contributions, or functions, made by its component parts (including social institutions like the family and the educational system) to the operation of the total social system.

Subsequent interpretations of the functionalist perspective have acknowledged that the unity mentioned previously is seldom achieved in real-life human societies because what is beneficial, or functional, for some groups is often injurious, or *dysfunctional*, for other groups in the same society or in other societies. For example, Herbert Gans (1972, 1995) argued that the affluent in the United States benefit from the conditions of life that are decidedly injurious for the poor. The existence of poverty ensures that dirty and dangerous work (e.g., cleaning homes, offices, and streets; selling sex and illegal drugs; or providing the recruits for the lower levels of the armed services who do most of the actual fighting) is done at low cost to the affluent but at high cost to the poor. Poverty creates a vast array of jobs for the middle-class managers and professionals, including judges, lawyers, social workers, psychiatrists, and teachers who staff the criminal courts, drug treatment centers, homeless shelters, "special" schools, and job retraining programs whose "clients" are mainly poor people. Poverty also provides employment for upper-class philanthropists and the charitable organizations they found and direct. Finally, the poor provide a market for inferior goods that cannot be sold to the better-off groups in society (food past the sell-by date, used clothing, faulty appliances, and so on). In chapter 10, we'll see how the international adoption market functions to provide babies purchased at low cost (sometimes stolen) from some of the poorest families in some of the world's poorest counties to affluent families in the world's most prosperous countries and how similar markets provide poor children from poor countries for labor at menial (often dangerous and/or illegal) jobs for low or no wages in affluent countries. Heated debates have arisen over the question of whether foreign adoptions are functional or dysfunctional for the provider coun-tries and families and for the children concerned. In chapter 12, we'll discuss "intervention" programs to teach parenting skills to poor mothers that provide well-paid jobs for the middle-class profession-als who design and administer them without increasing the mothers' access to the resources that would enable them to escape from poverty.

One of the major mechanisms that function to maintain and repro-duce societies is *socialization*. This is the aspect of the functionalist per-spective that is most relevant to our concerns. Socialization has been variously defined as follows:

- "The development of the individual as a social being and partici-pant in society" (Clausen 1968, 3–4)
- "The process through which children, and in some cases, adults, learn to conform to social norms" (James et al. 1998, 23)
- "The method by which societies get their individual members to think and behave in a proper fashion" (Lemert 2002, 37)
- "The imposition of social patterns on behavior" (Aberle, quoted in Clausen 1968, 3–4)

Some definitions stress the individual learner, some stress the process, while others put greater emphasis on the social apparatus that shapes the process.

By the 1970s, functionalism had come under increasing attack for being conservative and overly deterministic, for assigning children a predominantly passive role in their own socialization and viewing childhood as only a period of preparation for future adulthood.[1] While relatively few sociologists now identify themselves as function-alists, most still react to it to some degree, even if only to reject it. As we'll see in chapter 5, recent research on socialization in the family gives considerable attention to *shifts* in parents' aspirations for their children and modes of child rearing and how they reflect economic and demographic *trends* as well as *changes* in basic cultural values. There is also an emerging consensus that socialization is a dynamic process in which children socialize adults as well as being socialized by them.

Conflict Perspective

Influenced by the theories of Karl Marx and Max Weber, this perspective is critical of functionalism on the grounds that it gives insufficient attention to the social forces that precipitate social change. Many of its adherents view conflict as endemic to any society because social institutions are basically inequitable. The families, schools, and other institutions that enable societies to sustain themselves over time and transmit their culture from one generation to another also perpetuate age, gender, and social class inequalities and enable elites (disproportionately White adult males) to maintain a disproportionate share of power and other advantages.

Though most adults prefer to think of parent–child relations as benign and adult control over kids as justified on the grounds that adults know what's best for them, *age stratification*, a basic characteristic of family structure, results in uneven distributions of resources and power that may cause antagonism and dissension between family members of different ages (Foner 1978). As a social group, children are arguably the most powerless group in almost any society, though we'll see in chapters 6 and 7 that like other relatively powerless groups, kids have discovered many ways to resist, undermine, or circumvent adult authority. We'll also see that conflicts within and between groups appear to be as common among children as among adults.

Exchange Perspective

Influenced by economic theory, animal psychology, and behavioral psychology, exchange theorists also fault functionalism for its "oversocialized" conception of human beings. They perceive individuals as rational and calculating beings who actively endeavor to maximize their "social capital" by engaging in social activities and relationships that seem to offer them the most rewards at the lowest costs and avoiding those that do not appear to be cost effective (Wells 1978, 127). This may explain why, as we'll see in chapter 5, as the costs of raising children continue to rise in the industrialized nations of North America, western Europe, and East Asia, more and more adults, especially those with good educational and occupational credentials, are postponing or forgoing marriage and kids.

Until recently, sociologists have not paid much attention to exchanges among kids or between kids and adults—probably because adult researchers did not view children as having the capacity for the kind of rational, calculating behavior posited by exchange theory. However, in a paper titled "Kids and Commerce," Viviana Zelizer synthesizes a host of recent studies documenting kids' active engagement in a broad range of economic activities as producers, consumers, and distributors. The exchanges of money, food, and other items observed in school lunchrooms, classrooms, and playgrounds indicate that children "fashion elaborate systems of distribution covering a wide variety of objects and representing both peer solidarities and their divisions" (Zelizer 2002, 387). In chapter 4, we'll discover that Norwegian children who were in charge of their homes while their parents were at work became adept at negotiating with their parents, agreeing to perform certain household chores in exchange for the freedom and autonomy they gained in return (e.g., having the house to themselves or being able to do things they knew their parents would disapprove of).

Age and Life Course Perspective

It may seem superfluous to point out, as does the English historian Harry Hendrick (2000), that age is the "distinguishing criterion for identifying childhood." But the sociological theories of age and the life course that have challenged long-held stereotypes of aging and the elderly and stimulated a flood of research on the later years of the life cycle have only recently been systematically applied to the earliest years of life. Among the important concepts borrowed from the life course perspective is that of *age cohort*, or *generation*. As Anne Foner (1978) has put it,

Each cohort is unique in that it is formed at a particular juncture of history; its members share the same slice of history, and can look forward to a similar future segment of time. Each cohort bears the stamp of the historical context through which it flows [so that] no two cohorts age in exactly the same way. The most familiar example is the life course of persons coming to adulthood in the Depression as this compares with the life course of persons coming of age in the affluent 1950s. They differ in their work histories, family cycles, and in political and social attitudes. (343)

In other words, at birth all children become members of an age cohort, each of which experiences childhood differently. This does not mean that all children of a given age are the same. In any era there are cultural and subcultural variations in what is expected of children and how they are treated, and individual children are variously affected by their social surroundings and by social change. The boundary between childhood and adulthood also varies, though some societies are more internally consistent than others.[2]

It might be argued that the social change most affecting the status and treatment of children in modern societies is the drastic shift in the age structure due to the extension of the human life span combined with declining birthrates. The industrialized nations of North America, western Europe, and East Asia are often referred to as *aging societies*, where for the first time in history, children are a numerical minority. United Nations figures show that at the middle of the twentieth century, the proportion of children in these nations was about double that of older persons; by the end of the twentieth century, the proportions of older persons and of children were about the same (each about 20 percent); it is predicted that by the mid-twenty-first century, the proportion of older persons will increase to above 30 percent, while the proportion of children will decline to about 15 percent. The German sociologist Jurgen Zinnecker notes that the changing demographic balance among age-groups has already precipitated conflicts over the division of labor and distribution of resources between young and old. The status of children is weakened, he posits, when "parents only make up a small fraction of the adult population. Those adults who do not have children are less interested in transfer services to children or families with children," especially when these children are viewed as "other people's (in particular, immigrant or minority) children" (Zinnecker 2001, 13–19).

Matilda White Riley, a pioneer in the sociology of the life course, points out that relations between the generations are also negatively affected by the rigid *age differentiation* characteristic of modern societies such that formal education is assigned primarily to the young, work to those in the middle years when family responsibilities are also heaviest, and retirement and leisure to older people. Age differentiation may occur even *among* children; for example, most schools now have an age-homogeneous grade structure that gives children few opportunities for interaction with older or younger schoolmates. Riley (1997) advocates loosening these age barriers so that contacts between younger and older people are facilitated and opportunities for education, work, and leisure are more evenly distributed among people of different ages.

Interactionist Perspective

This perspective has its roots in *symbolic interaction theory* as formulated by the American scholars George Herbert Mead, Charles H. Cooley, and W. I. Thomas during the first half of the twentieth century. Like the exchange and conflict perspectives, interactionism faults functionalism for its overemphasis on the influence of social institutions on individual behavior. In this case, the focus is on the process by which individuals create themselves and their social worlds through *social interaction* with cultural objects and ideas as well as with other people. Society then is the *framework* within which social action takes place, not the *determinant* of that action.

The centerpiece of Mead's analysis is the development of the *self*, an entity that is distinct from the physical body and that enables the individual to "be the object of his own actions" and "act toward himself as he might act toward others"—for example, getting angry with himself, arguing with himself, taking pride in himself, telling himself to "do this" or not to "do that," setting goals and making plans for himself, and so on (Blumer 1978, 92). Mead conceptualized play and games as major mechanisms for self-development, propelling a child toward "taking the attitudes of other individuals toward himself within a social environment or context of experience and behavior in which both he and they are involved" (Mead 1934, 138). By playing with an imaginary companion or playing at being a mother, a teacher, a policeman, or a puppy, a young child learns to assume different roles, and by joining other kids to play "family" or "good guys versus bad guys," she learns how to behave in multirole situations. Later, through organized games, older children not only enlarge their repertoire of roles but also learn how the different roles are related to each other and how to "take the attitudes of everyone else involved in that game." Participation in a baseball game, for example, requires each player to be "ready to take the role of everyone else" since he "must know what everyone else is going to do in order to carry out his own play." Moreover, each of his own acts "is determined by his assumption of the action of the others who are playing the game. What he does is controlled by his being everyone else on that team." Thus, each player incorporates in himself the *other*, defined as "an organization of the attitudes of those involved in the same process." With enough experience in games with complex rules and multiple players, the self assimilates "the attitude of the whole community," which Mead called the *generalized other* (151–54).

In chapter 5, we'll see that what is usually called *child rearing* is a reciprocal process involving a myriad of interactions between parents and kids:

> While parents influence children, the effectiveness of this influence depends in great part on how children, and particularly adolescents, perceive and react to their parents' efforts to help them, socialize them, and monitor them. Even a very young child can choose to ignore requests made by parents. *Parents actually need a child's cooperation in order to raise him or her.* (Ambert 1997, 240)

Thus, we'll talk about *parent* rearing as well as about *child* rearing. In parts III and IV (chapters 6–9), we'll examine a number of empirical studies that document the extent and complexity of children's face-to-face peer interactions. For example, her studies of the play, games, and verbal interactions of working-class African American and Latina preadolescents led Goodwin (1990) to postulate that far from being "a defective version of the adult world into which [they] will eventually be socialized," children's friendship and play groups are the primary settings where they socialize each other and "create and recreate for themselves their own socially organized world of meaning" (13). However, Goodwin views peer group interaction not as occurring in a social vacuum but as, at least to some extent, "shaped by the historic, economic, and social conditions within which it is embedded" (20).

Social Construction Perspective

In the introductory essay of a volume that is viewed by many as marking the beginning of this field of sociology, Alan Prout and Allison James proposed a new paradigm that has stimulated and shaped much subsequent research, including many of the studies discussed in this book. The Prout and James paradigm incorporates the following principles:

1. "Childhood, as distinct from biological immaturity, is neither a natural or universal feature of human groups but appears as a specific structural and cultural component of many societies. . . . Comparative and cross-cultural analysis reveals a variety of childhoods rather than a single and universal phenomenon."
2. "Children's social relationships and cultures are worthy of study in their own right, independent of the perspective and concerns of adults."
3. "Children are and must be seen as active in the construction and determination of their own social lives, the lives of those around them and of the societies in which they live. Children are not just the passive subjects of social structures and processes."
4. "[To] proclaim a new paradigm of childhood sociology is also to engage in and respond to the process of reconstructing childhood in society" (Prout and James 1990, 8–9).

The justification for a separate field of sociology of children and childhoods offered in chapter 1 as well as our designation of context, comparison, and change as basic terms for the analysis of children's social lives reflect the first and second principles. The third principle echoes certain aspects of the interactionist perspective—there is indeed considerable overlap between these two perspectives. It also implies that implementation of the new paradigm requires new ways of studying children, in particular, modes of gathering data that enable kids to speak for themselves about their own lives, about the people who are important to them, and about their social surroundings. (We shall take up these methodological issues in chapter 3.) The fourth principle proposes a redefinition of the researcher's role. In comparison to other sociological theories, this perspective demands from researchers a high level of *reflexivity*, that is, a willingness to examine their own biases as well as to challenge the "taken-for-granted" meanings attached to children and childhood.

PERSPECTIVES FROM OTHER DISCIPLINES AND INTERDISCIPLINARY FIELDS

Psychological Perspectives on Human Development

As mid- to late-twentieth-century sociological theory was dominated by the functionalist perspective, psychological theory of the same period was to a great degree shaped by developmental theories, Piaget's model of stages of individual development in particular. Recent criticism of these theories has claimed that "Piaget's experimental context and tasks were so out of the ordinary compared to children's normal, everyday experience that they found them difficult to relate to and understand" (Woodhead and Faulker 2000, 24). Harsher critics have complained that "developmentalism inevitably serves to diminish the status of the immature child when measured against adult standards and reasoning" and that universal, standardized development stages and targets tend to "pathologize" kids who do not achieve them and "show little awareness of the possibility that these concepts are socially and culturally defined" (Davis, Watson, and Cunningham-Burley 2000, 205). Subsequent empirical research has shown that in more familiar circumstances, many kids perform tasks well beyond their capacities by Piagetian standards. In a South African squatters' community in which most children scored dismally on standardized tests of cognitive development, the anthropologist Pamela Reynolds (1989) found that these same children engaged in rich fantasy play, constructed elaborate child-size towns from scraps of metal and wood scavenged from the debris scattered throughout their community, and performed an extensive repertoire of complicated choral music with little or no adult assistance.

In Piaget's defense, it is only fair to point out how much current sociological research on children takes for granted aspects of his approach that were highly innovative, even radical, at the time, in particular his "emphasis on encouraging children to talk freely, thus allowing their thinking to unfold and reveal itself to an attentive researcher [who] did not belittle their explanations" (Woodhead and Faulker 2000, 25). (For an excellent reassessment of Piaget's contributions to sociological theory, see Tesson and Youniss 1995.)

A major redirection of developmental theory can be found in the work of Urie Bronfenbrenner, who proposed a new theoretical, methodological, and substantive approach to the study of children that he named *ecology of human development* and defined as

> the scientific study of the progressive, mutual accommodation, through-
> out the life span, between a growing organism and the changing immedi-
> ate environments in which it lives, as this process is affected by relations
> obtaining within and between these immediate environments, as well as
> the larger social contexts, both formal and informal, in which the settings
> are embedded. (Bronfenbrenner 1977: 514)

Bronfenbrenner's conceptualization of the dynamic relationship between individual development and sociocultural context has stimulated
research in all the social sciences. A number of recent psychological
studies reject the assumption of a universal and decontextualized "child"
in favor of cross-cultural comparisons of beliefs about children, child-
rearing practices, and children's behavior (e.g., Goncu 1999), and sociological research based on the social construction perspective shares
many of the same basic premises. (Bronfenbrenner's influence on figure
1.1 and our discussion of context in chapter 1 have already been noted.)

Biosocial and Genetic Perspectives on Human Development

Any sociologist studying children and childhoods must at some point
confront the ongoing debate over genetic influences versus environmental influences (or "nature versus nurture"). It is generally agreed
that children's development is a combination of physical, psychic, social,
and cultural components that are themselves interrelated, but there is
less agreement on the relative importance of genes and environment on
each type of development. Even height, an indicator of children's physical development that can be easily and accurately measured, involves a
complex interaction of genes and environment. While each child carries
a "genetic blueprint that guides his or her growth pattern," nongenetic
environmental effects ranging from diet, health care, and socioeconomic status to exposure to war, infectious diseases, and family trauma
affect children's growth patterns and their eventual adult height. Height
of parents, part of a child's genetic inheritance, provides at best "a shaky
prediction," since the parents' physical development was also "molded

by a life course of outside influences" (Small 2001, 67–69). Though children's growth rates are fairly regular in societies where their basic nutrition, health, and safety needs are met, under less favorable conditions, a child's biological potential may never come to fruition. For example, a study of North Korean refugee children (Paterniti 2003) found that because of the huge gap between North Korea and South Korea in economic development and distribution of material resources (food in particular), by the age of seven there is a 4.7-inch difference in height between North Korean children and their South Korean counterparts, a difference that increases another three inches by late adolescence. An anthropologist who has worked with these refugee children fears that the stunted *physical* development resulting from their impoverished early environments will "become a *social* stigma affecting many generations to come" (Paterniti 2003, 51, emphasis added).

In a review of recent research on the brain development of babies and young children, the noted psychologist Jerome Bruner describes the connections between biological and social development as follows:

> Babies begin life with "start-up" knowledge inherited from our evolutionary past, knowledge that provides the means for making a first shot at representing what they encounter. Once they have done this, infants are in a position to repair their first "edition" in the light of new experience, which in turn, alters previous knowledge in such a way as to make new experience possible. In short, new experience leads to new knowledge which then permits new experience, the cycle is never ending. But most important, the cycle requires the involvement, even the collusion of others, whose minds and ways of thought we come to take for granted. (Bruner 2000, 28)

The importance of context, including the "involvement of others," was also underscored by Noam Chomsky, the noted scholar of language development, in a lecture delivered at the Massachusetts Institute of Technology in 1988. "Any organism," he said, "needs a rich and stimulating environment in order for its natural capacities to emerge." Under optimal conditions, a child's biological endowment is "awakened by experience," and "sharpened and enriched in the course of the child's interactions with the human and material world"

(Chomsky 1988:33–34). An illustration of the reciprocal effects of nature and nurture can be found in Ambert's discussion of "resilient" children—those kids who manage to survive and thrive even in the face of war, poverty, family violence or abuse, and other adversities. While resilient children appear to have inherited the *potential* to make the most of difficult circumstances, they can do so only if the environment offers them at least a chance of improving their situation. As Ambert (1997) points out, "*opportunities have to exist*, however minimal they may be, again indicating the importance of the environment in interaction with personality" (35–36). In chapter 10, we'll consider how the grossly uneven distribution of environmental opportunities among the world's children prevents millions of them from realizing their genetic potential; in chapter 12, we'll review some strategies for improving the odds.

A review of research on the interactive effects of biological and social processes on family relationships and the behavior of children and parents emphasizes the difficulties of specifying the source and extent of genetic contributions:

> Some genetic influence is passive, derived from the fact that parents and children share genes. Smart kids live in parent-designed, intellectually challenging environments. Some genetic influence is reactive, stemming from the way parents and others respond to genetically influenced behavior. Antisocial behavior may cause parents to be less affectionate. Finally, some genetic influence is active, that is, genetically influenced behaviors cause children to seek and create environments that in turn affect their behavior. The risk-taking child may seek like-minded individuals as friends . . .
>
> [In addition, there are] factors that moderate by amplifying and reducing genetic influences [which] include historical and cohort variables, as well as parenting practices. For example, authoritative parenting may reduce genetic influences, whereas laissez-faire practices may increase them. (Booth, Carver, and Granger 2000, 1020–21)

While they advocate a "biosocial" perspective on the family, these authors acknowledge that our knowledge about the ways genes influence behavior and interpersonal relationships is still very limited.

Historical Perspectives on Childhood

Sociologists attempting to identify critical shifts in perceptions of childhood and to trace their effects on the treatment of children are indebted to historical research on the family. Important elements of the social construction perspective on children and childhoods might be said to have originated in Philippe Aries's *Centuries of Childhood*, published in 1962. In this book, Aries advanced the dramatic hypothesis that "the very concept of childhood was a product of modern thought. Before the seventeenth century, though children existed, childhood did not." Premodern children "lived in the margins of adult life, with little or no distinctive cultural identity of their own. Their clothes were miniaturized versions of adult wear, they had no special culture of play, no children's literature, there was no Wordsworthian idealization of the innocence or carelessness of childhood." Though the reasons for this absence were complex (many children died young; most homes lacked the resources, including privacy, needed for an intimate family life; and children of all classes were sent away from home early), this all "changed decisively, Aries believed, in the seventeenth century, with the arrival of a new and sentimentalized conception of family, in which the cultivation of the affections and the shaping of childish character now had each their privileged place" (Duffy 2002, 61).

Subsequent historical research has challenged and eroded Aries's hypothesis, offering empirical evidence—from toys, games, books, and distinctive clothing to religious and secular laws requiring special treatment of children—that well before the turning point proposed by Aries, "adults regarded childhood as a distinct phase or phases of life, that parents treated children as children as well as like adults, that they did so with care and sympathy, and that children had cultural activities and possessions of their own" (Orme 2002, 5). Family records and correspondence provide evidence that "as far back as we can tell, most parents loved their children, grieved at their deaths, and conscientiously attended to the task of childrearing" (Pollock, quoted in Duffy 2002, 62). From his analysis of a vast array of documents and artifacts relating to the lives of children in medieval England, Orme concludes decisively that "there is nothing to be said for Aries's view of childhood in the middle ages, nor indeed of a major shift in its history during the sixteenth and seventeenth centuries. . . . Aries's views were mistaken: not simply in detail but in substance. It is time to lay them to rest" (9–10).

The debate over the degree of continuity in family life over time is far from resolved, as is the parallel debate over whether "notions of family and childhood have progressed over time, resulting in more humane treatment of children" (Hendrick 2000, 39). A recurring theme throughout this book is the profound implications of the disagreement between those who view the invention of childhood as a major cultural achievement and believe that children should enjoy a special status and should not be initiated too soon into the adult world versus those who view this protective attitude as a cover for the maintenance of adult control over children and argue that children's welfare is better served by extending their civil rights and enhancing their participation in society.

Other historians have called attention to the need for more systematic comparisons of children and childhood in different cultures (both Aries and Orme based their arguments on study of a single European country) and the need to address "issues not on Aries's agenda," such as explaining the origins and continuing ubiquity of child poverty, child labor, and the worldwide "gulf in life experience separating the children of the wealthy from the children of the poor" (Cunningham 1998, 1208). Work by scholars who have attempted to fill in the gaps identified by Cunningham will be included in chapters 8 and 10.

Perspectives from Gender Studies and Minority Studies

Although relations between generations differ from one time and place to another, a universal characteristic of child–adult relations is asymmetry of power. Sociologists who believe that children as a social group can be classified as a subordinate minority group comparable to other minority or subordinate groups have looked to such interdisciplinary fields as gender studies, Africana studies, Latino studies, and Asian studies for concepts, hypotheses, and findings applicable to the study of children and childhoods.[3]

Comparisons of the status of women and children by Barrie Thorne (1987), Leena Alanen (1994), and Ann Oakley (1994) have been especially fruitful. An important—perhaps the most important—lesson to be learned from feminist research is the significance of *standpoint*. Alanen argues that there is no such thing as impartial or disinterested research because "knowledge always contains a perspective from one or another location, a *standpoint* from which the world is known" (Alanen 1992, 50). Patricia Collins and other Black feminist theorists have pointed out that standpoint is shaped by race as well as gender and by the interaction between them and that the impact on research is considerable: "Because elite White men control Western structures of knowledge validation, their interests pervade the themes, paradigms, and epistemologies of traditional scholarship" (Collins 2000, 251).

Of all minority and subordinate groups, children are most likely to be confined to the *private domain*, to have the greatest difficulty in gaining access to the world outside the home and immediate neighborhood and the least scope for public action. "Only very occasionally—in school strikes, playing games, and as 'delinquents'—have children appeared through their *direct* actions in historical accounts" (Hendrick 2000, 43). The examples of children's participation in major social movements included in the box in chapter 1 (see page 5) and discussed more fully in chapters 10 and 12 suggest, however, that at least some kids have moved beyond games and delinquency and into the public arena. Moreover, while acknowledging the very real constraints on children's agency, James et al. (1998, 30–31) argue that the very act of defining children as a minority group "politicizes" childhood, thereby challenging the existing power relations between kids and adults.

Some go so far as to claim that children are not merely *a* minority group but "*the* minority group *par excellence*; it is they who provide the minority paradigm for other minority groups, in that the latter are stigmatized as children." When women, racial and ethnic minorities, and senior citizens "have undertaken to liberate themselves from their minority status, one of their goals at the symbolic level has been to free themselves of stigmatization as children. Thus they gradually acquired the universal civil rights [that] have bit by bit been extended to more and more groups of citizens. . . . The only remaining population group that systematically and generally is denied civil rights is children" (Qvortrup 1987, 10–11). Children can also be distinguished from other minority groups by the fact that they are the only such group whose status is both *universal* and *temporary*. *All* adults *have been* children, and if they survive childhood, *all* children *become* adults.

CONCLUSIONS

In this chapter, we have taken a fast tour through a huge body of scholarly work of daunting complexity. We hope that this brief review of theoretical perspectives has conveyed the range of alternative ways of thinking about children and childhoods, the extent to which the findings that emerge from any empirical study are shaped by the researcher's perspective (personal as well as theoretical), and, conversely, how new findings stimulate researchers to reconsider and revise their perspectives.

By documenting some of the ways in which society's youngest members shape and are shaped by their social surroundings, recent research on children has offered a more dynamic view of socialization than the functionalist perspective originally conveyed. Close examination of children's social worlds has revealed that they engage in a variety of economic activities, generally assumed to be an adult prerogative but consistent with the exchange perspective. Similarly, applications of the conflict perspective have shown that children, like adults, are sensitive to the unequal distributions of power and other resources between older and younger generations and that conflict among kids is common as well. Age and life course perspectives shed light on the problematical status of children in modern industrial societies and the unanticipated consequences of segregating kids in age-homogeneous groups. Finally, sociologists using the interactionist and social construction perspectives have generated a vibrant picture of childhood, one in which kids are actors as well as spectators, whose ideas, activities, and experiences have a reality of their own, distinct from and at least partially independent of adult social worlds and adult concerns *about* children.

From other disciplines, sociologists have gained insights into the ways in which perceptions of childhood and the treatment of children have changed over historical time; the complex interaction between biological, psychological, and social influences; and the ways in which children as a social group both resemble and differ from other minority or subordinate groups.

How researchers think about children influences how they study them—and vice versa—and the findings of any empirical study are to a considerable degree determined by the researcher's choice of theoretical perspectives and research methodologies. In the next chapter, we'll review various methods of gathering and analyzing empirical data or evidence about children and childhoods.

NOTES

1. For criticism of the shortcomings of functional theory for the study of children and childhoods, see Waksler (1991, chaps. 1 and 2), Corsaro (1997, chap. 1), and James et al. (1998, chap. 2).

2. In Japan, for example, on Adult Day (January 14), *all* Japanese citizens who have reached their twentieth birthday during the previous twelve months are accorded voting and all other adult rights. In the United States, in contrast, citizens have the right to vote and enlist in military service at age eighteen but cannot purchase alcoholic beverages until age twenty-one. There is some variation from state to state in the age at which one can marry without parental permission (eighteen in most but not all states), obtain birth control services, and drive. Recent murder convictions for persons as young as twelve have provoked heated controversy about the age at which one can be tried for capital offenses as an adult, which now varies from one jurisdiction to another. Qvortrup's mode of distinguishing children from nonchildren acknowledges that the boundary between childhood and adulthood is vague, variable, and often arbitrary: "A person is a child until he reaches majority, or you may follow the Convention of the Rights of the Child and define children as those human beings who are below 18 years of age; or you may as I prefer suggest children to be all those people who have not yet passed the age of obligatory schooling—i.e., obtained the right to make important decision on their own" (Qvortrup 2000a, 1).

3. As defined by Louis Wirth, a minority group is "any group of people who because of their physical or cultural characteristics are singled out from others in the society in which they live for differential and unequal treatment, and who therefore regard themselves as objects of collective discrimination. The existence of a minority in the society implies the existence of a corresponding dominant group with higher social status and greater privileges. Minority status carries with it the exclusion from full participation in the life of the society" (quoted in Qvortrup 2000a, 8).

3

STUDYING CHILDREN
AND CHILDHOODS:
RESEARCH METHODOLOGIES

Given the basic premise of this book that kids are active participants in their own upbringing, not just passive recipients of adult socialization, it follows that the most direct way to learn *about* children is to learn *from* children. This principle has been summarized in William Corsaro's often-quoted statement that "children are the best sources for understanding childhood" (1997, 103), which we'll refer to hereafter as *Corsaro's Rule*.

Such a perspective requires rethinking research methodology as well as theory, and a major contribution of researchers like Corsaro is their attention to the nature of evidence or data about children and child-hoods. Challenging the conventional role of children in social science research—that is, as passive objects of adult scrutiny—these researchers remind us that *how* we study kids affects *what* we learn about them. As the most powerless of all groups in society, children's voices are least often heard directly. While women and members of racial and ethnic minorities have fought for and (to varying degrees) gained the right to define themselves rather than simply being objects of research by their social superiors, children rarely study themselves and just as rarely have any say in how they will be studied. This tendency to obtain, analyze, and interpret data about children from the perspective of nonchildren has been termed the *adult ideological bias*.

DATA-GATHERING MODES

Corsaro's Rule requires that, wherever possible, at least some of the data be gathered directly from the children who are the subjects of the research, and it implies that the views of children and the views of adults should be *compared* rather than assuming that they are the same or that the adult view is the correct one. This means that the study of children requires not special techniques for gathering and analyzing data but rather "a rigorous application of the general methodological requirement, true of studying adults or children, that the techniques used should reflect the concrete particularities of the persons being studied" (Prout 2000, xi). In the following chapters, we'll include studies utilizing one or more of the following methods of data collection:

- Surveys
- Observation
- Interviews
- Experiments
- Analysis or reanalysis of data routinely gathered by public and private agencies
- Analysis of physical materials or artifacts, including photographs, children's clothing, toys, and games, stories, and artwork produced by or for kids

Quantitative and Qualitative Data

Quantitative data include public opinion surveys, demographic data, and statistics gathered by government and nongovernmental organizations. Qvortrup (1990) has argued that many children and children's problems have been rendered invisible because of the absence of "child-specific" statistics in conventional methods of government record keeping. For example, child poverty rates come out higher if the calculations are based on children than if they are based on families.

Social indicators, or statistics gathered periodically, usually from multiple sources, can be used to track patterns or trends over time—for example, to monitor the ups and downs of the economy, the incidence and spread of diseases, or student achievement in a nation's school systems.

Social indicators have been developed to provide comparable quantitative measures of children's status and well-being. About half of each edition of UNICEF's annual *State of the World's Children* is devoted to statistics on the conditions of life for children (e.g., rates of infant and child mortality, malnutrition, poverty, disease and disease prevention, and school attendance) in all nations for which data are available.[1]

In the United States, researchers at Duke University and the Foundation for Child Development have constructed the Child Well-Being Index (CWI), a composite of twenty-eight measures representing seven quality-of-life "domains" (including material well-being, emotional well-being, health, safety, and social relationships) that will, it is hoped, enable researchers and policymakers to "track overall well-being at the national level on an annual basis" (Land 2000). A graph of CWI scores since 1975 shows a dip in scores throughout the 1980s, hitting bottom in 1993, then rising to a point slightly higher than the initial score, leading the researchers to conclude that, overall, American kids are faring about 5 percent better now than they were in 1975 (Guzman et al. 2003).

It's hard to know just what to make of these results, indeed whether it's possible to quantify the quality of children's lives. In general, social indicators can tell us the rates at which certain behaviors (e.g., delinquent or criminal acts) or circumstances (e.g., poverty) have gone up or down though not about the causes and effects of these changes. They can also help identify areas where people's beliefs do not correspond to the empirical evidence. Comparisons of social indicators with opinion data reveal, for example, that American adults tend to think that the child poverty rate is much higher than it actually is and to believe that violent crime among teenagers is rising when in fact it has dropped sharply during the past decade (Moore, Brown, and Scarupa 2003; Moore and Redd 2002). Whether an index like the CWI can help policymakers, teachers, and parents make more informed decisions about children remains to be seen.

In South Africa, a research team that is developing the nation's first social indicators to measure and monitor the welfare of children and youth is also the first to involve children in the process. In a series of sessions with children in three different provinces, it was learned that the child participants defined their well-being somewhat differently than did the adult staff, tending to "focus on relationships rather than specific content. For example, they are more interested in talking about whether they like their math teacher than about how much math they are learning" (Child and Youth Research and Training Programme 2003, 2). Following these sessions, children *and* adults will present their views and findings directly to South African policymakers.

A common rationale for quantitative studies is that they are more "scientific" than qualitative studies because they are more likely to be based on the large samples and systematic data gathering and analysis necessary for generalizing and drawing inferences.

At the same time, even the most rigorously designed quantitative studies may be inaccurate or misleading. For example, a reexamination of the 1990 U.S. Census found that it undercounted or somehow missed at least 2 million children (3.2 percent of the actual total of the country's children), that children were a disproportionate percentage of those who were missed, and that minority and disadvantaged children were more likely to be missed than Caucasian and advantaged children (*New York Times*, August 26, 1999). Moreover, even the most ambitious quantitative studies provide only "partial snapshots," not the whole picture, of any aspect of childhood, and findings from different studies may contradict each other. For example, the voluminous research on the effects of mothers' employment on children's cognitive, emotional, and social development has yet to provide a conclusive answer to the question, Is home care or outside-the-home care better for young children? Finally, critics of a strictly quantitative approach are concerned that

> coming away with nothing but numbers (or worse, standardized numbers) has told us little about the day-to-day interactions of children. It has led us to believe that such interactions can be reduced to computations. Those aspects of children's lives that cannot be readily measured, but that instead must be described in text and *interpreted*, have been ignored or operationalized in very suspect fashion. (Graue and Walsh 1998, 23)

Researchers who favor *qualitative* methods of data gathering do not view themselves as detached, objective experts employing systematic procedures that will produce unbiased knowledge. Though they may use quantitative data to provide background or context for their studies, their own data are usually gathered by direct observations and informal discussions with participants on their own turf. Studies of the same group(s) of chil-

dren in a natural setting over a fairly long period of time using a variety
of qualitative methods supplemented by background data and physical
materials are often referred to as *ethnographic studies*. Good ethnographic studies are rich in detail and provide a sense of "flesh and blood"
reality. For this reason, ethnography has been chosen by many researchers who have adopted the interactionist or social construction theoretical perspective. A major weakness of ethnographic studies is that because most are intensive examinations of a single or small number of
cases, it is difficult to generalize, even from those studies that seem to
mirror the reality of children's lives most convincingly. In addition, some
researchers have expressed concern that "ethnographic work among children often 'othered' the world of children" by highlighting "a separate
children's culture with belief systems and social methodologies foreign to
an adult's eye" (James, Jenks, and Prout 1998, 181).

While it has been suggested that one might choose *quantitative* methods for projects that attempt to "map childhood as a large-scale phenomenon" and *qualitative* methods for projects that attempt to "document the
doings of children in context" (Prout 2000, xi), neither is inherently a "better" way to study children, and there are usually advantages to using both
approaches. For example, a cross-national study of media access and use
by European children (Livingstone and Bovill 2001; to be discussed in
chapter 5) used a multimethod design that combined a survey of a large
sample of children in twelve different countries, in-depth interviews with
a smaller subset of survey participants, and background data on the countries obtained from government statistics and reports.

Experiments

Although the experiment is held up as the model for rigorous scientific research, the requirements of experimental design (especially, the
random assignment of subjects to experimental and control groups and
the application of experimental "treatments" with unknown effects) can
rarely be met in real-life research with human subjects, especially children. For many inquiries of interest to scholars, experiments must be
ruled out for ethnical reasons. We don't, for example, permit researchers to implant electrodes in the brains of randomly selected children or place children in dangerous environments in order to study the

effects on their social and emotional development. By today's standards, some of the most influential social science experiments of the twentieth century (e.g., Sheriff's studies of boys' behavior in experimental camps that were designed and manipulated for research purposes, to be discussed in chapter 7) would almost certainly fail to be approved by a government or university human subjects committee.

Valuable data on the effects of children's social environments can sometimes be obtained by studying *natural experiments*, when events or interventions that were not created for research purposes may impinge on kids' lives in significant respects—for example, growing up in a utopian community like the Israeli kibbutz (see chapter 12), spending a portion of one's infancy or early childhood in an extremely impoverished orphanage or children's home, or taking part in a political protest movement (to be discussed in chapter 10).

In North Carolina, the opening of a casino on a Cherokee reservation provided the setting for a natural experiment on the effects of being suddenly lifted out of poverty. The correlation between poverty and psychopathology is well documented, but the causal relationship remains hypothetical. Does poverty *cause* psychic and behavioral disorders? Or is poverty *caused by* psychopathology? Or are both caused by some other variable(s)? Ethical considerations preclude controlled experiments in which babies are randomly assigned to grow up in poverty or in more affluent circumstances, but a Duke University Medical School research team was able to take advantage of an unplanned intervention—the casino distributed a portion of its profits to all Cherokee families living on the reservation, enabling some to rise above the federal poverty line. Children who were between the ages of nine and thirteen at the beginning of the study were given annual psychiatric assessments for eight years. At each testing after the opening of the casino, there was a sharp drop in the incidence of behavior disorders among the children whose families broke the poverty threshold. By the end of the study, the incidence of temper tantrums, stealing, bullying, and vandalism had dropped 40 percent, to the same levels found among children whose families had never been poor. The payments had no effect on the behavior of children whose families were unable to rise from poverty or on children whose families had not been poor to begin with (Costello et al. 2003).

The researchers can only speculate on what happened in these families that explained the changes in their children's behavior (some posited that having a secure income gave parents more time to spend with their children, while others felt that the psychological benefits were a by-product of the better jobs generated by the casino, improving the general outlook of the entire community), but the importance of this natural experiment is that it provides empirical evidence in support of the hypothesis that economic insecurity was the cause rather than the effect of children's behavioral disorders and that moving families out of poverty can bring about a reduction in deviant and aggressive behavior.

CHOOSING APPROPRIATE RESEARCH METHODS

A number of recent discussions of research on children and childhoods have called for the use of "child-friendly" methods of gathering data, by which is generally meant that they are fun for kids as well as congruent with their interests and competencies. Samantha Punch, whose ethnographic study of children growing up in rural Bolivia will be discussed in chapter 10, objects to the term "child-friendly" on the grounds that it is patronizing and inconsistent with a perception of children as able and entitled to speak for themselves. "If children are competent social actors," she asks, "why are special 'child-friendly' methods needed to communicate with them?" In partial answer to her own question, she acknowledges that, at least for the time being, research with children *isn't* the same as research with adults "mainly because of adult perceptions of children and children's marginalized position in adult society" (Punch 2002, 321). Thus, she recommends that researchers adopt a multimethod approach that combines traditional modes of gathering data, such as participant observation and interviews, with techniques that enable children to communicate their views of themselves and their social worlds.

Following are some strategies for adapting research methods to the subjects' interests, experiences, and expertise:

- Study kids in familiar settings rather than in laboratories, school offices, or classrooms where adults dominate. It has been found, for example, that babies and young children display more sociability and social competence when observed in their own homes than in experimental settings. A Norwegian sociologist learned about the daily routines of four-year-olds by having them take her "literally step by step from bedroom, to bathroom to kitchen and so on, in order that these familiar places could provide triggers for children's accounts." A Finnish researcher gathered data from schoolchildren while walking home with them after school or accompanying them to the places where they spent their free time (Mayall 2000, 131–35).

- Use small groups in which children outnumber adult researchers rather than one-on-one interviews for discussion of controversial topics or sensitive areas of kids' lives. Washington (2002) succeeded in obtaining detailed data on their attitudes and knowledge about AIDS and AIDS prevention from focus groups of African American male teenagers, who are seldom consulted even though they constitute a group at high risk of contracting AIDS. In the United Kingdom, groups of nine-year-olds from a range of family backgrounds and cultures were given vignettes of five different family lifestyles, ranging from married couples with and without children to nonresidential fathers and children, and asked to discuss and if possible reach a group consensus on whether each of the five was a "real" family (O'Brien, Alldred, and Jones 1996).

- Give children whose lifestyles violate conventional adult assumptions about what constitutes a proper childhood opportunities to describe their lives as *they* see them. Woodhead and Faulkner (2000) set up workshops in Bangladesh, Ethiopia, the Philippines, and Central America where children in occupations ranging from lead mining, fireworks manufacturing, and street vending to fishing and agricultural work were "encouraged to represent their feelings and beliefs in whatever ways were meaningful to them, including drawings, mapping, role play as well as group discussion. At the heart of the protocol were a series of semi-structured activities and games focusing on key themes in children's lives, about family circumstances and parental expectation, experiences of work and school (positive and negative), self-esteem and personal identity. As far as possible children's own words shaped the preparation of the report" (29).

- Allow children to describe and assess their experiences through activities that they enjoy and do well. After finding to his chagrin that the

Italian preschoolers he was studying were considerably more accomplished than he was in art and language, Corsaro turned his incompetence to his advantage by encouraging the child "experts" to teach him how to paint a picture or pronounce Italian words correctly (Corsaro and Molinari 2000). Robert Coles, whose work will be discussed in chapter 10, collected thousands of drawings from children without permanent homes or living in impoverished and dangerous environments. Pictures with accompanying text created by Sami children living in remote areas of Norway that were heavily contaminated by fallout from the 1986 Chernobyl nuclear disaster provided valuable data on how the decimation of the reindeer herds that were their livelihood affected the cultural identity as well as the health, diet, work, and daily routines of an indigenous minority people (Stephens 1995b). Several years after the atomic bombing of Hiroshima, a Japanese scholar compiled a collection of essays by child survivors who provided detailed and often harrowing accounts of what they observed and experienced during the bombing and its aftermath. Originally published in Japanese in 1960, *Children of Hiroshima* has been translated into many languages and continues to influence medical and psychological research and to inspire nuclear disarmament movements (Osada 1982).

CONTROLLING FOR ADULT IDEOLOGICAL BIAS

A major impediment to implementing the new research paradigm is the reluctance of many adults, including sociologists, to take children and their ideas seriously. In a *New York Times* story on the intensification of civil defense instruction for Israeli schoolchildren, the author noted the thoughtful questions asked by the students. He also reported that a special telephone line set up to answer children's questions had received thousands of calls and that many of the callers asked how they could help their parents in case of a poison gas attack, leading an official to comment that in many cases the "children were the leaders of the house." Despite his own evidence of the active involvement of many young Israelis in safeguarding themselves and their families, the author concluded that "in the end [they] were still *only children*" (*New York Times*, January 3, 2003; emphasis added).

Another impediment is that all adults are outsiders to the social worlds of children. Two sociologists who have specialized in participant observation with children point out that "like the white researcher in Black society, the male researcher studying women, or the ethnologist observing a distant tribal culture, the adult [researcher] who attempts to understand a children's culture cannot pass unnoticed as a member of the group" (Fine and Sandstrom 1988, 13).

At the same time, a unique characteristic of research on children is that *all adult researchers have themselves been children*. By contrast, the attributes of race and sex are permanent. Except in exceptional cases, usually of misclassification or reclassification, males have never been females, and Whites have never been Blacks. Some attributes can be changed. Individuals may change their religion (through conversion) or nationality (through emigration), and in many parts of the world today such changes are relatively frequent, but they're still not universal. *Some* but not all Americans are former Russians, *some* but not all Muslims are former Christians, but *all* adults are former children.

Having actually experienced the status they are studying does not, however, guarantee an unbiased view of childhood. The "tales of former children are seldom to be trusted," says Lillian Hellman in her memoir *Pentimento*, because they have been colored by personal experience and tend to be exaggerated. "Some people supply too many past victories or pleasures with which to comfort themselves, and other people cling to pains, real and imagined, to excuse what they have become" (Hellman 1973, 92). The lesson for researchers: "To learn *from* children, adults have to challenge the deep assumption that they already know what children are 'like,' both because, as former children, adults have been there, and because, as adults, they regard children as less complete versions of themselves" (Thorne 1993, 12).

Initial efforts by adult researchers to minimize their influence on child subjects took the form of making themselves as unobtrusive as possible. They were advised to observe from a concealed location and to back up their observations with video- or audiotaping. If this was not possible, "mingling with the children in their natural habitats" until they "become accustomed to the observers' presence and therefore are less likely to 'perform' for them or alter their behavior in any significant way" was recommended. In reality, researchers were as likely to find themselves "backed-up against a corner of the classroom or playground, trying to ignore children's invitation to join in the game, and kidding themselves they can appear like the metaphoric 'fly on the wall'" (Woodhead and Faulkner 2000, 15).

In a highly influential paper published in 1988 and often reprinted, Nancy Mandell urged sociologists to cast off their traditional roles as detached observers and to adopt what she called the *"least-adult"* role, defined as "responsive, interactive" and "fully involved" while "neither directing nor correcting children's actions." In order to accomplish this in her own research, Mandell (1991) says that she

> assumed the role of learner, and allowed the children to teach me their ways. As a neophyte, I either attached myself to small groups of children or I placed myself strategically in activity areas. In both instances I stayed close physically, watched carefully, said very little, and closely followed their behavior. Once admitted to their social exchanges, I interacted freely with the children, making full use of the physical space and equipment provided by the centers. As a member of the children's social world, I both observed and participated in rule stretching and breaking. . . . [O]ver time I became an active participant, not merely a peripheral, passive, or reactive observer. (42)

However appealing in principle, the least-adult role model presents as many difficulties in practice as the fly-on-the-wall approach. Apart from their physical size precluding their "passing" as kids, few adults can throw themselves into kids' activities as fully as Mandell appeared to do. James et al. (1998, 183) propose a middle ground between the detached-adult and least-adult models that they term "semi-participant or friend." An excellent application of this strategy can be found in a recent ethnographic study of children's racial attitudes, assumptions, and behavior in a racially diverse preschool that we'll discuss in chapter 8 (Van Ausdale and Feagin 2001). As the principal data gatherer, Van Ausdale, a White female adult, "established herself as a combination of playmate and listener for the children and as a teacher's aide for the adults." In situations where children seemed in danger of physical harm, Van Ausdale brought the situation to a teacher's attention but avoided exercising authority herself:

> She never threatened the children with sanctions for their words or actions, nor did she try to influence them to change their behaviors. She

did not engage children in directed questioning of their racial attitudes or behaviors, nor did she direct their activities or design activities to elicit racial or ethnic responses. Significantly, thus, children would often use "potty language" in her presence or would enlist her in evading teacher sanctions. In no case did she ask any children predetermined questions; she let issues come up naturally. (Van Ausdale and Feagin 2001, 45–46)

A direct way to avoid or correct adult ideological perspective is to involve children as co-researchers, though studies in which this is actually done are still rare. In a study of six communities in northeastern United States in which children between the ages of four and eight were interviewed about their daily routines, their contacts with other people in their homes and neighborhoods, and the rules and restrictions that governed their lives, half the interviews were conducted by ten- to twelve-year-old kids who were paid for their work and received the same training as the adult interviewers (Boocock 1981). While child and adult interviewers proved to be equally competent, there were a few differences in the data obtained. For example, the child subjects were more likely to tell a child interviewer than an adult interviewer about engaging in forbidden activities (e.g., sneaking candy or other prohibited snacks or watching violent or late-night television programs). Since the data gatherers were not present when these activities reportedly occurred, it is unclear whether kids were overreporting deviant behavior to other kids or underreporting deviant behavior to adults—the point, however, is that the interviewers' ages did appear to affect how their subjects responded to some questions. When Scott (1999) showed the videotapes she had made of African American first-grade girls on the school playground to the girls who were taped and to other girls who were not, she discovered that the girls' interpretations of the video data often differed from hers as well as from what she was told by teachers and other school personnel.

Clearly, the practical problems of increasing children's participation in research cannot be overlooked. In a detailed and thoughtful discussion, Alderson (2000) cautions that problems of coercion and exploitation resulting from the unequal power of children and adults are not resolved simply by adding kids to the research team. If they are to become real members of a research team, questions like the following need to be answered: How much and what kinds of input should be solicited from child researchers? How much responsibility is it fair to expect children to carry? How much should adults intervene, and how can they avoid manipulating children? Should child researchers be paid? If so, how much? If not, what should they receive for their work? Who should have final control over the data and how the research findings are reported?

ETHICAL ISSUES

Attempting to control or reduce adult ideological bias does not mean ignoring or downplaying very real ethical issues that arise in research with children. Indeed, concern for the rights and protection of *all* human subjects, children or nonchildren, clearly merits the attention it has received in recent years. Moreover, we believe that according children more active roles in the research process is an important step in the direction of protecting their rights as human subjects as well as acknowledging their competence to speak for themselves. Christensen and Prout (2002) recommend adherence to the principle of *"ethical symmetry,"* by which they mean that

> the researcher takes as his or her *starting* point the view that the ethical relationship between researcher and informant is the same whether he or she conducts research with adults or with children. [Application of this principle means that] researchers do not have to use particular methods or, indeed, work with a different set of ethical standards when working with children. Rather, it means that the practices employed in the research have to be in line with children's experiences, interests, values, and everyday routines. (482)

Priscilla Alderson, who has done pioneering work on children's consent to surgery (to be discussed in chapter 12) and on increasing children's participation in research, has proposed the ten topics shown in the box on page 46 as ethical guidelines for social research with children.

ETHICAL GUIDELINES
FOR RESEARCH WITH CHILDREN*

1. Purpose of the research

   If the research findings are meant to benefit certain children, who are they and how might they benefit?

2. Costs and hoped-for benefits

   Might there be risks or costs such as time, inconvenience, embarrassment, intrusion of privacy, sense of failure or coercion, fear of admitting anxiety?

3. Privacy and confidentiality

   When significant extracts from interviews are quoted in reports, should researchers first check the quotation and commentary with the child (or parent) concerned?

4. Selection, inclusion, and exclusion

   Have some children been excluded because, for instance, they have speech or learning difficulties? Can the exclusion be justified?

5 Funding

   Should the research funds be raised only from agencies which avoid activities that can harm children?

6. Review and revision of the research aims and methods

   Have children or their caretakers helped to plan or commented on the research?

7. Information for children, parents and other caretakers

   Are the children and adults concerned given details about the purpose and nature of the research, the methods and timing, and the possible benefits, harms, and outcomes?

8. Consent

   Do children know that if they refuse or withdraw from research, this will not be held against them in any way? How do the researchers help children know these things?

9. Dissemination

   Will the children and adults involved be sent reports of the main findings?

10. Impact on children

    Besides the effects of the research on the children involved, how might the conclusions affect larger groups of children?

* Summary of topics and questions proposed by Priscilla Alderson. Reprinted from Pia Christensen and Alan Prout. 2002. Working with ethical symmetry in social research with children. *Childhood* 9: 490, by permission of Sage Publications Ltd.

Gaining access to children and obtaining informed consent from the appropriate persons is more difficult in some societies than in others. For example, in Finland, a country with very low levels of crime and social disorder, Alanen had little difficulty securing general consent from parents to her walking home with children after school and accompanying them to the places where they spent their free time. By contrast, in the United Kingdom and the United States, where crime rates are much higher and adult fears for children's safety are often realistic, gaining consent is more difficult and becoming ever more so (Mayall 2000, 131–35).

CONCLUSIONS

Our brief review of methodological issues relating to research on children and the range of methods used in recent studies tells us that there is nearly always more than one way to study any aspect of children's childhoods, there is seldom a "best" method for any study, and there are usually advantages to using multiple methods of data collection and analysis. The research studies discussed in the following chapters represent a diversity of theoretical and methodological approaches.

We believe that this research also makes a compelling case for Corsaro's Rule, that children are the best sources for understanding children and childhood. It is important, though, to keep in mind that asking children *their* opinions and taking their answers seriously, a revolutionary idea in the 1970s, remains controversial today. The romanticized notion of childhood innocence, vulnerability, and incompetence maintains a strong hold on adult thinking about children and childhood. Though the following chapters will include examples from the small but growing body of research in which children are active participants as subjects and, occasionally, as co-researchers, most of the studies we'll refer to were designed, executed, and written by nonchildren.

NOTE

1. The most extensive compilations of social indicators on American children can be found in Federal Interagency Forum on Child and Family

Statistics, *America's Children: Key Indicators of Well-Being* (www
.childstats.gov); U.S. Department of Health and Human Services, *Trends in
the Well-Being of America's Children and Youth* (http://aspe.hhs.gov/hsp/
00trends/); and research reports and online data resources of Child Trends,
a private Washington, D.C.–based research center (www.childtrends.org
and www.childtrendsdatabank.org).

II

KIDS AND THEIR FAMILIES

4

CHANGE AND DIVERSITY: THE TWO CONSTANTS OF FAMILY LIFE

A family is a group of people which all care about each other. They can cry together, laugh together, argue together, and go through all the emotions together. Some live together as well.

—Thirteen-year-old (England)

The two-parent, multiple-child family that typified mid-century America is now complemented by many other forms and structures. The "traditional" family of today includes families headed by grandparents, same-sex couples, single parents, and step parents.

—Nancy Kropf and Denise Burnette

We're a normal divorced family.

—Thirteen-year-old (England)

For most kids, life as a social being begins at home. In all societies, the primary social institution responsible for the care and upbringing of children is the family, and most children spend their earliest years in a household in which they develop intimate and long-lasting relationships with one or both or their biological parents and one or more siblings, sometimes with other relatives as well.

In chapter 2, we noted that as a result of the combination of declining birthrates and extended life spans that characterizes modern industrialized societies, children are, numerically, a smaller proportion of the total population—and perhaps a diminishing "presence" in society as well. The changing composition of the population has been accompanied by transformations in family structure and family relations. Donald Hernandez, formerly chief of the Marriage and Family Statistics Branch of the U.S. Bureau of the Census, characterizes the vast shifts during the past half century in family size and composition, parents' education and employment, modes of child care, household income, and distribution of human and material resources to children and their families as "revolutions" (Hernandez 1993).

In this chapter, we'll examine the demographic trends relating to family composition that seem to have the strongest impact on children's well-being and their experience of childhood.

THREE KINDS OF FAMILY REVOLUTION

The Shrinking Family and the *Rarefaction*[1] of Children

Whatever term is used to characterize the growing "shortage" of children in industrialized countries resulting from declining fertility and longer life expectancy, sociologists agree that this trend is affecting the social atmosphere as well as the intergenerational balance in such countries. The majority of U.S. households have *no* children, and less than a quarter consist of married couples with children. Census figures for 2000 showed that among families that did have children, 21 percent had three or more and 37 percent had two, while 42 percent had only one; the number of one-child families had doubled since 1970. To look at it from a child's perspective, at the beginning of the twentieth century, about three-quarters of Americans grew up in families with five or more children, and fewer than 10 percent had two siblings or less; by the end of the century, only 6 percent of all American children had five or more siblings, the majority had either one or two, and a growing minority had none (Bureau of Statistics 2003, 63; see also Lerner, Sparks, and McCubbin 2000; National Marriage Project 2003).

We also noted in chapter 2 that the striking declines in fertility and family size that have occurred in virtually all societies can be explained by exchange theory—or, as Hernandez (1993) puts it, by "the desire of individuals and couples to improve their relative social and economic standing, or to keep from falling behind, in competition with other couples and in light of changing economic opportunities, assisted during recent decades by technical refinements in birth-control methods" (40).[2] Having fewer children allows parents to spend more money, time and other resources on each. Having fewer siblings may reduce competition among brothers and sisters for their parents' attention, but fewer children will have the experience of caring for younger siblings or being cared for by older ones, and more children will have to look outside the home for playmates. Over the long run, Hernandez found, children from smaller families tend to have greater opportunities for advanced education and for obtaining occupations with relatively high income and social status, though family size appears to have little effect on their psychological well-being as adults (19).

Some European population specialists believe that the *rarefaction* of children is leading to a future in which a majority of kids will be only children. Despite this trend, there has been little research on only children since the 1970s. Though some of these earlier studies were flawed by presuppositions about only children's greater susceptibility to psychological disorders, most found both positive and negative outcomes. In one of the rare studies in which children's own opinions were solicited, a third of the only children interviewed stated that the greatest advantage was receiving more attention from their parents; however, almost the same proportion of respondents cited greater attention from parents as the major *disadvantage* of being an only child. From a kid's perspective, that extra attentiveness from mom and dad could be viewed as either comforting or suffocating—or both (Golini and Silvestrini 1997). As the first nation to legislate and (to a certain extent) enforce a one-child-per-family policy, China offers a unique setting in which to compare children's development in one-child and multiple-children families. Despite dire predictions of oncoming generations of spoiled "little emperors," the most extensive surveys show little or no difference between only children and other children on a variety of personality and academic performance measures (Poston and Falbo 1990).

Employment and Education Revolutions

Beginning in the late nineteenth century, the large farm family that was the model American household was replaced by the smaller "breadwinner-homemaker" family as many men left home to work in factories and offices while mothers remained at home to care for the children and perform other household chores. Hernandez identifies the year 1890 as the "great divide," when there were approximately equal proportions of children living in two-parent farm families and in nonfarm breadwinner-homemaker families. Less than a century later, mothers followed fathers into the labor force so that by the 1980s, the "woman's presence in the household during the day [was] just about like that of the man's in the 1880s" (Coleman 1987, 32–33). In the fifty-year period between 1940 and 1990, dual-earner families (i.e., two-parent families with both parents in the labor force) increased sevenfold, from 5 to 38 percent.

British and American children questioned about their parents' employment expressed generally positive opinions, though many wished their parents earned more money, were less often tired and stressed, and had more time to spend with them. An interesting serendipitous finding was that the more kids knew about their parents' jobs and the more they believed that their parents liked and were committed to their work, the more highly they rated their competence as *parents* (Galinsky 1999, 234–44; Loissis and Noller 1999).

Because of the expansion of state-supported educational systems throughout the twentieth century, each succeeding generation received more formal schooling than its predecessors. Compared to the 1920s, when only about 60 percent had at least eight years of schooling and less than 20 percent were high school graduates, virtually all American parents now have completed at least an elementary education, and more than 80 percent have completed high school or more. The average number of years of education completed is still lower for African American and Latino parents than for European American parents, though the gap has narrowed. Children too are staying in school for ever more years. For parents, this means additional education expenditures and less availability of children for household labor; for kids, it generally means more years of economic dependency (Lerner et al. 2000).

Child Care Revolutions

When the United States was a primarily agricultural country, both child care and economic production could be carried out in the same place by the same people. The transformations in parental employment just described resulted in a decline in parental availability and a growing demand for alternative forms of child care. The large increase in school enrollment following fathers' employment outside the home constituted the first child care revolution. Having their kids in school facilitated mothers' labor force participation, which in turn fostered a second revolution in which nonparental care was extended to younger children. Between 1940 and 1987, "the proportion of preschoolers who did not have a parent at home full-time nearly quadrupled from about 13 to 50 percent, and by 1987 about 40 percent of preschoolers were regularly cared for by someone other than their parents" (Hernandez 1993, 11). Who this someone was depended on the family's income; for preschoolers from poor families, the substitute caretaker was likely to be a relative, while preschoolers from more affluent homes were cared for primarily by nonrelatives (Smith 2000). In chapters 6 and 12, we'll compare data from several nations on the effects on children's development and well-being of parental care versus nonparental care.

The reduced availability of parents and scarcity of older siblings also accounts for recent increases in *self-care*. A study by Child Trends (Vandivere et al. 2003) reported that more than 3 million American children under thirteen were left to care for themselves at least a few hours a week. To date, the hazards of self-care have received the most publicity, from the disasters befalling Macaulay Culkin in the *Home Alone* movies to newspaper accounts of children who died in home accidents while their mothers, usually single moms whose babysitters had not shown up and who feared losing their jobs, were at work—leading some reformers to call for legislation prohibiting parents from leaving their children alone in the home and penalizing those who violate the prohibition. Research that is both free from ideological preconceptions and well designed is in short supply, and the findings are mixed. Though some studies have found susceptibility to fear, loneliness, depression, and overeating to be greater among unsupervised children, others show no differences between children cared for by adults and those who care for themselves, and there is no consensus about the earliest age at which children can safely be left alone (Mertens, Flowers, and Mulhall 2003; Rodman 1990). The Child

Trends report reflects Americans' ambivalence about kids not under adult supervision, warning that self-care may put children at risk but then acknowledging that it not always harmful and that it is normal for children to become more independent and to take increasing responsibility for themselves as they progress through childhood. An unexpected finding was that for children age nine or younger, those from higher-income families were *more* likely to be left unsupervised than their counterparts from lower-income families. (A difference in the same direction was also found in a recent ethnographic study comparing the parenting practices of affluent middle-class families and working- or lower-class families [Lareau 2003], to be discussed in the next chapter.)

Comparisons of American "latchkey" children with their counterparts in other times and places offer alternative perspectives on self-care. For example, in a study of Norwegian "home-stayers" (the author's term for latchkey children), Anne Solberg (1990) found that most used their home-alone time to do their school homework, to perform certain household chores, and to have fun with friends. They rarely reported feeling lonely or afraid and generally considered taking on some household responsibilities in return for having the house to themselves a satisfactory trade-off. Solberg argues that while an adult may view a home without adults as "empty" or even dangerous, from a kids' perspective such a home may offer independence and freedom to use the time and space as they choose. Anthropologist Meredith Small (2001) reminds us that historically most child care was performed by children and that looking after oneself, younger siblings, and sometimes other people's babies and young children remains customary in many parts of the world today. The differences between the American and Norwegian research findings undoubtedly reflect societal differences in the safety of children's homes and neighborhoods as well as cultural differences in beliefs about children's capabilities and needs.

DIVERSITY PLUS CHANGE: CONSEQUENCES FOR CHILDREN AND THEIR FAMILIES

There is no doubt that family structure matters for children, and there is ample evidence that the type of family that most benefits children is headed by both biological parents with adequate income in a low-conflict marriage (Moore, Jekielek, and Emig 2002, 6). The problem is that this kind of family is in increasingly short supply. Although the married-parents-with-kids family still accounts for the majority of households with children, this proportion has been declining in North America and most European nations, with a corresponding shift toward a variety of *alternative*—generally smaller, more heterogeneous, and less stable—family forms. In the United States, increasing numbers of children lived with the following:

- Mother only or father only
- Unmarried biological parents
- A biological parent and stepparent
- A biological parent and unmarried partner
- Same-sex parents
- Grandparents or other relatives
- Nonrelatives, including foster parents

We had hoped to include tables showing changes in the numbers and percentages of children living with their continuously married biological parents compared to those living in the various alternative family forms listed here. We soon discovered, however, that even if we limited our tabulations to the United States, some of the figures we sought were not readily available or not in the form we wished, and constructing tables that were accurate without being insuperably complicated was virtually impossible, at least in the time at our disposal. The situation was summed up by a U.S. Census Bureau staff member and coauthor of a special report on American children and the households they live in (Lugaila and Overturf 2004) who told us, "There are hundreds of different ways of presenting the data and we cannot show them all" (Julia Overturf, personal communication).[3]

What can be generalized about recent changes in family structure in the United States and other industrialized nations appears to boil down to the following: as a result of shifting patterns of adult living arrangements, relatively more children are characterized as follows:

- They are born to unmarried women (from 5 percent of all American children born in 1960 to 12 percent in 1970 to almost a third by the end of the twentieth century).

- They will spend at least part of their childhood in at least one of the alternative family forms listed previously—though they are much *less* likely than in the past to experience the death of a parent.
- They will experience multiple changes in family composition, partly because families headed by single, cohabiting, or remarried parents tend to be less stable than families headed by continuously married parents (Teachman, Tedrow, and Crowder 2000).

Given the complexity and fluidity of alternative family forms, we will not attempt an assessment of each type. In the next section, we'll consider the *economic* consequences for children of living in alternative families. Then we'll consider the *social and emotional* consequences of family dissolution by reviewing the continuing debate on the effects of divorce. Next we'll consider how children are faring in two of the fastest-growing but least studied alternative family forms: those headed by gay or lesbian couples (the most controversial type of family in nearly all societies) and those headed by grandparents (a new version of the traditional extended family). We'll end this chapter with findings from studies that offered kids the opportunity to express their views about alternative families.

The "Alternative Family Structure = Economic Disadvantage" Equation: Which Comes First?

A general finding of studies comparing traditional and alternative families is that kids whose parents are single, separated, divorced, or absent are more likely to be economically disadvantaged than kids whose parents are and remain married to each other. In the United States in the 1990s, annual income for two-parent families with children averaged more than three times the annual income of single-mother families with children, and the gap continued to widen as married parents tended to benefit more than single parents from the economic expansion and greater prosperity of the 1990s, especially if both parents were in the paid labor force (Amato 2001; Coontz 1997). In Canada during the same period, 21 percent of all children were poor, but the proportion rose to 65.8 *percent* for children living in single-mother families (Ambert 2002, 18). The income gap between single-parent households and married-parents households is a worldwide phenomenon, though it is wider in some countries than in others (more about this later).

While there is general agreement about the association between non-traditional family structure and financial instability, there is less agreement about which causes which and whether other variables also affect the equation. Indeed, there is evidence in support of each of the following four claims:

1. *Family structure is a direct cause of economic advantage or disadvantage*: In the first year after divorce, Canadian women's household income drops by about 50 percent and men's income by about 25 percent (when these figures are adjusted for family size, men's income actually increases slightly, though women's drops by 40 percent). The proportion of Canadian women in poverty "rises from 16% before divorce to 43% after divorce. Even three years after divorce, women's income remains far below what they had during marriage and far below their ex-husbands' current income" (Ambert 2002, 17–18). Estimates based on data from a national longitudinal study of "fragile" U.S. families suggest that marriage to the father of their child could "substantially improve the economic status of unmarried mothers," although it would not bring them up to the level of mothers who were married at the time of the child's birth (Bendheim-Thoman Center 2002, 2).

2. *Economic advantage or disadvantage is a direct cause of family structure*: The same longitudinal study that found that marriage to their child's father improved the mother's financial circumstances also found that fathers' employment status and wages were predictive of their marital status: employment raised the probability that unmarried parents would marry or at least live together with their child, men who had earned $25,000 or more during the past year had more than double the rates of marriage of those who did not, and "an increase of one dollar per hour in wages increases the odds of moving into marriage by five percent" (Bendheim-Thoman Center 2003b, 2). Other studies have found that as a family's economic situation *worsens*, parents are *less* likely to marry or stay married. As well as weakening marital bonds, "persistent poverty and financial distress erode parents' ability to provide consistent involvement,

support, nurturance, empathy, and discipline [and] increase the oc-
currence of coercive and punitive parental behavior" (Demo and
Cox 2000, 881).

3. *The relationship between family instability and financial instability is interactive or reciprocal*: Yet other empirical findings indicate that a change in *either* side of the equation affects the other
   side. While it is true that single parenthood can lower earning capacity and worsen poverty, it is also true that poor parents and job-
   less parents are more likely to divorce and less likely to marry in
   the first place than parents with secure jobs and incomes. All too
   often, this reciprocal process ends in a downward spiral, with low
   income leading to family dissolution leading to even lower income
   and so on since "single parenthood and family instability intensify
   preexisting financial insecurity, throwing some people into economic distress and *increasing the magnitude of poverty for those
   already impoverished*" (Coontz 1997, 140; emphasis added).

4. *The equation is also affected by other variables*: While growing up
   in a single-parent home increases the risk of child poverty, school
   failure, juvenile delinquency, and teen births, it is "just one among
   many factors that put children at risk of failure, just as lack of exercise is only one among many factors that put people at risk for heart
   disease" (Seccombe 2000, 1105). Unmarried parents differ from
   their married counterparts in ways that translate into disparities in
   employment prospects and earning capacities. For example, children in single-parent and cohabiting families are more likely to be
   poor than children in married-couple families because unmarried
   parents tend to be younger and to have less formal education. The
   "fragile families" study is finding out that the childhood disadvantages associated with not living in an intact two-parent family are
   not solely the result of living with unmarried parents but also resulted from the host of economic, health, and other problems that
   deterred them from marrying (Bendheim-Thoman Center 2003a,
   2003b). The income gap between single-mother and two-parent
   families is also exacerbated by 1) women continuing to be paid less
   than men for comparable work and 2) the decline in wages relative
   to prices and the cost of living, necessitating more than one earner
   in most households with children. Coontz estimates that more than

one-third of all *two-parent* families with children would be poor if both parents didn't work and that even if all single mothers were married to the fathers of their children, the economic benefits to children would not be great—"two-thirds of the children who are poor today would *still* be poor" (Coontz 1997, 140).

Another variable that affects the equation is the extent of *public support* for children and families. Although the income gap between single-parent households and married-parents households is a worldwide phenomenon, it is less pronounced in western European nations with universal entitlements like children's allowances, paid parental leaves, and job and income security (Kennedy, Whiteford, and Bradshaw 1996; Smeeding and Torrey 1988).

In sum, the relationship between family structure and economic advantage or disadvantage is strong and clear, but explanations for the relationship are various and contradictory, allowing social scientists and policymakers with very different views about what is good for children and their families to point to empirical evidence in support of their position. As we'll see in the final chapter, this divergence of views has led to very different strategies for strengthening families.

The Divorce Debate[4]

Recent books by two prominent psychologists, both based on extensive clinical data gathered longitudinally, illustrate the divergence of expert opinion about the long-term effects of divorce on children. From her analysis of data on some 1,400 families (roughly half divorced and half not) gathered over the course of twenty-four years, Hetherington (2002) concluded that 75 to 80 percent of children whose parents divorced adapted well enough to the change so that five years later their emotional adjustment and self-image were about the same as children from intact families. In contrast, Wallerstein, Lewis, and Blakeslee (2000) found that the fears and anxieties children developed when their parents divorced often persisted even twenty-five years later, causing these individuals to suffer in adulthood as well as in childhood. Reflecting the deep divisions of opinion among Americans about what harms and helps kids, both books have been praised by some reviewers and vilified by others—Hetherington is accused of being overly optimistic, while Wallerstein is criticized for overgeneralizing from a sample of sixty affluent White families who were referred to her clinic because of their family conflicts.

Debate about the effects of divorce on kids has been prolonged and acrimonious. The most comprehensive syntheses of current knowledge can be found in the very thorough reviews prepared periodically by Paul Amato and various coauthors (1993, 2000, 2001) and by Anne-Marie Ambert (2002), both of whom report that children with divorced parents score lower on measures of academic achievement, psychological adjustment, self-concept, and quality of relations with parents and peers and are more likely to exhibit emotional disorders such as depression and anxiety and behavioral problems, including aggressiveness, hostility, and delinquent acts. Amato (2001) noted, however, that 1) "mean effect sizes tended to be modest," 2) "more methodologically sophisticated studies tended to yield weaker effect sizes," and 3) effect sizes tended to diminish with time and to fluctuate over time in response to economic trends and shifts in social values (355–57).

Ambert and Amato agree that no single factor accounts fully for the negative outcomes for children associated with parental divorce. In addition to the *poverty and economic hardships* associated with marital dissolution (discussed in the previous section of this chapter), the most frequently cited and well documented explanations are the following:

- *Conflict* between parents *prior to and during* the dissolution process. Children whose parents separate or divorce are more likely than other children to have been exposed to parental conflict.
- *Diminished parenting.* As a result of increased stress, parents have less time to interact with their kids, are less nurturing, and use more extreme (either extremely harsh or extremely permissive) or inconsistent modes of discipline.
- *Accumulation of stressful life events*, such as moving, changing schools, and losing contact with friends and relatives, that exacerbate *preexisting* psychological, behavioral, and educational difficulties. Ambert (2002, 23–24) notes, in addition, that parents who divorce are likely to be troubled people who may pass on their difficulties to their children via *genetic inheritance* and kids so predisposed may be especially disturbed by a family crisis like divorce.

Amato (2002, 1282) concludes that divorce is not a panacea, but neither is it inevitably harmful to children. Predicting its effects in advance is difficult since, as another sociologist who has done extensive research on the subject points out, "no one as yet has a formula that can tell parents how much pain they must bear, how much conflict to endure, before ending a marriage becomes the better alternative for themselves and their children" (Cherlin 2000, 68). It has also been pointed out that divorce is just one kind of family change and that it would be useful to compare its impact with that of other major family transitions. Using data from a national longitudinal survey of American youth, Kowaleski-Jones and Dunifon (2004) found, for example, that when characteristics of parents' and children's personality and mental health were controlled, the birth of a sibling had greater impact on the home environment than did parental divorce; that the effects of both differed before, during, and after the event (an impending birth was associated with increased emotional support provided to children, but this support decreased with the arrival of a new sibling); and that the effects differed for boys and girls (during some periods, their parents' divorce was associated with a slight increase in emotional support to girls but not to boys).

Same-Sex-Parent Families

By some estimates, about one-third of the cohabiting couples in the United States are same-sex partners and as many as 14 million children are being raised by at least one parent who is a lesbian or a gay man. Though same-sex marriages have been legalized in some European countries and civil unions of same-sex partners legally recognized in others, such initiatives are more recent in the United States, where they face strong organized opposition.[5] Even though gay or lesbian families are accepted grudgingly or not at all by many Americans, the empirical evidence on families headed by same-sex parents contradicts lingering stereotypical beliefs and fears, showing few differences between children of same-sex parents and other children and suggesting that what differences exist "stem largely from the social stigma attached to homosexuality and consequent social rejection outside the home" (Ambert 2003, 12). The most comprehensive literature reviews (Ambert 2003; Demo and Cox 2000; Patterson 2000) and an assessment of 415 U.S.

families headed by same-sex parents in thirty-four states (Johnson and O'Connor 2003) consistently show the following:

1. No significant differences between children raised by gay or lesbian parents and children raised by straight parents on measures of intelligence, school performance, and peer relationships.
2. No significant differences between children raised by gay or lesbian parents and children raised by straight parents on measures of personality characteristics, emotional adjustment, or behavior problems.
3. No significant differences between children raised by gay or lesbian parents and children raised by straight parents in their likelihood of becoming gay or lesbian. One exception to the general pattern was Ambert's (2003) finding that "young people raised in same-sex-parent families are more tolerant of same-sex experimentation [and] develop a homosexual identity slightly more often than do children in other families," though she concluded that the relative and possibly interactive effects of heredity and learning are "impossible to evaluate at this point" (12).
4. No significant differences between homosexual households with children and heterosexual households with children in family stability. Despite their ambiguous legal status, gay or lesbian couples with children were no more likely than heterosexual couples with children to break up, and male couples were slightly more likely than married couples to have a parent staying at home to care for the children.

Custodial-Grandparent Families

In North American and most European countries, the proportion of three-generation households declined throughout most of the twentieth century. Several studies of American grandparents (Cherlin and Furstenberg 1992 is probably the most comprehensive) found that most wanted to enjoy their grandkids without being responsible for them and that few took an active role in their upbringing and discipline, leading the authors to characterize the preferred grandparent–grandchild relationship as "recreational." However, examination of intergenerational relations in Western industrialized countries over the past half century also indicates that, contrary to the stereotype of older people as a financial drain on their younger relatives, grandparents are more likely to provide material support than to receive it. In addition, a significant and steadily growing number of grandparents are assuming primary, sometimes sole responsibility for raising their grandchildren. In the United States, about 15 percent of all grandmothers have been the major caretaker of one or more grandchildren for six months or more. The number of children living in the home of a grandparent doubled between 1970 and 2000 (from 2.2 million to 4.4 million), and over a third of these children were being raised solely by their grandparents. Major precipitating factors in the creation of "no-parent" families are the parents' young age (many are themselves children), drug addiction, divorce, or desertion (Bureau of Statistics 2003, 42; Kropf and Burnette 2003; Lugaila and Overturf 2004; Mitchell 2000, 214–15; Pruchno and Johnson 1996).

Research shows both benefits and costs to custodial grandparents. On the positive side, "grandparents who are raising their grandchildren consistently report that the experience adds joy and meaning to their lives and provides them with companionship and a purposeful social and familial role. In addition, their caregiving role serves an important kin-keeping function for their family and the larger society" (Kropf and Burnette 2003, 363). On the other hand, several studies have documented negative effects on custodial grandparents' physical health (including increased risk of heart disease, hypertension, and diabetes) and psychological well-being (including increases in stress, depression, and insomnia); diminished opportunities for meaningful, sustained social relationships outside the family; and legal and financial difficulties. Unless grandparents are legally recognized as primary caregivers by the states where they live, they often cannot register children for school or get medical care or government assistance. Kids living in a grandparent-headed household without a parent present were twice as likely as kids in three-generation households to be living in poverty and much less likely to be covered by any kind of health insurance (Fields 2003; Kropf and Burnette 2003; Lee et al. 2003).

There is little comparable research on the effects of custodial grand-parenting on *children*, though one study found that kids reared solely by their grandparents were not significantly different from kids raised in traditional families except in academic performance (Pruchno and John-son 1996, 3). Since grandparents generally become primary caretakers when families are already in trouble, difficulties experienced by the kids may reflect the family stress and disorder that prompted the grandpar-ents to step in and educators' lack of knowledge and experience in deal-ing with surrogate parents more than the grandparents' deficient child rearing (Dannison and Smith 2003).

KIDS' PERSPECTIVES ON ALTERNATIVE FAMILY LIFESTYLES

A burgeoning number of studies, especially in the United Kingdom, provide empirical evidence congruent with the basic premise of this book that, given the opportunity, many kids are willing and able to speak for themselves. We'll consider here a few studies in which children re-port on their experiences in traditional and alternative families and about how they cope with major family transitions.

Children's construction of family and kinship was the topic of a series of studies in which kids between the ages of seven and fourteen living in several different London neighborhoods met in ethnically diverse groups to talk about their own daily lives at home and school. One of the tasks was to assess five hypothetical families described in vignettes, or brief descriptions, illustrating a range of contemporary family lifestyles. Younger children were also asked to draw their own families, and older participants were given diaries to complete at home over the next week (O'Brien, Alldred, and Jones 1996). Most of the children had definite opinions about what constituted a "proper family." The married-couple-and-children-living-together model was the most strongly endorsed of the family vignettes—most of the participants felt that it takes children to make a family and that the parents should be married. They were di-vided on the relevance of consanguinity. Single-mother-and-child households were generally considered the best substitute for a two-par-ent family; mothers and children were felt to be emotionally close be-cause "they have the same blood." But the ties of blood may become secondary in the face of parental absence or disregard. A nine-year-old boy said he didn't count his father as family because "he can't even remember our birthdays." In a lively group discussion on what they would do if their mother became seriously ill and "you knew where your father was," a boy who rarely saw his father maintained that he would phone for an ambulance but not for his dad.

The group discussions revealed, however, that "individual opinions were not totally fixed. Children could persuade each other to change position, particularly after listening to accounts where other had relevant experience, [and they] used the group to examine the boundaries of acceptable parenting." The researchers concluded that "children, like adults, can hold contradictory principles of what makes a family" and that in the wake of breakdowns in traditional family structures, children are already developing new survival strategies to accommodate them (O'Brien et al. 1996, 94).

Kids' perspectives on life after parental separation or divorce is the subject of a review of empirical studies, mainly from English-speaking countries (Pryor and Rodgers 2001, chap. 4) and an in-depth study of postdivorce family life based on a series of qualitative interviews with 117 British children and youth aged four to twenty-two conducted in their homes or at another location of their choice (Smart, Neale, and Wade 2001). The most frequent initial reaction to their parents' separation was sadness; subsequent feelings ranged from anger to bewilderment to ambivalence to relief. Children who had witnessed severe parental conflict and domestic violence were especially likely to experience conflicting emotions. For some, the separation experience was mainly negative; for others, it provided an opportunity to "escape from the war zone." Asked what he considered the best postdivorce household arrangement, one teenager suggested that "the least disturbance would be if one of the parents ran away!" A nine-year-old girl stated frankly that her father had caused so much trouble that she was happier without him around. On the other hand, a number of respondents felt that their relationships with both parents were better now than before the divorce (Smart et al. 2001, 70–76, 120).

A major complaint was lack of communication from adults. The studies reviewed by Pryor and Rodgers (2001) showed that few children felt they were adequately prepared. Only about a quarter even knew about the separation in advance, and most received the news in the form of a blunt statement with little or no explanation of why their parents were separating. In this respect, British, Australian, and New Zealand kids did not differ markedly from a sample of Botswana kids of separated or divorced parents, nearly all of whom felt that their mothers had not provided enough information about the separation; that their views, in particular about contact with their fathers, had not been sought; and that, in general, they had had no choice but to submit to arrangements made *for* them by adults (Maundeni 2002).

The inconveniences that followed many family breakups, in particular, commuting back and forth from one parent's home to the other, soon became routine for most kids. A sixteen-year-old girl said, "I'm just so used to it I can hardly imagine it any other way." A nine-year-old girl who spent half of each week with each parent even felt that "it must be a bit *boring* for children who don't have separated parents." A sixteen-year-old girl who traveled to Holland with her hockey team was surprised that some of her teammates were homesick. She claimed not to miss either parent; not having them both around had, she said, made her more independent than most of her friends (Smart et al. 2001, 81, 127, 135–40). A New Zealand girl reported that she became the "man of the house" after her father left, learning how to change fuses and do other household repairs (Pryor and Rodgers 2001, 118). The main complaint about coparenting was that spending "quality time" with each parent could leave kids less time for favorite activities or make them feel guilty about hanging out with friends rather than keeping their parents company.

Despite the pervasive lack of good communication, many kids in the studies reviewed were influencing the divorce process as well as being influenced by it. Having learned to manage difficult emotions and situations, some "began to question their parents' attitudes, values and expectations," and having begun "to think for themselves about their place in the family, it is not surprising that they should want to have more say in matters that affect them" (Smart et al. 2001, 82–83). Not that their concerns were always attended to in any of the countries studied. Smart et al. (2001, 160–68) note that policy decisions and legal proceedings in the United Kingdom are dominated by judges, lawyers, social workers, and other adult "experts," while most of the children involved preferred to keep family problems within the family and did not appreciate having to share their personal problems and feelings with people they considered outsiders. The authors' warning against a "slide into increased intervention" and "enforced intimacy" with strangers is mirrored in a New Zealand girl's objection to the compulsory counseling imposed on her: "I felt manipulated into saying things I didn't really feel [and] almost violated by the way I was having to reveal myself . . . there was a whole lot of unnecessary trauma associated with it" (Pryor and Rodgers 2001, 120).

CONCLUSIONS

If they agree on little else, sociologists concur that the past half century has seen fundamental changes in family structure and relationships, that these changes are occurring throughout the world and are likely to continue, that in many societies there is no longer a single dominant family form, and that a majority or a substantial minority of kids will experience a variety of family settings as they pass through childhood and adolescence. A major point of disagreement is whether these trends benefit or harm children.

On one side are those who emphasize the harmful effects of diversity and instability, comparing contemporary families unfavorably with the supposedly stronger families of the past. Proponents of this view point to research documenting the advantages to children of growing up in an intact family headed by two biological parents, though most recognize that family stability is linked to job security and adequate income and acknowledge that "there is not yet a proven approach for building strong marriages, particularly for disadvantaged unmarried couples" (Moore et al. 2002, 7).

On the other side are those who view change and diversity as inevitable and not necessarily detrimental to children's welfare. They believe that promising new forms of childhood are emerging in the twenty-first century, that dilution of parental power and more open communication between kids and parents are indicators of a desirable democratization of the family, and that new forms of family life may complement rather than conflict with the married-parents-multiple-children model. Rather than defining kids who spend at least part of their childhoods with stepparents, single parents, gay or lesbian parents, or grandparents as victims of social change, why not view them as social pioneers from whom we have much to learn?

Paul Amato (2000) observes that both of these views are partly true but that both "represent one-sided accentuations of reality. The increase in marital instability has not brought society to the brink of chaos, but neither has it led to a golden age of freedom and self-actualization." Every kind of change in family structure and functioning probably "benefits some individuals, leads others to experience temporary decrements in well-being that improve with time, and forces others on a downward cycle from which they might never fully recover" (1282). Pryor and Rodgers (2001) also refer to an unattainable golden age but one in the mythical past. Their conclusion: since we can neither return to that bygone age nor halt social change in the present, "our energies are better used in supporting children and their parents in diverse family structures" (277).

In the still rare instances in which their views are sought, kids have plenty to say about what constitutes a proper family and a satisfying family life, how to deal with parents' problems and weaknesses, and how to weather major family transitions. Taking children's knowledge seriously would, of course, require a fundamental shift in policymaking and professional practice, replacing the current adult ideological model, "based on theorizing a 'common good' for all children and then imposing it in a downwards fashion," with a more "ground-up, research based process" in which kids' perspectives and preferences are taken into account (Smart et al. 2001, 123–24).

NOTES

1. This term was coined by two Italian demographers (Golini and Silvestrini 1997) to describe the situation in "aging" European countries where birthrates have dropped to record lows.

2. Morgan (2003) offers a biosocial explanation for the fertility decline: "having few children and heavily investing in them 'fits' well with our evolutionary inheritance and with the neural wiring in our and our children's brains" (593; see discussion of biosocial and genetic perspectives in chapter 2).

3. The diversification and fluidity of family forms has occurred so recently and rapidly that consensus on terminology has not yet been reached, and es-

timates of the numbers of children living in various types of households depend on how they are defined and measured. Definitions of family composition and methods used to compute their statistical frequency rates change over time and vary from one country to another, sometimes in different parts of the same country.

Several new categories were added to the 2000 U.S. census to reflect the increased complexity of American households, allowing a more nuanced representation of children's living arrangements but making comparisons with earlier time periods more difficult. Yet even the most recent census calculations do not distinguish the percentage of married-parents households that contain stepparents as opposed to continuously married parents, and despite the dramatic increase in families headed by unmarried partners (up 71 percent during the 1990s), this category does not differentiate between children living with single parents and those living with unmarried partners or tell us whether unmarried partners are of the same or opposite sex. Divorce rates, which vary from one country to another, are sensitive to changes in a population's age distribution (e.g., the number of divorces tends to go down as older people become proportionately more numerous even if younger people are divorcing at a high rate). Moreover, "an unknown number of couples separate but never divorce. This type of conjugal dissolution may be as real as a divorce, yet it does not appear in divorce statistics" (Ambert 2002, 2–4). On the other hand, a given category of family structure may encompass a diversity of family lifestyles reflecting differences in social class, race or ethnicity, and other characteristics of family members and with differing consequences for the children involved (Demo, Allen, and Fine 2000, chaps. 8–10).

Finally, some respondents may misunderstand or be reluctant to answer questions about their household arrangements. In the United States, fewer people identified themselves as cohabitors (about 3 million) than were classified as such by the Census Bureau (over 4 million), perhaps because of the social disapproval associated with this type of family (Seltzer 2000, 1259–60).

We are indebted to Dr. Overturf for helping us find our way around the 2000 census and for patiently answering our many questions about changes in family composition.

4. Increase in marital dissolution is a worldwide trend. The U.S. divorce rate, long the world's highest, was surpassed in the late twentieth century by Russia and some of the former Soviet republics. Demographic analyses suggest that the rate may have peaked in some industrialized nations, including the United States and the United Kingdom, though it continues to rise, sometimes sharply, in other industrialized and many developing nations (Neft and Levine 1997; Seager 1997). Ambert (2002) points out that the rise and fall of divorce

rates depend on a number of factors, including demographic trends as well as changing lifestyles and social values.

5. At this writing, the first same-sex marriages are being performed in a few states or municipalities, and others have enacted legislation enabling same-sex partners to register as "domestic partners" with some but not all the rights and obligations of married couples. These developments are strongly opposed by religious conservatives who are pressing for a constitutional amendment banning same-sex marriage. Three states (Florida, Mississippi, and Utah) still prohibit adoption by gays, though the Florida ban is being challenged in a federal court.

5

KIDS AT HOME: SOCIALIZATION AND THE ALLOCATION OF FAMILY RESOURCES

The way I see it you can only ever have one person that's . . . like your dad, or your mum, doing dad or mum things.

—Twelve-year-old (England)

My fathers, you must shape the vision of tomorrow, but in order for that vision to become a reality, you must rededicate yourselves to a new beginning. Go back to your families. Go raise and teach your children.

—Ayinde Jean-Baptiste, age twelve, from speech delivered at the 1995 Million Man March, Washington, D.C.

Parents are the products of the children born to them.

—Julius Segal and Herbert Yahraes

In their definitive work on intergenerational relations, Alice and Peter Rossi explain the unique qualities of the relationship between children and their parents as follows: "No other human relationship has as long a history as that between a parent and a child, [and] no other adult figures are as important to the qualities children will bring to their adulthood as parents are, from the shared genes to personality characteristics, status attainment, basic values, and perhaps, the parenting styles the children bring to the rearing of their own children" (Rossi and Rossi 1990, 252). The same basic point was made even more succinctly by the boy, quoted at the beginning of this chapter, who said there's no one like your parents for "doing dad and mum things." In this chapter, we'll examine this unique relationship through a review of recent research on the family socialization process, on the way in which household resources are allocated among the various family members, and on the contributions made by children to their households.

THE TWO-WAY PROCESS OF FAMILY SOCIALIZATION

As we saw in chapter 2, functional theorists identified socialization as the major task of the family, and interactionist theorists later argued that socialization is not just something that is "done" to children but is an interactive process that affects the socializers as well as the socialized. Through their efforts to raise their children in accordance with their values and aspirations, parents are themselves changed. And, as we'll see, kids alter their parents' lives from—indeed even before—birth, and by the time they are able to express themselves verbally, they are likely to characterize their relations with their parents as interdependent rather than unidirectional and to define themselves as providers as well as recipients of care and support. In this section, we'll examine both sides of the socialization process: on the one hand, *child rearing* as practiced by parents and other adults, and, on the other, the reciprocal process, which we'll call *parent rearing*.

Child Rearing

Raising children is both a private and a public task. The day-to-day care of most infants and young children is carried on in the relative privacy of the family, where parents "make literally thousands of choices that affect the development of their children and their well-being" (Alwin 2001, 101). At the same time, families are expected to instill in children their society's basic values, attitudes, and modes of behavior; as Small (2001) has noted, the way we bring up children "often reflects more about our social history and our folkways and our traditions than what babies and children might need and expect" (3).

Until recently, advice to parents was communicated mainly by word of mouth, from relatives and neighbors (especially older females), religious leaders, and other members of the community believed to have special knowledge or wisdom. By the mid-twentieth century, however, traditional ideas and practices were increasingly rendered obsolete by the radical societal changes precipitated by industrialization and urbanization. Cut off from familiar sources of advice and assistance, often lacking practical experience in the care of infants and young children, modern parents became increasingly dependent on new kinds of experts, many of whom dispensed their advice through the rapidly developing mass media. Dr. Benjamin Spock's *Baby and Child Care*, the most popular child-rearing manual in history, first published in 1946 and now in its eighth edition, has been translated into over forty languages and has sold over 40 million copies around the world. More recent modes of dissemination include television programs hosted by the authors of bestselling manuals and websites where parents can offer advice as well as receive it (Boocock 1999; Grant 1998; Hulbert 2003).

A number of sociologists have noted changes in parental aspirations and expectations during the past fifty years. Comparing American research from the early to late twentieth century, Alwin posits that the most significant shift is in the direction of greater emphasis on children's *autonomy* and less emphasis upon their *obedience* to adult and institutional authorities. He believes that this shift in parental attitudes reflects "fundamental changes in our culture, in the expression of our basic values, and in some areas a clear shift in values" (Alwin 2001, 100). The German sociologist Jurgen Zinnecker (2001) has hypothesized a similar trend in parent–child relations that he describes as a shift away from *coercion* and toward *negotiation* and *individualization* and that he views as part of the more general process of *modernization*. These shifts in social values and parental aspirations are reflected in the most widely read child-rearing manuals. For example, later editions of Spock's *Baby and Child Care* favor a more lenient handling of misbehavior than earlier editions. A comparative analysis of the content of best-selling manuals in the United States, France, Japan, and the People's Republic of China published during the last decades of the twentieth century revealed a kind of globalization of expert opinion.

Despite cross-national and within-nation differences in some of the details of recommended parenting practices, endorsements of open expression of affection, flexible child care routines sensitive to the character and needs of the individual child, and less punitive modes of discipline appear to be worldwide trends. By the 1990s, the majority of experts in all four countries recommended against spanking—though in each country there was also vigorous resistance by conservatives who espoused stronger parental authority and stricter discipline (Boocock 1999).

The negative effects of harsh modes of discipline have also been investigated by historians (e.g., Greven 1991) and sociologists (e.g., Strauss 1994), and a recent review of six decades of psychological research on the effects of corporal punishment concluded that the risk of subsequent aggressive or antisocial behavior and mental health problems far outweighed the short-term benefit of "instant obedience" (Gershoff 2002). Not surprisingly, surveys of children (e.g., Galinsky 1999) have found that those whose parents used the harshest modes of discipline are the most likely to express negative feelings toward them. Yet anthropologists remind us that discipline is a product of culture. While slapping, spanking, yelling, and other negative punishments don't appear to work well—in fact, they tend to beget more bad behavior—with many Western or westernized kids, there are societies in which corporal punishment or ridicule are normative and others in which punishment of any sort is unknown (Small 2001, 154–59).

Changes in parenting practices may reflect technological innovations as well as cultural beliefs and social and economic trends. In a recent article by a University of Colorado professor of pediatrics, it was reported that while more than half the children in the world are toilet trained at about age one, in the United States, toilet training tends to be delayed until age two or even three. Why? Because the widespread availability and affordability of disposable diapers in combination with the growing number of busy dual-career families has reduced incentives for earlier toilet training. The author also noted that delayed toilet training has been wholeheartedly endorsed by those who benefit from it financially, in particular, companies that manufacture disposable diapers and other baby paraphernalia (Schmitt 2004).

Is There a "Best" Way to Raise Children?   In addition to the authors of child-rearing manuals, psychologists and other scholars of human development have created a substantial body of research on the outcomes of alternative modes of child rearing. During the past three decades, a high degree of consensus has been reached among North American and western European researchers on the benefits of a particular mode of parenting, generally termed *authoritative*. Authoritative (not to be confused with *authoritarian*) parenting is generally characterized as combining the following:

1. A high level of *support*, reflected in such behaviors as helping children with everyday problems, praising their accomplishments, and showing affection
2. A high level of *monitoring*, reflected in such behaviors as supervising children's activities, keeping track of their school work and their friendships, and requiring conformity to family and communities norms
3. *Noncoercive* methods of discipline (such as discussing the consequences of misbehavior) rather than harsh and punitive methods

A number of empirical studies have produced empirical evidence that authoritative parenting is more effective than more *authoritarian, permissive,* or *neglectful* modes of parenting in achieving desirable personality, academic, and behavioral outcomes for children. (A concise summary of this research can be found Demo and Cox 2000, 880–82.)

Some scholars have expressed doubts about the universal appropriateness of the authoritative model on the grounds that high levels of parental warmth and support and avoidance of harsh punishment may work for White, married parents living in middle-class neighborhoods with ample social capital but that poor parents living in dangerous neighborhoods need to exercise greater control and stronger modes of discipline in order to ensure their children's safety and success. This criticism was explored in a study by Amato and Fowler (2002) of 13,017 adults and 3,808 children chosen randomly from a national sample of American families and households and interviewed in 1987–1988 and again in 1992–1994. At least in this sample, the effectiveness of authoritative parenting did not vary significantly by family structure or parents' race, ethnicity, education, income, or gender, leading the authors to conclude that "a core of parenting practices appears to be linked with positive outcomes for children across diverse family contexts" (703).

The claims made for authoritative parenting have been more fundamentally challenged by scholars who argue that child-rearing practices are *socially constructed*, resting on "complex, changing, and competing ideas about the essential nature of children and their appropriate place in society" (Davis 1994, 133). Jerome Kagan's reviews of biological and psychological research led him to conclude that 1) the absolute needs of human infants are few (adequate protection from hunger, cold, disease, and severe physical pain), 2) those needs can be met in a variety of ways, and 3) there is little or no scientific support for much of the advice given to parents by child-rearing experts:

> *Children do not require any specific actions from adults in order to develop optimally*. There is no good evidence to indicate that children must have a certain amount or schedule of cuddling, kissing, spanking, holding or deprivation of privileges in order to become gratified and productive adults. The child does have some psychological needs, but there is no fixed list of parental behaviors that can be counted on to fill these critical requirements. (Kagan 1980, 429–30)

Of course, what parents actually *do* may diverge from their stated beliefs about good parenting as well as from expert opinion. Several surveys carried out during the 1990s reported that American parents continued to spank their children even if they were aware that most child-rearing experts advised against it. In one survey, 90 percent said that they did; in another, 42 percent of the mothers of children younger than four said they has done so during the previous week (Halle 2002, 14; Strauss 1994). However, few studies are based on direct observation of what actually goes on in children's homes. (Most of the research comparing authoritative and other modes of parenting depends on what parents *said* they did.) We'll devote the next section to a recently published study in which the researchers, by overcoming what Hulbert (2003) calls "the difficulty of finding out what is happening behind those closed doors" (7), gathered a unique body of data on current American child-rearing practices.

A Rare Look inside the Home   In *Unequal Childhoods*, Annette Lareau (2003) presents detailed ethnographic accounts of nine third-grade children and their families, selected from a total sample of 88 children (thirty-six middle- to upper-middle-class children who attended school in a small suburban district and twenty-six working-class children and twenty-six children whose families were supported by public assistance and/or sporadic employment who attended school in a large urban district). The sample contained roughly equal numbers of Blacks and Whites and girls and boys. Lareau and her associates observed the kids and their families for extended periods of time in their homes and accompanied them on their daily rounds of outside activities.[1] The book's central theme is the persistence of social class–based differences in family relationships, modes of child rearing, organization of daily life, and relations between the family and the school and other social institutions and the extent to which these differences not only shape children's behavior but also determine their chances of success in school and later life. Lareau distinguishes between two modes of child rearing: the "concerted cultivation" model, characteristic of middle- to upper-middle-class child rearing, and the "natural growth" model, characteristic of working- to lower-class child rearing. Features of the concerted cultivation model include the following:

- Organization of family life around children's extensive schedules of school and extracurricular activities. Even the latter are adult organized and chosen for their educational value.
- Encouragement of children's verbal fluency through interaction with adults in which they are allowed, indeed encouraged, to express their own opinions and can expect to have their views taken seriously.
- Precedence of children's scheduled activities over kinship time and ties. Relations with siblings are not close and are often acrimonious.
- Close monitoring of homework by parents, who also intervene frequently and assertively at school on behalf of their children.

In contrast, the *natural growth* model is characterized by:

- Greater separation of children's and adults' spheres and more "free-flowing" time when kids can create their own amusements and set their own pace in pursuing them.

- Stricter discipline and more frequent resort to physical punishment. Obedience and respect toward older people is expected and generally obtained. Kids may display considerable verbal fluency with friends, but they mainly *listen* to adults.
- More frequent contact and closer and warmer relationships with kin of all generations. Sibling relationships are generally close and cordial.
- Parental deference toward teachers, little interference with school affairs, and few demands made on behalf of their children.

Since the sample contained approximately equal numbers of Black and White families in each of the social class categories, Laureau was able to examine the intersection of race and class. Regardless of their present class status, all the African American parents had themselves experienced racism and were vigilant for signs of racial discrimination against their children—a problem that White parents were seldom obliged to confront. Yet in this particular sample, social class appeared to account for more of the differences in children's daily lives and behavior than race. "Black and white middle-class children were given enormous amounts of individualized attention, with their parents organizing their own time around their children's leisure activities, [and] it was the middle-class children, Black and white, who squabbled and fought with their siblings and talked back to their parents," behavior that was "simply not tolerated in working-class and poor families, Black or white" (Lareau 2003, 241).

Each of the two child-rearing models had advantages and disadvantages. On the one hand, "daily life for working-class and poor children is slower paced, less pressured, and less structured than for their middle- and upper-middle-class counterparts," who spend considerable time in transit and often seem to rush from one scheduled activity to the next, only to wait around for their share of a busy coach's attention, for their parents to pick them up, or for their siblings to finish *their* team practice (Lareau 2003, 76). Despite the middle- and upper-middle-class preoccupation with educational enrichment and personal development, the long stretches of unsupervised free time available to less privileged kids may be more conducive to creativity, initiative, and enjoyment. The fierce competition between siblings and the children's right to question adult decisions could make middle-class family life exhausting, and one can share Lareau's regard for working-class families under constant financial strain who were nevertheless "raising children who are polite and re-spectful and do not whine, needle, or badger their parents" and who have deep and abiding ties with their grandparents and other kin (160).

What Lareau and her associates learned, however, is that the accom-plishments of the working-class and poor families did not translate into advantages in the larger society, while the skills and experiences ac-quired by middle- and upper-middle-class kids through dialoging with their parents and from their often hectic round of team sports, music lessons, and performances gave them confidence and ease in dealing with adults and societal institutions. Although *all* the parents were deeply concerned about their kids' education and wanted to see them succeed in school, the concerted cultivation model of child rearing was more congruent with professional educational ideology and standards, and the middle-class moms' skills in networking and information pro-cessing enabled them to work the educational system to their kids' ad-vantage. The lower-status parents' deference and their very lack of de-mands were defined by school personnel as a lack of interest and involvement in their children's schooling. Poor parents even feared—not unrealistically in some cases—that they would be "turned in" to "the authorities" and have their kids taken away from them, a fear that afflu-ent parents never expressed (Lareau 2003, 228–32).

Unequal Childhoods, an example of ethnographic research at its best, illustrates both the strengths and the weaknesses of this methodology. The vividly detailed portraits of a memorable cast of characters make compelling reading. We come to care about them even if we don't always agree with what they say and do. The data also fill in a major gap in the quantitative research documenting the wide and widening gulf, on every indicator of education, occupational, and financial success, between those on the higher and lower rungs of the social ladder. By attending to the minutiae of everyday social interactions, Lareau is able to identify the *process* by which higher- and lower-status children are placed on differ-ent paths that diverge ever more over time. The study also offers an un-conventional view of childhood and child rearing. If her conclusions are correct, they call into question some of the assumptions underlying mainstream research on social status and expert advice on child rearing, for example, about the superiority of middle-class modes of child rearing and the deficits of lower-class families, about the universal powerlessness of children (the middle- to upper-middle-class kids in Lareau's sample did not behave like subordinates in many of their dealings with parents and other adults), and about the inevitability of overscheduled kids and frenetic family life.

On the other hand, Lareau's sample was small, and neither the children nor the communities were randomly selected. To what extent can we generalize from these findings? Would we find the same patterns in other communities or other regions of the United States? How do we know there is not something that sets these children (or some of them) apart from other children or American children in general? The members of the research team were chosen to ensure racial and gender diversity, but none of them had children of their own at the time. How much did this affect what they saw and heard?[2] Only more studies in other settings and employing a variety of research methods will allow a fair assessment of Lareau's provocative hypotheses.

One such study carried out at the same time as Lareau's but using a larger sample and different modes of data gathering offers some theoretical and empirical support for its basic argument. For a comparative analysis of community *social capital*, Bould (2003; introduced in chapter 1) gathered quantitative and qualitative data from 291 neighborhoods in the northeastern and mid-Atlantic United States. Suburban neighborhoods that contained all or disproportionate numbers of White, upper-income, two-parent nuclear families were likely to be rich in social capital. Though few had extended kin in the household or even in the neighborhood, informal networks of neighbors looked out for each others' kids, and there was ready access to public and private services in cases of emergency. In contrast, in the urban neighborhoods where most lower-income and disproportionate numbers of racial minority and single-parent families lived, residents had limited access either to informal social capital or to public or private emergency services. In fact, given the lack of law enforcement and other means of controlling disorder, Bould classified some of these neighborhoods as having *negative social capital*. In such neighborhoods, "parents must be entirely self-sufficient in order to protect their children. They must create a 'family as fortress' style of parenting" (57). The two quite different patterns of daily life identified by Bould in a larger sample of communities paralleled the class-related modes of child rearing and family lifestyle posited by Lareau. That Lareau had to draw her higher-status and lower-status families from different school districts is also congruent with the differences in neighborhood social capital discovered by Bould.

Parent Rearing

Defining children as active participants in their own upbringing challenges the traditional assumption that socialization is largely a process of internalizing adults' knowledge and skills. As the primary agents in their children's social and emotional development, parents (especially mothers) are responsible for any problems their kids may have. As its title suggests, this assumption is challenged in an important book, Anne-Marie Ambert's *The Effect of Children on Parents* (1992, revised edition 2000). Reversing the usual way of thinking about cause and effect in family relationships, Ambert examines the evidence for children's influences in multiple areas of parents' lives. Citing a study of newborns in which it was found that the babies initiated four out of five of the mother–infant interactions observed, she argues that the shaping of parents' behavior by their kids begins at birth. Rather than concluding, as many do, that "children who exhibit an overly dependent personality do so because their parents treat them restrictively," isn't it equally plausible "to conclude that parents treat them restrictively *because* the children are dependent?" Assuming that abusive parental behavior causes premature babies to cry more than other babies ignores the possibility that "fussy children or babies who cry a lot are more likely to be targeted than are placid infants who do not arouse their parents' negative behavior" (17–19). Similar examples have been provided by other scholars. The correlation "between severe punishment and children's aggressiveness is often taken to show that harsh discipline produces aggressive children; yet it could show instead that aggressive children evoke harsh child-rearing methods in their parents" (Skolnick 1978, 54–55). Although childhood autism was long thought to be caused by emotionally "cold" mothers, "many years and large number of wrongly stigmatized mothers later, it was concluded that cause and effect had been confused" (de Winter 1997, 12).

Over time, Ambert concludes, being a parent can affect one's health, income and career trajectory, values and attitudes (they tend to become more conservative), feelings of control over one's life (they generally decline), and life plans (they tend to become more changeable and un-predictable) and the quality of interpersonal relations within and out-side the family.

In the late 1990s, a new round in the never-ending debate over who affects whom opened with the publication of a highly controversial book titled *The Nurture Assumption* (Harris 1998), in which the author up-dated and expanded a lengthy review of literature that had been pub-lished in a prestigious psychological journal (Harris 1995) and had won a prize from the American Psychological Association. Countering widely accepted psychological theories that explained children's development and developmental problems as a result of how they were treated by their parents, Harris contends that most of the research purporting to show the power of parental nurture fails to establish the direction of em-pirical causation. Her interpretation of the same research is that parent-ing styles are as likely to be the effect as the cause of a particular child's temperament and that parents' influence on their children is limited at best, especially when compared with effects of heredity and children's peer groups. The qualities, physical and psychic, that children are born with can strongly influence how their parents treat them (see discussion of genetic theories in chapter 2). And on a wide range of attitudes and behaviors, kids tend over time to become more like their friends and less like their parents (we'll come back to this issue in the next chapter).

Because the very idea of children socializing adults is still strange to most adults (and threatening to many), there is little research examining the process by which this occurs. In the rare instances when they are consulted, children claim to do a fair amount of *parent rearing*, and most see nothing unnatural about this. A national survey of American third through twelfth graders found the following:

- 17 percent said they take care of their fathers often or very often.
- 26 percent said they take care of their fathers sometimes.
- 29 percent said they take care of their mothers often or very often.
- 24 percent said they take care of their mothers sometimes.

Through experience, these kids learned how to relieve their parents' stress and fatigue by listening to their complaints, telling them funny stories, or helping with housecleaning and cooking (Galinsky 1999,

240–42). Similarly, most of the British kids interviewed by Smart, Neale, and Wade (2001)

> did not find being supportive of parents an onerous, anxiety-laden or bur-
> densome activity, but regarded it as an everyday family practice and ex-
> pression of relatedness. Interestingly, children often spoke of parents in
> affectionate terms that mirrored those of a parent speaking of a child.
> They expressed concern about whether a parent was eating properly (es-
> pecially in the case of fathers living alone) and whether they were taking
> proper care of themselves. (75)

Children have on occasion written their own manuals offering other kids advice on how to deal with common parent-rearing problems. In one such manual, titled *The Kids' Book about Parents* and written by eleven- to fourteen-year-old students at a Massachusetts school with the assistance of one of their teachers, readers are advised to develop a realistic attitude about the things parents do "that are wrong and that drive us crazy." Some parental flaws can be corrected "with a little bit of help from kids, along with the will to change from the parents," but flaws that are part of a parent's basic personality cannot, and the authors recommend learning to live with them. One confided, "I have never dealt with any of my parents' flaws because I don't think they will change, and that's part of their charm" (Students at Fayerweather Street School and Rofes 1984, 23–24).

The students offer thoughtful suggestions for coping with even the most serious family problems, including parents who are drunk, neglectful, or abusive. Most of their advice, however, is about resolving the mundane difficulties experienced by all kids. They provide a list of common warning signals that parents are stressed or unhappy: they overeat, chain-smoke, stare blankly at the TV, slam doors, snap at everyone, clean excessively or not enough, or drive too fast and yell at other drivers (Students at Fayerweather Street School and Rofes 1984, 93). Two general strategies are offered for dealing with stressed or unhappy parents. One is simply to stay out of their way until they get over it. The other, more proactive strategy (which mirrors advice to parents on how to handle a cranky child) is to try to improve their mood by

> doing anything they ask (especially lots of chores), being cheery and opti-
> mistic with them, and not losing your patience with them. It's a good idea

not to ask them silly questions or bother them with little matters. You might do some nice things for them without being asked—take the dog for a walk, bring them coffee in bed, make them some food, and take care of younger siblings. Some parents just need to be told to go to their room and lie down. (93–94)

HOW FAMILIES ALLOCATE SCARCE RESOURCES

According to the adult ideological perspective, parents make sacrifices for their children, and family life is organized around their needs. Withholding valuable family resources from children is unthinkable, except perhaps in very poor or "backward" societies. However, data from several British studies reveal that, contrary to common belief (or what we would *like* to believe), inequitable distribution of family resources is not uncommon and children are sometimes the losers. Even regarding something as basic as food, O'Brien (1995) found that the kids' share was often of lesser quantity and quality than the adults' share. In an effort not to "waste" expensive food, some mothers routinely gave children smaller servings or none at all. When family finances were tight, eggs and cheese, whole fish, and the more expensive cuts of meat were often reserved for adult males, while children were given more breakfast cereal, fish fingers, crisps, and baked beans.

Space

In a mid-twentieth-century survey of the housing situation of Swedish families conducted by the Nobel Prize–winning economist Alva Myrdal, it was found that 60 percent of all children lived in overcrowded dwellings compared to 47 percent of the total population, leading Myrdal to conclude that, intentionally or not, Swedish housing standards were lower for children than for adults. In the late 1980s, similar calculations made for a European Centre for Social Welfare Policy and Research study of nineteen countries showed that while the general housing situation had improved considerably in the intervening half century, there was still "a striking difference between children and adults" in the likelihood of living in substandard housing (Qvortrup 1990, 91–92).

O'Brien's findings regarding kids' access to space in the late twentieth century parallel findings from research on European and American cities earlier in the century. Because of a scarcity of indoor space at home, boys from poor families met their friends, organized their games, and earned money on the streets, though girls, "whatever their social background, had more limited and controlled access to outside space. They were more likely to be sheltered, protected, chaperoned and kept under surveillance than boys" (O'Brien 1995, 510–11). Over the century, children's access to outdoor play space has been increasingly restricted because of a loss of open spaces to building construction, increased traffic congestion, and the growing dangers (or perceived dangers) of street crime and violence (historical data on American city children's play and play space can be found in Children's Aid Society 1978; Dargan and Zeitlin 1990; Nasaw 1985).

In affluent societies and households, children's access to indoor space tends to increase with age. Having a room of one's own has become normative for middle- and upper-class children and is increasing among working-class children as well. As noted in the box in chapter 1, teenagers' bedrooms in North America and western Europe are likely to be equipped with TVs and cable hookups, phones or phone extensions, personal computers, and video games. A comparative study of children's media use in eleven European countries and in Israel (Livingstone and Bovill 2001) posits that the extension of "personal space" via electronic modes of communication, by enabling kids to entertain themselves and each other in virtual as well as in real time and space, is not only affecting family relationships but also producing a new peer culture that can transcend community or even national boundaries. The designers of a national survey of American kids from ages two through eighteen conclude that children's personal space is characterized by a superabundance of media and an absence of adults. Though they now have access to "more media with more channels or outlets within each medium, offering more (and more varied) content, more vividly than even the most 'outlandish' mid-century science-fiction novels once predicted," a combination of technological and social changes may be creating environments in which kids "use these media largely independent of adult supervision or comment—indeed, often in the absence of adult awareness" (Roberts and Foehr 2004, 5).

Time

The most comprehensive quantitative study of time allocations in American homes can be found in the analysis by sociologists at the University of Michigan Institute for Social Research of time diaries collected from national samples of children and parents in 1981 and 1997 (Hofferth and Sandberg 2001). Children surveyed in 1997 spent *more* time in school (or preschool) and doing homework, *more* time in organized group activities like team sports, and *more* time doing household chores and assisting their parents with grocery and other shopping but *less* time eating, watching television, playing, and sleeping than their counterparts in 1981. Free time for unstructured play indoors or out dropped from 40 percent of a child's day in 1981 to 25 percent in 1997.[3]

Parents too experienced a "time crunch," spending more hours working, doing errands, and organizing their children's activities. It is also worth noting that despite the rise in the number of dual-earner families, children in these families spent as much time with their parents as did children in single-earner families, and the kids of working parents surveyed in 1997 received more parental attention than did the kids of working parents surveyed sixteen years earlier. (This finding was substantiated by a similar study of time diary data [Sayer, Bianchi, and Robinson 2004] that revealed that both mothers and fathers spent more time in child care activities in the late 1990s than in the mid-1960s.) Some dual-earner families managed this by "split-shift" arrangements whereby one parent cares for the kids while the other is at work. Others squeezed in more time with their children by sharing activities like shopping, cleaning house, preparing food, and reading; by supervising their kids' homework and attending their extracurricular activities; and by scheduling extra "quality" time on weekends—leaving them little time for leisure activities and sleep.

Though families with dual-working parents are increasing throughout the world, the time crunch is most severe in the United States. By the end of the twentieth century, Americans worked on the average more hours per week and per year than people in any other nation; moreover, between 1969 and 1987, the average employed American—irregardless of income, marital status, or occupation—worked an additional 163 hours annually on the job. Because time spent on domestic labor, including housework and child care, remained almost the same, this statistic means that Americans worked, on average, 1 extra month each year. The time that family members spent in the labor force continued to increase between 1989 and 1995, *with families raising children logging in the longest hours.* (Bogenschneider 2000, 1144; emphasis added)

No wonder that parents in some prosperous suburbs are trying to program a little "dawdle time" into their kids' crowded schedules or are working with school and religious leaders to organize occasional "family nights" when all team sports, homework, meetings, and other evening events are canceled.

Lareau's findings, however, suggest that the time crunch may not be ubiquitous even in the United States. While the middle- to upper-middle-class families that she and her associates studied certainly match the pattern reported by Hofferth and Sandberg, children in less privileged families enjoyed considerably more leisure time and greater freedom to organize their own activities. Bould (2003), who also found class-related variations in parenting practices and kids' behavior, cautions against a tendency to assume that what White middle- and upper-class, heterosexual two-parent families do is the behavioral standard, causing us to marginalize or overlook other kinds of family lifestyles.

ARE KIDS COST EFFECTIVE?

The Cost of Childhood

As we have seen, the worldwide birthrate decline appears to be the result of social, economic, and political changes that have combined to lessen the cost-effectiveness of having children. According to U.S. Department of Agriculture estimates, it now costs approximately $170,000 to raise a child to age eighteen, an increase of more than 50 percent over the past thirty years (Lino 2002). This figure does not include "extras" like music or swimming lessons, summer camp, or orthodontics or money put aside

for college, now attended by a majority of American high school graduates. Nor does it take into account the loss of family income due to one
or both parents leaving the labor force or working fewer hours in order
to care for their children. Married couples with children are far more
likely than childless couples to be late paying their bills, to face foreclo-
sure on their homes, and to file for bankruptcy. Though child-rearing
costs vary depending on family size and composition, place of residence,
and socioeconomic status, for most adults having a child isn't just a matter of minor lifestyle adjustments but is also one of accepting a lower
material standard of living (Calhoun and Espenshade 1988; Espenshade
and Calhoun 1986; Surowiecki 2003).

The explanation for the sharp decline in birthrates in most European nations offered by a Norwegian sociologist exemplifies the exchange perspective introduced in chapter 2: kids are coming to be
viewed "not only as a bad economic investment for the parents but also
as consuming time and representing barriers to the fulfillment of
competing, adult needs" (Jensen 1994, 62). A researcher at the National Institute of Statistics in Italy interpreted her nation's declining
fertility rate (1.2 births per woman in 2001) as follows: "People are
studying longer, and thus are finding work later, when there is work,
and then are marrying later, which doesn't necessarily mean having a
baby anymore." Explaining why she was still childless, an Italian
woman in her early forties put it more bluntly: "It's never been at the
top of my list. [In fact], it's never been in the top 200 things" (*New
York Times*, December 26, 2002).[4]

There is also an imbalance of costs and rewards between the family
and the state, with families bearing a disproportionate share of the
costs of raising children without gaining a direct financial return on
their investment, while the state, which benefits from healthy and well-
educated kids who become productive workers, leaves the bulk of the
expenses to the family. Predictably, government officials in countries
with low birthrates are urging women to have more babies, although the
continuing decline in birthrates indicates that they have failed to offer
adequate incentives to do so.

While both women and men seem to have less to gain from marriage
and children than in the past, gender differences remain.

The Cost of Motherhood

In a book titled *The Price of Motherhood*, Ann Crittenden (2001) argues that for most American women, having children imposes substantial costs—in fact, it's now the best predictor of female poverty. Mothers' earned income is lower than that earned by men or childless women, and the reduction of their lifetime earnings and savings resulting from interruptions to their careers—often referred to as the "motherhood penalty" or "mommy tax"—places them at higher risk of poverty in old age or in the event of divorce or separation. Testing the relationship between motherhood and wages across two cohorts drawn from the National Longitudinal Survey of Young Women, Avellar and Smock (2003) found that even after controlling for a number of individual variables, each additional child was associated with a negative effect on her mother's wages, and the "motherhood penalty" did not diminish over time.

Added to the economic disadvantages are the logistical difficulties of combining employment and child rearing and the discontinuities between attitudes and reality regarding working mothers. Although over half of American mothers are back in the workforce before a baby's first birthday and two-thirds of the mothers of preschool children are employed outside the home, polls continue to show that 70 percent or more of Americans believe that it's better if mothers stay home and take care of their children. Moreover, after the birth of a child, even couples committed to gender equality tend to revert to a more gendered division of labor. A 1981 study of first-time parents in the Baltimore metropolitan area found that many mothers who formerly worked outside the home "suddenly find themselves tied to the house doing unpaid and largely menial work, while fathers continue much as before," devoting more of their time and energy to work than to family (Entwisle and Doering 1981). A 1998 replication of this study in a different part of the country produced the similar conclusion that "whatever egalitarianism once existed between [first-time parents] falls away as they move from being a man and a woman to inhabiting the roles of mother and father" (Walzer 1998, 363). At the same time, standards for mothering continue to rise, calling for ever more

careful attention to the minute idiosyncrasies that make children individuals; constant nurturing of a child's physical and cognitive development; and the consistent elevation of children's needs above virtually all other of life's demands, [all of which require] copious amounts of physical, mental, and emotional energy on the part of the individual mother. (Stevens 2001, 75, 103)

In addition, mom continues to bear the lion's share of the blame when things go wrong. Walzer (1998) found that not only did mothers worry about not providing the correct mix of nurturing and stimulation, but they "also worried that they weren't worrying about their children enough" (363).

The Cost of Fatherhood

Since the 1970s, social scientists and popular writers have heralded the arrival of the "new father," as indicated by the following:

- An increase in the number of men who attend childbirth, from almost none thirty years ago to less then 10 percent twenty years ago to over 90 percent today
- An increase, though small, in the number of men switching to less demanding jobs so that they can spend more time with their children or turning down promotions that involve relocation so as not to uproot their families
- An increase in the number of single fathers raising children (over 2 million in 1998, triple the number of father-only families in 1975, and now one in every six single parents)

For all the talk of a new American father, the vanishing father is still a more frequent phenomenon. Most breakups of families with children involve the father moving out, and nonresident dads find it difficult to maintain a close relationship with their kids. Several longitudinal studies that followed nationwide samples of U.S. children in disrupted families for more than a decade found that only about a quarter of them saw their fathers at least once a week, more than a quarter had not seen them at all during the previous year, and few of those who did maintain contact with their fathers had the opportunity to spend extended periods of time with them. Financial support from nonresident fathers was meager, averaging about $3,000 a year, and only about half of divorced mothers and a quarter of unmarried mothers received any support at all (Crowell and Leeper 1994; Furstenberg and Harris 1992; Seltzer 1991). No wonder that Ayinde Jean-Baptise, the twelve-year-old boy quoted at the beginning of this chapter, urged the men at the Million Man March, "Go back to your families. Go raise and teach your children."

Though single-father-with-children families are one of the fastest-growing family types in the United States, some sociologists posit a "male flight" from marriage and children. Pointing out that the median age of first marriage for men has reached twenty-seven, the oldest in U.S. history, Popenoe (National Marriage Project 2002) argues that men are more reluctant to "commit" than in the past because they face fewer social pressures to marry, they can enjoy sex and companionship with women without marrying them, or they haven't met a woman for whom they're willing to give up the benefits of single life and take on the costs and inconveniences of family life. Furstenberg and Cherlin (1991) argue that marriage and parenthood are a "package deal" for men. Strong marriages exert a pull on men to take on the role of father, but if the marriage weakens or dissolves, men's commitment to fatherhood also attenuates. However, an empirical test of the male flight model using U.S. census data that traced trends in parenting since the late nineteenth century concluded that recent declines for *both men and women* are simply extensions of a prevailing tendency for over a century rather than a new "crisis" in family life (Hogan and Goldscheider 2001, 173).

When working fathers do shoulder a greater share of responsibility for child care and household chores, they experience the same conflicts between the demands of home and work that make the lives of working mothers so difficult. A California father who quit a management job in one hotel to work as a bell captain in another, taking a cut in pay as well as in hours, had mixed feelings about his decision. On the one hand, spending more time at home was better than working sixty- to seventy-hour weeks and seeing his kids so rarely that they "didn't seem to know who I was." On the downside, he has little time for his wife, his friends, or himself, and he envies his coworkers who are receiving promotions and interviewing for better jobs (*New York Times*, April 26, 1998). Like their female counterparts, fathers with heavy domestic responsibilities complain about the relentless demands of young children, the lack of adult company, and the boredom and tiring physical labor associated with housework. In addition, the couple relationship is likely to be affected—and not always positively. A British study found that many mothers begrudged their partners a greater share of hands-on parenting, criticized them for being too soft on the kids, and resented it when the children went to dad for comfort and cuddling. They were particularly irritated when other people praised him for his involvement in child care—no one had called *them* bloody marvelous when *they* were their kids' primary caretakers (Russell 1986).

Attempts to promote gender parity via public or corporate policy have had mixed results. Sweden's proactive policy, offering leaves to all parents at close to their current salaries with extra compensation to couples who divide the leave time equally between father and mother, has resulted in small but steady increases in fathers' participation. In one Swedish city, many of the fathers who took parental leave not only were their children's primary caregivers but reported increased time in other household tasks as well (Chromholm 2002; Furst 1999). In the United States, paternity leaves are not universal entitlements, few of the men who are eligible take them, and corporate culture still inhibits men from taking fuller family roles. Doubts remain whether men who care for kids—their own or other people's—are engaged in "real" work, and fears remain that men left alone with young children will molest them or at least leave them with confused sexual identities (Crowell and Leeper 1994; Hochschild 1997).

OTHER WAYS OF LOOKING AT CHILDREN'S VALUE

If raising kids is so costly, why do people continue to have them, especially when effective methods of birth control are widely available? One answer is that economic benefits are not the only or the most important ones. The trouble with the cost-benefit model, according to Qvortrup (1990), is that kids are "turned into items on *parents'* budgets, and are thus made into expensive objects, similar to the dwelling, the car and domestic appliances" (94).

Emotional Rewards

In her classic work on the social value of children, *Pricing the Priceless Child*, Zelizer (1985) argued that the economic value of children has been replaced by enhancement of their emotional value. In an often-quoted phrase from this book, American children are now viewed as "economically worthless but emotionally priceless." Zelizer's hypothesis has been supported by data from other nations as well. In a series of surveys of mothers in Japan, South Korea, Thailand, France, Britain, and the United States, it was found that happiness, love, companionship, self-development, and other emotional rewards of having children took precedence over utilitarian values such as "additional work power" or "security in old age" or discharging family obligations such as carrying on the family line or performing traditional religious rituals (Youth Development Headquarters 1981). A more recent review of studies on the value of children (Nomaguchi and Milkie 2003) found that children were both "a source of joy and a source of burdens" for their parents and that in most cases the new demands on parents' time and the drain on their physical and emotional energies were balanced by enhanced *self-efficacy* (the feeling that life was working out the way they wanted it to) and *social integration* (the strengthening of existing social ties with relatives, friends, and neighbors and broadening of social networks to encompass a wider range of people and community organizations).

Economic Contributions

Another answer to the question of why people continue to have children is that cost-benefit analyses tend to look only at adult inputs and overlook children's contributions to the household economy. In a study of 730 English secondary school children between the ages of eleven and sixteen, Morrow (1994) found that 40 percent had regular home responsibilities, from looking after younger siblings to helping with housecleaning, laundry, and meal preparation, and that almost as many helped out in a family business or earned money outside the home (e.g., delivering newspapers, babysitting, car washing, and yard work). The Norwegian "home-stayer" children discussed earlier in this chapter not only performed household chores but also, by caring for themselves, enabled their parents to work outside the home. As noted in chapter 4, a substantial amount of child care in many parts of the world is performed by children, and in a reversal of the conventional adult–child relationship, a not insignificant number of children in affluent European nations are the major (though usually unpaid) caretakers of disabled parents or other family members (Becker, Dearden, and Aldridge 2001).

In immigrant families, children who are more fluent in the new language than their parents often assume the role of interpreter in family dealings with government officials, school personnel, and shopkeepers. A study of the preadolescent children of Spanish-speaking immigrants (Orellana, Dorner, and Pulido 2003) found that many kids helped their parents fill out job, credit card and social security applications, and income tax returns. A few managed family bank accounts or were responsible for major household purchases. While serving as their families' language brokers was empowering for some children, for others it could be time consuming and stressful. One child who tried unsuccessfully to intercede for a sibling who was being held back in school felt she had let down her whole family:

> I felt bad that I couldn't understand why, that I couldn't explain to the teacher that my mom wanted to know why. And 'till this day, we really don't know what happened. Because my sister was not a horrible student, so my mom's convinced that we misunderstood something in the process. (517)

The most comprehensive review of American research on children and housework (Lee, Schneider, and Waite 2003) indicates that when mothers are employed outside the home, kids are more likely than their fathers to take up the slack. In general, the more hours mothers work outside the home, the more hours children work in the home (fathers do not increase their share of domestic work proportionately). The amount and type of housework vary by children's age (older kids do more than younger kids), race and ethnicity (African American and Latino kids do more than European American and Asian American kids), and gender (girls do more and different kinds of domestic chores than boys, and the gender gap is even more pronounced for minority kids) and by the mother's marital status (kids do more household chores in single-parent and divorced-parent homes than in two-parent homes). Ironically, the unequal amounts of household work performed by girls and boys and the sex typing of chores suggest that as mothers challenge stereotypical sex roles outside the home, they may be reinforcing them at home.

Although household chores for children are often defended (nearly always by adults) on the grounds that they teach valuable skills, inculcate a sense of responsibility, or enhance self-esteem, Lee and colleagues (2003) found little empirical evidence in support of these claims. If asked, few kids defined their chores as an educational opportunity; many did them mainly to avoid punishment. Disagreements over chores are among the most frequent sources of family conflict, especially between adolescents and their parents. Attitudes toward household work varied with the nature of the task. Caring for other family members or working with them on a home repair or decorating project might enhance feelings of family cohesiveness, but repetitive routine housecleaning seldom produced, in kids or adults, a heightened sense of responsibility or the satisfaction of making a valued contribution, and almost any household chore that was always assigned to the same person was viewed as onerous.

CONCLUSIONS

Given the pace of social change and the diversity of contemporary family structures and lifestyles, the usual experts can no longer be relied on to provide blueprints for successful parenting. While some research points to the benefits of a particular mode of parenting, other research suggests that children's basic needs can be met in a variety of ways and that no particular parenting practices will ensure the survival and well-being of all children. Moreover, the socialization of children is a two-way process in which parents and children shape each other's attitudes and behavior. Not only are parents changed by parenting, but, as we'll see, parental influence is tempered by the effects of the following:

- Children's peer groups, the subject of chapter 6
- Children's social position as determined by their race, ethnicity, gender, and socioeconomic status, to be discussed in chapters 8 and 9
- Societal or global trends that affect parents' power not only to support their families economically but also to raise their children in accordance with their own values and beliefs, to be taken up in chapters 10 and 11

Though kids are commonly viewed as financially burdensome to their families, recent research indicates that the majority of children contribute some form of labor to their households and many make financial contributions that are not trivial. An anthropologist who has specialized in the interaction of biology and culture in child rearing estimates that in some societies kids "essentially pay for themselves, as a result of the money they bring in, services they provide, and goods they produce, by the time they are seven years," and she goes on to hypothesize that "kids' work may have contributed to our very success as a species" (Small 2001, 30–31; we'll come back to this point in chapter 10). Many children, it appears, are both emotionally priceless and economically useful.

NOTES

1. Appendix A of *Unequal Childhoods*, which should be required reading for all researchers in our field, is an impressively thorough and candid discussion of how the research team faced such dilemmas as obtaining a diverse sample of children in a society whose educational system is stratified by class and race, obtaining consent and establishing rapport with the families, recognizing and restraining their own biases, and coping with the stress and exhaustion induced by long hours of intensive observation of intimate and sometimes contentious family life.

2. A sharp contrast is provided by Patricia and Peter Adler's *parent-as-researcher* method of ethnographic research (Adler and Adler 1998; to be discussed in chapter 7), in which their study of preadolescent peer culture was carried out in the community in which they resided, and the informants included their own children and their children's friends and schoolmates. One wonders how researchers who were resident parents would have interpreted the communities studied by Lareau or, conversely, how outsiders might have interpreted the lives of the children studied by the Adlers.

3. The authors of an ethnographic study of fourth-grade children's time use caution against oversimplifying the distinction between "structured" and "unstructured" activities: "lumping together all lessons, camps, and sports as 'structured activities' may obscure as much variance as categorizing all free time as 'play' or 'passive leisure'" (Chin and Phillips 2003, 173). They found, for example, that summer programs attended by the children in their sample varied from a highly intensive basketball "clinic" featuring rigorous daily drills in drib-

bling, passing and shooting, competitive games, and a constant flow of advice and correction from the coaches to a day camp where kids spent day after day on the same school playground and passed most of the time in informal peer interaction with little adult supervision. Conversely, kids watching television, generally assumed to be a "mindless" activity, were sometimes deeply absorbed and could describe in detail the programs they watched, and most of the kids who played video games did so "with a strong desire to win, which meant acquiring and applying a great deal of knowledge and a wide range of motor skills—skills at which our fieldworkers often failed" (157).

4. Even the assumption that children strengthen a marriage has been called into question by a considerable amount of quantitative data since the mid-1970s, when a national survey on perceived quality of life carried out by the University of Michigan Institute for Social Research showed that "members of childless marriages report greater marital satisfaction than those with children; among marriages with children, the greater the number of children the lower the satisfaction reported by the parents; and on a variety of marital satisfaction indices, satisfaction drops sharply with the birth of the first child, sinks even lower during the school years and goes up markedly only after the exit of the last child" (Boocock 1976, 258). The ups and downs of parents' satisfaction with their marriages and relations with their children have been traced empirically in a number of subsequent studies, one of which concluded that the "initially stabilizing and later destabilizing effects of children combine over the course of the marriage to give parents only a modestly higher chance than childless couples of reaching their twentieth wedding anniversary" (Waite and Lillard 1991, 930; see also Demo and Cox 2000; Hernandez 1986; Nomaguchi and Milkie 2003; Twenge, Campbell, and Foster 2003).

III

SOCIAL WORLDS
BEYOND THE FAMILY

6

KIDS IN GROUPS

Childhood truly begins when one can escape from one's own home and play freely with one's chums in the streets and surrounding neighborhood, out of sight of adults and free of their control.

—Marie Rouanet

Children have many environments. Their mission is to learn how to get along in all of them.

—Judith Rich Harris

Remembering her girlhood in mid-twentieth-century France, the author quoted at the top of this page observes that children's lives change when they join other kids in social spheres outside their homes. Corsaro and Eder (1990) elaborate on the nature of that change: "Informal activities with siblings and playmates, participation in organized play groups, and attendance at nursery schools all lead to children's joint production of an initial peer culture. Such experiences serve to launch children on a path involving their production of and participation in a series of peer cultures in which childhood knowledge and practices are gradually transformed into the knowledge and skills necessary for participation in the adult world" (204). This does not mean that childhood is only "a period of apprenticeship that prepares children for competent membership in adult society." It is also a period during which they "creatively appropriate information about the adult world to produce their own unique cultures" (Corsaro and Eder 1990, 199–200).

In this chapter, we'll examine children's experiences in children's and adults' social worlds outside their families. Kids "leave home" for many reasons but most importantly to be with friends (informally or in organized play groups), to go to school and after-school activities, and to engage with other kids in the exchange of knowledge and goods and in the creation of distinctive cultures that are often concealed from nonchildren. Beginning with infancy and early childhood and then proceeding to middle childhood and adolescence, we'll examine evidence on the behavior of kids when they get together outside their homes, where they learn how to make friends and participate in the creation of kid culture.

GROUP LIFE OF BABIES AND PRESCHOOL CHILDREN

Age may be the first characteristic by which young children categorize other human beings. There is considerable evidence that even before they are a year old, babies are interested in and attracted to other babies. Sustained attachments between one baby and another have been recorded in day care centers and other settings where infants are cared for with others of about the same age and are mobile enough (usually by eight to ten months of age) to approach a desired playmate on their own. (Preference for playmates of one's own sex and race does not appear to begin until about ages two and three, respectively, though scholars disagree about the exact ages.) There is also evidence that babies and young children display more cognitive and social skills (and display them earlier) with other kids than with adults (Harris 1995; Thompson and Grace 2001; Van Ausdale and Feagin 2001).

Learning from Each Other

Data on babies' inventiveness and sharing of skills were provided by a *natural*, or unplanned, experiment in a New York day care center. When the mother of a ten-month-old boy picked him up one afternoon, she was surprised to be told that other mothers had been complaining that her son had taught their children how to unzip the Velcro straps of their winter hats and take them off. Unzipping hats and throwing them on the floor was definitely not part of the center "curriculum," nor had either of the boy's parents showed him how to do this. Rather, he had learned this entertaining routine by trial and error, and other babies watching him began to try it out themselves—and to continue practicing their newly acquired skill at home.

The serendipitous finding that babies can learn from other babies and can repeat what they have learned in other settings led to a more systematic experiment in which one-year-olds were shown toys made especially for the experiment and trained by the adult experimenter on how to use them. When the trained babies demonstrated the toys to other ("learner") babies, most of them played "correctly" with the toys most of the time. In a later phase of this experiment, the learner babies watched the trained babies play with the toys but were not allowed to play with them until the toys were brought to their homes two days later. Even after a forty-eight-hour delay, most could reproduce accurately what they had observed but not practiced in another setting (*New York Times*, July 21, 1995).

Children of preschool age teach each other not only cognitive skills but also how to get along with each other—that is, how to be social. The major socialization mechanism is *play*. Whether the children he was observing were Italian or American, from higher- or lower-income families, or in public or private preschools, Corsaro (2003) found that during free play, they tended to cluster in small transitory playgroups, with constant movement between clusters and relatively brief interactions. Despite the fragility and fluctuation of play clusters, children developed rules and rituals governing who may join an existing group or activity and strategies to avoid disruption by adults or other kids. They also had a clear if rudimentary understanding of friends and friendship, summarized by Corsaro (2003) as follows: "the kids you are playing with are your friends, while those not playing are often seen as a threat to friendship" (40). The following passage illustrates how a savvy preschooler learns the necessary language and behavior to gain entry into the ongoing play of two classmates:

> Debbie comes up to the sandbox and stands near me, closely watching the other two girls. After watching for about five minutes, she circles the

sandbox three times and stops again and stands next to me. After a few more minutes of watching, Debbie moves to the sandbox and reaches for a teapot. Jenny takes the teapot away from Debbie and mumbles "no."

[Debbie backs away but after a few more minutes of observation says to the second girl]: "We're friends. Right, Betty?"

Betty, not looking up at Debbie and continuing to place sand in the pan, says, "Right."

Debbie now moves alongside Betty, takes a pot and spoon, begins putting sand in the pot and says, "I'm making coffee."

"I'm making cupcakes," Betty replies. (Corsaro 2003, 41–42)

Fantasy Play   By engaging in *shared fantasy play*, young children produce routines and rituals that enable them, in the security of the group, to explore, explain, and deal with the fears, conflicts, and unknowns in their lives. Some of the richest descriptions of children's fantasy play can be found in the work of Vivian Paley, a nursery school and kindergarten teacher at the University of Chicago Laboratory School. Paley is a rare example of an adult who not only listens to young children but also takes them seriously enough to *learn from them* and to incorporate their perspectives into her own teaching practice. Rejecting the conventional role of classroom teacher, Paley constructed a new role that is a combination of a colleague and an outsider who must listen to her subjects with the care and objectivity of an anthropologist. She taped each day's events for later transcription and analysis and has drawn from these materials to write a series of highly acclaimed books that combine detailed descriptions of the children's play, lengthy verbatim quotations of their conversations, and reflections on her own development as a teacher of young children.

In *Wally's Stories*, Paley (1981) passes on some of the lessons she learned from a five-year-old who entered her kindergarten class preceded by his reputation as a "bad boy" whose restless, hyperactive, noisy, and uncooperative behavior had caused him to be expelled from his previous nursery school. Only when she redefined Wally as a valuable informant rather than a behavior problem could Paley appreciate his fantasy play virtuosity and his ability to interpret his classmates' concerns and behavior, both displayed in the following passage:

As Wally changes from dinosaur to superhero to lion, Fred keeps an eye on him. He examines Wally's behavior and then watches my reaction.

Wally, however, never watches me. He seldom takes his cues from adults, bringing forth his own script for being a five-year-old. He is never bored, except when he's on the time-out chair, and even then his head dances with images and stories.

"Whoever sits in the time-out chair will die for six years until the magic spell is broken," he says one day after a session on the chair.

"They turn into a chair," Eddie decides, "and then God breaks the spell."

"Not God," corrects Wally. "God is for harder things."

"Fairies could do it," says Lisa. "Not the tooth kind."

"It *is* a fairy," Wally agrees. "The one for magic spells."

The children like Wally's explanations for events better than mine, so I give fewer and fewer interpretations each day and instead listen to Wally's. The familiar chord he strikes stimulates others to speak with candor, and I am the beneficiary. (6–7)

Resisting Adult Authority

Corsaro postulates that from their earliest years, children challenge adult authority and attempt to gain control over their lives. His classic analysis of nursery school "underlife" (1988) provides many examples of preschoolers' skills at secrecy and subterfuge. For example, kids in Italian and American preschools evaded rules prohibiting guns and shooting by using hands, shovels, blocks, and other "make-does" when out of sight of a teacher. They also smuggled forbidden toys into school. In one nursery school, kids got around the rule by bringing small personal objects— toy animals, Matchbox cars, candies, and chewing gum—that they could conceal in their pockets. "While playing, a child would often show his or her 'stashed loot' to a playmate, and they would carefully share the forbidden objects without catching the attention of the teacher or TA. Although such small deceptions may seem insignificant to an adult, as they were to the TAs who would often chuckle and ignore them, they were not trivial to the children and were important moments in the sharing of peer culture" (197). In a 1998 interview, Corsaro reflected on the way in which opposition to adult culture strengthened children's social bonds with each other: "What I found interesting was not that the kids wanted to bring their own toys but that when they smuggled them in they never played with them alone. They played with them collectively. . . . They wanted others to know that they had them. They wanted to share the toys with others. They are not only sharing the toy but sharing the fact that they are getting around the rule" (Gladwell 1998, 61).

Because much of the content of peer culture is about things that kids are not supposed to know about, secrecy is an important resistance mechanism. Research on African children indicates that, like the Italian and American preschoolers studied by Corsaro, they "have a private language for describing intimate parts of the body, using words that are forbidden in the presence of adults" (Harris 1995, 470). Though all of the preschools studied by Corsaro had rules prohibiting "bad" language, he recorded "swearing routines" filled with references to sexual activity and the legitimacy of one's parentage—indeed, swearing was appealing *because* it was taboo. A particularly memorable experience for Corsaro (1988) was hearing a four-year-old girl utter a fourteen-word string of curses that "contained some words I had heard only a few times, and two or three I had never uttered in my life." A second girl to whom the swearing routine had been addressed responded with her own string of curses, repeating several of the "bad" words from the first string but adding some of her own. The routine "continued for three more rounds, with the girls producing many of the words over and over and giggling at their bit of naughtiness." As Corsaro interprets the incident, the girls were not expressing anger or hostility toward each other but mutual pleasure in sharing forbidden words (197–99).

Conflict among Kids

Though young children may at times present a united front against adult rules and authority, peer conflict is also a basic element of group life. During 140 hours of observation of one- to five-year-olds enrolled in a university day care center, Baumgartner (1992) recorded 476 conflicts or disputes involving over sixty children, an average of 3.4 disputes per hour. Though most of the time most of the kids are *not* involved in conflicts, disputes erupt frequently and suddenly. "Children who are playing contentedly alongside each other one moment may become embroiled in heated confrontation the next. Conflicts tend to end as abruptly as they arise, and to persist for only brief periods of time" (6). Over a third of the conflicts occurred when one child attempted to take a toy away from another child. Other sources of conflict were unwanted proximity or touching, accidental injury inflicted during rough-and-tumble play, contested places in line or seats at worktables, and complaints that others kids were too noisy, too slow, or too selfish (7). In all age-groups, both girls and boys engaged in all forms of conflict and conflict resolution.

Violence occurred in 43 percent of the conflicts, though in many cases children who were hit did not hit back. Some conflicts simply dissipated because the children gave up simultaneously or the dispute morphed into another mode of interaction, as in the following example:

> As the Preschool I children lined up outside the bathroom after washing their hands for lunch, Jimmy bumped into Melanie and knocked her down, apparently by accident. Melanie scrambled to her feet and confronted Jimmy angrily, calling him a "peanut butter face." Jimmy retorted that Melanie was a "hot dog face." The two children then exchanged a series of insults, each constructed by adding the word "face" to the word for some sort of food. ("Pretzel face," "cheese face," and "French fry face" were among the jibes.) At first, the children were quite angry and their exchange hostile. After a while, however, the mood changed and the dialogue took on a game-like character. Soon both children were laughing and the quarrel was forgotten. (Baumgartner 1992, 22)

The predominant modes of managing disputes were 1) *aggression*, typically brief and unilateral; 2) *submission* to the authority of adults; or 3) *giving up*, abandoning the issue in dispute and retreating to another part of the room or playground. The disputants rarely resolved their conflicts by negotiating. Other kids rarely intervened as allies, mediators, or peacemakers, and when they did, the intervention was limited, as in the following example:

> In the Toddler I classroom, Paul walked over and grabbed a toy from Naomi, at which point Naomi began to cry. Noelle, who had been playing by herself nearby and who had witnessed the incident, hurried over and hit Paul. Paul did not react to this and Naomi continued to cry until one of the teachers finally asked her what was wrong. Before she could answer, Noelle, who had remained at the scene, pointed wordlessly at Paul, who then held out the toy and offered it back to Naomi. (Baumgartner 1992, 27)

Compared to Corsaro, Baumgartner found little peer culture and virtually no resistance to adult authority. Most of the time, the kids seemed pretty independent of, even indifferent to, each other while being extremely dependent on their powerful adult teachers. She posits that it is only to be expected that in social situations where

> authority is extreme and highly salient, connections between the children are tenuous, fortuitous, and situational. While a lack of social integration can arise from many sources, in this case the dominant presence of the teachers does much to account for the weak ties that the children have with each other. . . . There is not much at stake in relationships between the children. (25)

Baumgartner argues that there is nothing distinctly "child-like" about the way these preschoolers handled their disputes. Adults who are members of subordinate groups use similar modes of conflict resolution, including submission to those with more status and power, low rates of negotiation, mediation and alliance, and occasional outbursts of violence.

Is Day Care Good or Bad for Young Children?

Social science research does not provide a conclusive answer to this question, partly because, as we saw in chapter 3, research results depend on *who* is doing the research and *how* they are studying the problem. Two British researchers who suggest that day care may enrich children's daily lives simply by exposing them to other children caution against "focusing exclusively on baby's relationship with a single adult— generally the mother [and] assuming that children at nurseries are deprived of mother's care." By doing so, they argue, researchers not only underestimated the capabilities of babies and young children but also failed to test the alternative hypothesis that "children at home are deprived of other children's company" (New and David 1985, 243–45).

Research on the child care systems developed in Nordic countries, which are based on a *dual socialization* model that defines a normal childhood as one in which young children have the daily experience of both home and center care, shows generally positive outcomes. Several rigorously designed longitudinal studies of Swedish children found that elementary and secondary students who had been enrolled in day care scored higher on a wide range of academic and social skills than class-mates who had been cared for at home and that the earlier a child entered day care, the higher the scores, leading the director of one of these stud-ies to conclude that "early entrance into day care tends to predict a cre-ative, socially confident, popular, open, and independent adolescent" (Andersson 1992, 32–33). Observations of Swedish children being delivered to day care centers and picked up at the end of the day record few in-stances of kids clinging to their parents; most run off happily to join their playmates, and many are reluctant to leave when their parents return to take them home. When children's views were solicited, most rated being with their friends as the best part of day care, much more important than the toys, equipment, adult staff, or any particular activity (Dencik 1995).

In contrast, in the United States, opponents of outside-the-home child care can point to empirical evidence of its detrimental effects on children's development. For example, a recent government-funded as-sessment (Early Child Care Research Network 2003) reported that the more time children spent in nonmaternal care during the first four and a half years, the more behavior problems they exhibited during those years and later in kindergarten. This conclusion is, however, challenged by researchers who argue that the *quality* of child care matters more than whether it is provided by Mom or by someone else and that Amer-ican kids who attend *high-quality* day care and preschool programs are more successful in kindergarten, elementary school, and beyond. The problem is that so much of the nonparental care available in the United States is of mediocre or poor quality (Barnett and Hustedt 2003; Es-pinosa 2002). We'll come back to this problem in chapter 12.

GROUP LIFE OF SCHOOL-AGE CHILDREN AND ADOLESCENTS

By the time they enter school, most children are seasoned veterans of group life, and the fluctuating clusters of young children have evolved into more durable, rule-governed entities whose members have learned how to do the following:

- Join a group and participate in group activities
- Create and transmit group culture

- Conceal "forbidden" aspects of group culture and activities
- Resist and subvert adult rules and authority

In contrast to romantic views of children as natural egalitarians with little sense of status and power differentials, sociological research indicates that children as young as five are aware of status differences within their groups and that age is a major differentiating characteristic. From a qualitative study of children aged five to ten attending a summer camp near Chicago, Passuth (1987) concluded that age "was the single most important factor—over gender, race, social class, and geographic location—in understanding children's lifestyles and perceptions of their competencies" (200). The crucial boundary was between "big kids" and "little kids":

> No matter where they were on the age ladder, children saw themselves as bounded by the big kids on top who were older and had higher age status, and the little kids below them who had lower age status. Power and prestige were unequally distributed between the two groups, [and the] most salient feature of children's distinction between big and little kids was the big kids' greater power. This power was demonstrated in four ways: (1) bossing younger children, (2) excluding them, (3) defeating them in games, and (4) physically hurting them. (193)

Kids who did not "act their age"—especially if they tried to pass as an older kid—were "out-ed" and brought back into line.[1]

Peer Culture

Decades before many sociologists began to gather data *about* children directly *from* children, Iona and Peter Opie observed and questioned some 5,000 schoolchildren in various parts of England, Scotland, Wales, and Ireland, gathering detailed accounts of their favorite games, songs, rhymes, riddles, and jokes; the pranks they played on each other; and the multitude of ways in which they ridiculed and circumvented teachers, police, and other adult authorities. In *The Lore and Language of School Children* (1987), originally published in 1959, the Opies claim that children's culture is the world's oldest continuous culture. In support of their claim, they traced some of the playground games they observed as far back as Roman times.

In 1991, students in a Rutgers University honors seminar carried out a small-scale replication of the Opies' study and found that some of the songs and games they recalled from their own childhoods were also familiar to 1) classmates who had been brought up in other countries or other parts of the United States and 2) New Jersey elementary school children interviewed in playgrounds and at Boy Scout gatherings. They also discovered that New Jersey schoolgirls were jumping rope to chants that had also been sung by the students in the university seminar and by their middle-aged professor and that some of the chants were variations of ones collected by the Opies and traced by them to the eighteenth century (Parse and Heffron 1989). Although many elements of children's culture have been passed on for so long and disseminated so broadly that the authorship of the originals is unknown, kids tend to believe that the songs, rhymes, or jokes exchanged among friends were invented by contemporaries. Of a rhyme she had just learned that was in fact more than a hundred years old, an English girl told the Opies, "Here's one you won't know because it's only just made up" (Opie and Opie 1987, 12). Similarly, a Rutgers student collected a song from a twelve-year-old Boy Scout that he remembered singing when *he* was a Scout—each had thought he was learning a "brand new" song.

The speed with which kids' culture can be transmitted often defies researchers' efforts to trace the process. Within days of the beginning of the 1991 Persian Gulf War and despite warnings to parents and teachers from therapists and TV pundits to protect children from troubling information about the death and destruction brought about by the war, kids throughout New Jersey were singing or chanting similar derogatory rhymes about Saddam Hussein—and occasionally President Bush. Though children's culture has traditionally been passed on orally, the widespread availability of e-mail now facilitates transmission at even higher speeds and across greater distances.

A Culture of Secrecy   Because the creation and transmission of children's culture is an important way of dealing with adult power and oppression, much of it is scatological, subversive of adult authority, or both. The usual way for a child to learn the culture is from another child, often in secret and with instructions not to tell anyone, especially not an adult. The following song was transmitted by a New Jersey Boy Scout to a Rutgers University student researcher with a warning not to share it with his teachers:

> Dogs wear collars; horses wear bits. Lulu wears a sweater to cover up her t——s.
>   Lulu has a bicycle; the seat is made of glass. Every time she hits a bump, a piece goes up her a——s.
>   People work in factories; others work in stores. Lulu works in a funhouse with forty other wh——s.

It is almost a truism that kids are more likely to receive their sex education from their peers than from their parents or teachers. American girls interviewed by Lamb (2001) were aware that sexual play is "not at all acceptable or part of regular public life for girls. Nevertheless, they liked to 'practice' with each other, play with each other in sexual ways, and find some sexual pleasure in their games." Fantasy play with Barbie dolls was a popular means of communicating sexual lore. One group of friends updated the concept of "bosom buddies" by referring to themselves as "best vagina pals" (48, 59–60).

Adolescents too are adept at concealing their sexual activities from adults. A study based on data from the National Longitudinal Study of Adolescent Health found that half the mothers of sexually active American teenagers mistakenly believed that their kids were still virgins. Though close parental monitoring is often recommended as the most effective way to control adolescent behavior, a study of some 450 adolescents in grades 8 through 10 found that having a mom who kept track of where they were and with whom did seem to discourage sexual activity among eighth-grade girls but that by tenth grade the reverse was true—that is, close maternal monitoring was associated with *increased* sexual activity. Moreover, deviant behavior of peers was a better predictor of early sexual activity than level of parental supervision—kids whose friends were drug and/or alcohol users were more likely to be sexually active than other kids of the same age (Whitebeck et al. 1999).

Unknown Inventors

Some products of peer culture may go unnoticed by adults not because kids take great pains to conceal them but because they demonstrate talents and accomplishments that belie adults' expectations and are not reflected in the school curriculum or measured by standardized tests of ability or achievement. No one pointed out the discrepancy between the low scores on standard tests and the high levels of creativity and competence displayed in their everyday lives by children living in an impoverished South African squatters' settlement until Reynolds (1989; mentioned in chapter 2 in the section "Psychological Perspectives on Human Development") spent eighteen months in the community talking informally with the kids and observing their activities.

In the early twentieth century, children whose families immigrated to Hawaii from many different countries created a language of their own that was distinct both from any of their parents' native languages and from the rudimentary *pidgin* used by adult immigrants to communicate with their employers. Unlike pidgin, the children's invention was "a fully developed language, capable of expressing complex ideas." While the parents' pidgin varied according to their national origin, children of a given age cohort all spoke the same version of the children's language to the extent that "their national origins were no longer detectable in their speech, even by a linguist. On the other hand, because [the children's] language evolved over time, there were variations from cohort to cohort"—though all were independent of the languages spoken by their parents (Harris 1995, 469).

A more recent example is a sign language developed from scratch by deaf children in Managua, Nicaragua, being taught by older to younger children and becoming more complex and nuanced as it is passed on to succeeding generations of kids. Following their placement in the late 1970s in an elementary school special education class, the first wave of deaf children, absorbing little from the classroom instruction, which was conducted in Spanish,

> began to develop a new, gestural system for communicating with each other. The gestures soon expanded to form an early sign language. Through continued use, both in and out of school, the growing language has been passed down and relearned naturally every year since, as each new wave of children entered the community.
>
> [Researchers studying this language over the past twenty-five years found that] changes in its grammar first appear among preadolescent signers, soon spreading to subsequent, younger learners, *but not to adults*.

This pattern of transmission, when combined with the rapid and recent expansion of NSL, has created an unusual language community in which *the most fluent signers are the youngest, most recent learners.* (Senghas, Kita, and Ozyurek 2004, 1780; emphasis added)

Kids and Commerce

An important aspect of children's culture is the sharing or exchange of money, toys, and other valued items, transactions that are also likely to be concealed from adults. The major finding of a review of recent research on children's economic activities (Zelizer 2002) was that, "contrary to cherished [adult] images of children as economic innocents, we discover children actively engaged in production, consumption and distribution." Zelizer credits James McNeal (1999) with being the first to recognize the "vast stores of information on children still untapped in the files and publications of marketing experts," who saw the "multiple business potential of a growing 'kids market,' as primary markets (spending their own money), influence markets (shaping their parents' expenditures), and future markets" (377–79).

Marketing surveys show that purchases by American children between the ages of four and twelve tripled during the 1990s; by the end of the decade, children's annual income, from their own earnings as well as from allowances and gifts, totaled over $27 billion, of which they spent about $23 billion, over $7 billion of it for snacks and a similar amount for toys, games, and other play items. In addition, children's consumer power extended to influencing a substantial portion (about $188 billion) of their parents' annual spending for food, clothes, cars, electronic equipment, and recreation. At least half of all American teenagers (though more boys than girls and more high-income than low-income teens) have their own computers or access to one, and it is estimated that they will soon generate over $1 billion annually from online sales (Howe and Strauss 2000, 265–75; McNeal 1999). Studies of Chinese children during this period indicate that the huge demand for snack foods and fast foods marketed by multinational firms like McDonalds and Kentucky Fried Chicken was driven more by children than by their parents and grandparents, who were often schooled by their kids and grandkids about the desirability of these products (Jing 2000). Nor are children's economic activities limited to shopping. Zelizer points out that they also engage in negotiations with their parents about allowances, gifts, outside employment, and compensation for household work.

Other prime sites for economic exchanges are school playgrounds, lunchrooms, and classrooms. In both of the elementary schools she studied, Scott (2003) found that students shared food and money as a friendship maintenance mechanism. Since this involved breaking a school rule, kids hid their exchanges from adults:

> When the adults indicate "Snack Time," a girl with money will quickly purchase a snack, in order to get change. The change she quietly offers to her "best friend" by placing it on the table or slipping it into her hand while quietly saying, "I'll give you my money if you want." This movement is very rapid. At times, the recipient does not notice the initial stages of the process and misses the call for snacks. However, she always knows who to turn towards and give a quick "Thank you." She then either purchases her own snack or returns the money preferring to forgo a snack altogether or partake in her friend's purchase. This process depends upon the relation of the two girls and reflects the group norms for initiating and maintaining friendships. (188)

When money is not available, kids trade with whatever is at hand, including materials scavenged from scrap heaps in early twentieth-century American cities (Nasaw 1985) and in late twentieth-century South African squatter communities (Reynolds 1989). When the American troops left an isolated Italian island at the end of World War II, "their tents and rubbish tins were plundered, and for a decade these miraculous tin-openers no bigger than a razorblade were currency in the place of coins and penknives in the swaps and negotiations of the island's little boys" (de Bernieres 1994, 385–86).

Kids have demonstrated their entrepreneurial skills by creating and manipulating markets for trading commodities ranging from Beanie Babies to comic books and Pokemon cards. During the Pokemon fad of the late 1990s, when rare cards sold for as much as $375, individual child traders made and lost thousands of dollars (*New York Times*, January 20, 2001). On occasion, they venture into adults markets as well. A 1999 Merrill Lynch survey indicated that 11 percent of American twelve- to seventeen-year-olds owned stock, and a few teenage Internet entrepreneurs interviewed by Lewis (2001) handled millions of dollars for clients who were unaware that they were entrusting their money to a kid.

WHICH IS STRONGER? THE CONTINUING DEBATE OVER PEER INFLUENCE VERSUS FAMILY INFLUENCE

In the previous chapter, we saw how researchers like Anne-Marie Ambert and Jean Harris reopened the debate about the relative strength of parental and peer influences. Harris's group socialization theory posits that after controlling for differences in heredity (what kids get from their parents' genes), very little of the remaining variance can be attributed to differences in home environments and that the effects of the home are in any case transient. Achieving satisfactory relationships with parents and siblings is an important undertaking of early childhood, but what is learned from that endeavor may be of little use elsewhere. The older they get, the more children pick up behavioral cues outside their homes, so that, "by the end of middle childhood, [most children] will have at least two separate behavior systems—one for use at home, one or more for outside the home" (Harris 1995, 458, 479).

Group socialization theory can also explain a wide range of empirical phenomena that cannot be accounted for by other theories. For example, it explains why so many immigrant children who "learn one language at home and a different one outside the home become increasingly reluctant to speak the home language, even at home," and why the "language they speak with their peers will become their 'native language' when they are adults" (Harris 1995, 476, 482–83). Similarly, whether kids smoke cigarettes is more closely correlated with whether their peers smoke than whether their parents do—although experts continue to warn parents that *their* smoking will greatly increase the chances of their children taking up the habit. Group socialization theory can also explain the so-called Cinderella effect (that it is possible to be one person in one setting and a quite different person in another setting). Thus, a child who is shy and retiring at home may be a chatterbox in the classroom, and kids who absolutely refuse to eat broccoli at home may gobble it down at school if the other kids are eating it (Gladwell 1998, 58–59).

Finally, parents are themselves participants in peer groups whose members influence each other's child-rearing methods. Though it is commonly believed that child rearing is learned from one's own parents;

in fact, values and practices vary greatly from one generation to another, and women of the same age cohort are likely to be more similar to each other than to their parents in the way they raise their kids. In both industrialized and developing nations, peer groups of mothers form support networks that provide information and assistance to new mothers, and mothers who do *not* belong to such networks "find parenting more difficult and stressful and are more likely to violate societal norms by physically abusing their children" (Harris 1995, 467–68). Similarly, a comparison of fathers who were physically abusive with fathers of the same race and income level who were not found that the latter received more emotional support from their friends and had more friends and relatives who themselves had close relationships with *their* children (Coohey 2000).

Reviewers who have savaged Harris's book seem to be most offended by her rather cavalier claims that the way parents raise their kids doesn't seem to matter all that much,[2] that children's playgroups have longer-lasting effects than their families, and that peer culture is born from kids' efforts to distance themselves from adults. The dual socialization model on which Nordic child care systems are based assumes that family and preschool influences may be complementary rather than contradictory, and Scott suggests a more nuanced version of the group socialization model that underscores the variations and interactions of childhood influences: the relative power of parental and peer influence fluctuates over time, and "parents may inculcate long-term goals, while peers have strongest impact on immediate concerns" (Scott 1999, 18).

One reason peer influences are underestimated is that they are overlooked in much mainstream research or, if addressed, are treated as negative pressures to be controlled. The authors of a recent review of research on school adjustment and academic success reported only modest effects of families, noted almost as an afterthought that teenagers' friends also seemed to influence their educational success, but concluded that "it is difficult to make any causal conclusions about the influence their friends have on them" because 1) "teenagers select friends with similar interest and goals" and 2) "few rigorous studies address this issue" (Redd, Brooks, and McGarvey 2002, 3). Similar caveats were not raised regarding the influence of *adults*.

CONCLUSIONS

In this chapter, we have examined the multiplicity of children's social worlds outside the family. Getting along in all of them requires learning multiple sets of rules, mastering a variety of behavior repertoires, and knowing when to use which. From earliest childhood, kids obtain much of this knowledge from other kids.

The adult ideological perspective renders many adults clueless about what's going on in children's social worlds. This is partly because the lenses of age, like the lenses of gender or race, prevent them from seeing the full range of children's capabilities and accomplishments, partly because kids become adept at concealing many aspects of peer culture from nonchildren. Regarding the perennial debate over parental versus peer influence, it's probably fair to conclude that both are important but that their relative impact varies by situation and over time. The importance of parenting has probably been overestimated simply because it has been studied more than peer influence, in keeping with common adult-centered assumptions about how children are socialized.

In the next chapter, we'll see that the lines between adult social worlds and kid social worlds are even more strictly delineated when children enter school and learn that they must get along in both worlds.

NOTES

1. It should be noted that other empirical studies (Goodwin 1990; Horvat and Antonio 1999; Scott 2002, 2003, 2004) have challenged the centrality of age as the indicator of children's power in peer associations, suggesting that the combined and interactional effects of age, race, gender, and social class need to be taken into account.

2. Note that Kagan's argument (described briefly in chapters 2 and 5) that children have few absolute needs and that they can be adequately met through a wide range of parenting modes met similar resistance from developmental theorists.

7

THE TWO WORLDS OF SCHOOL

Mine eyes have seen the glory of the burning of the school.
We have tortured all the teachers; we have broken all the rules.
We plan to hang the principal tomorrow afternoon,
Our troops are marching on!
Glory, Glory, Hallelujah! Teacher hit me with a ruler.
Met her at the door with a loaded forty-four,
Our troops are marching on!

—Children's version of "Battle Hymn of the Republic"

Friends always come before school.

—Dutch high school student

Going to school now seems virtually synonymous with childhood, but universal compulsory schooling is in fact a relatively recent social invention. Only during the century between 1870 and 1970 did most national governments draft constitutions that specified the state's authority over education and obligation to provide it (Boli-Bennett and Meyer 1978). Almost everywhere in the world, children now have the right, indeed the obligation, to attend a state-controlled or -approved school to a certain level or until a certain age (from age five to seven until the mid- to late teens in affluent nations). Yet even today, a national education system does not ensure universal school attendance. According to estimates in the 1999 edition of UNICEF's *State of the World's Children*, approximately 130 million children of school age in the developing world, two-thirds of them girls, did not have access even to primary or basic education.

The adult ideological position that what children do in school is different from "real" work has been challenged by sociologists who argue that school work *is* real work. Although fewer children than in the past work directly alongside their parents or other adults, child labor did not end with industrialization. Rather, their workplace shifted from home or workshop to school, their work shifted from one useful type of labor to another, and the major beneficiaries of their labor shifted from the family to the larger society. Ambert (1995a) summarizes the argument as follows: "Schoolwork has become children's work and because its purpose is to train the future labor force, this work is beneficial to the economy of societies. . . . While children are no longer an economic resource to their parents, they remain so to adults in general" (x; see also Qvortrup 1995b, 50). In poorer nations where children's household or paid labor is still the norm (and still benefits their families directly), school attendance is likely to double their workload.

From a child's perspective, going to school means learning to navigate a complex environment in which two distinct social spheres coexist in the same physical space: on the one hand, the formal education, designed and controlled by adults, that takes place in classrooms, assemblies, gyms, and playing fields and, on the other, the informal (some would say underground) education, designed and controlled by kids, that takes place on the playground, in the halls and lunchroom, and even in classrooms when kids are out of earshot of adults. There is a bifurcation not only between the sphere controlled by adults and that controlled by kids but also between the adult worlds of home and formal schooling. Children must master the behavior appropriate to each.

In the next section, we'll consider the adult-controlled aspects of school life and the ways in which kids in their role as students learn how to get along in School 1. Then we'll turn to the parallel evolution of peer groups and peer culture in School 2.

SCHOOL 1: THE ADULT WORLD

In 1968, Philip Jackson, a former classroom teacher and school principal, published an exposition of school life from a child's perspective. Five distinctive features of life in the classroom, which Jackson calls "the daily grind," seem remarkably consistent with descriptions of their school experiences by late twentieth-century and early twenty-first-century students:

1. *Involuntary attendance*: A crucial fact about modern schools is that kids have to be there, whether they want to or not. Jackson points out that this is a characteristic that students share with the inmates of two other social institutions: prisons and mental hospitals.
2. *Living in a crowd*: Jackson also pointed out that "only in schools do thirty or more people spend several hours each day literally side by side" but without being allowed to interact freely. "Even factory workers are not clustered as close together as students in a standard classroom, [and once] we leave the classroom we seldom again are required to have contact with so many people for so long a time" (8). Because students greatly outnumber teachers and other school personnel and most did not choose to be there, crowd control is a constant concern. Students interviewed more recently in an Irish elementary school suspected that this was why they could not choose their seatmates, though one opined wistfully that "you should be allowed to sit beside your best friend" (Devine 2002, 310–11).
3. *Repetitive ritualized routines*: Variation in the forms of classroom activity is limited, but each activity is to be "performed according to rather well-defined rules which the students are expected to understand and obey—for example, no loud talking during seatwork, do not interrupt someone else during discussion, keep your eyes on your own paper during tests, raise your hand if you have a question" (Jackson 1968, 8). A fifth-grade boy in the Irish elementary school complained, "Every day we do the same thing and it gets boring. [The teacher] sticks to the same routine all the time." A second-grade girl in the same school said she often felt like a robot, "as if the teacher is in the middle of the room with a great big

remote control and you have to do everything she says" (Devine 2002, 310–11).

4. *Constant judgment of students' achievements and behavior*: Classroom evaluations may refer to students' academic attainment, institutional adjustment, or personal qualities, in some situations all three. For example, when a student is praised for answering a teacher's question correctly, "it may look as though he is simply being rewarded for having the right answer. [However, if] the teacher discovered that the student had obtained the answer a few seconds before by reading from a neighbor's paper he would have been punished rather than praised. Similarly, if he had blurted the answer out rather than waiting to be called on he might have received a very different response from the teacher. Thus it is not just the possession of the right answer but also the way in which it was obtained that is being rewarded"—or punished (Jackson 1968, 23–24). An American high school student described the evaluation system at her school as follows: "Be the best, above the rest. Lets' start with [the] whole grade-driven, norm-based (whose norm anyway?) system of determining how well you've learned. The only way I could get approval, attention even, was through grades, and all it took was shutting up. Staying sweet and silent and complicit on the surface" (Shultz and Cook-Sather 2001, 162). Or, as Jackson put it, "in schools, as in prisons, good behavior pays off" (34).

Students are aware that teachers' evaluations often reflect their biases regarding race, social class, and gender. A high school junior described one male teacher's method of grading female students: "On the day of presentations two girls presented the same topic. The one girl had on a skirt and a sweater and the other one had on a baggy sweater and jeans. I really listened to both reports and thought that their reports were really quite the same. They had close to the same facts and their visuals were both really good. I personally thought that the girl with the baggy clothes on did a little bit better on her presentation and the way she explained everything. But the next day when I asked both girls what they got, the girl with the baggy clothes got a B and the other girl with the skirt got an A" (Shultz and Cook-Sather 2001, 70).

5. *Learning to deal with authority*: Above all, school is a place where the line between the weak and the powerful is clearly drawn. Though schools are ostensibly created *for* students, they have little or no say regarding school organization or curriculum. An Irish fifth-grade boy demonstrated a clear grasp of the status hierarchy in his school: "Mr [principal's name] is the most important 'cos he runs the school, then Mr. [vice principal's name], then the teachers, and the children are last." A second-grade girl admitted that she might like to be a teacher because "you get to boss everybody around and tell them they are not so clever." In an American inner-city middle school, members of a research team who were allowed to observe seventh- and eighth-grade math classes in exchange for serving as math tutors found extreme status differences between adults and kids, exemplified by the principal announcing at the opening student assembly that "all adults have a right to tell students what to do, including the cleaning lady and the custodians." Rude, even abusive, treatment of students by adults was common, and more than one teacher expressed regret that corporal punishment was no longer permitted. Many teachers took advantage of their authority to lighten their own workloads, often coming to class late and leaving early. Homework was assigned sporadically and not always collected; grading was often done by having students mark each other's papers. Teachers were aware that students routinely cheated on homework and in-class assignments but did little to stop it and were not themselves averse to fabricating grades and test scores. Though school personnel maintained the fiction that teachers were teaching and students were learning, so little of either went on in the math classes observed by the researchers that they coined the term *counterfeit classrooms* to define them (Matthews 2003).

Because Jackson was concerned chiefly with the universal features of elementary and secondary school life[1] (he felt that few persons stumbling into a classroom anyplace in the world would fail to recognize it as such), he paid scant attention to differences among schools and classrooms. As we saw in chapter 5, the schools attended by kids in prosperous suburbs and those attended by kids in lower-income urban neighborhoods reflected vast differences in the combined home, school, and communities resources in the two types of neighborhoods and thus in the social capital available to school-age children and their families. Though the school lives of the working- and lower-class kids studied by Lareau and her associates closely approximated Jackson's daily grind, the middle-class students seldom had to endure such deadening classroom routines, were generally treated with patience and respect by teachers and administrators, and enjoyed considerable autonomy.

One feature of classroom life that has undoubtedly intensified since Jackson's analysis was published is the sheer magnitude of the pressures permeating school life. Although public opinion polls show that many or most respondents consider school violence the major problem in American education, some researchers, citing evidence that the number of killings, suicides, and other violent acts in U.S. schools has in fact been declining steadily since the early 1990s, argue that we should be more concerned about widespread though less visible forms of violence against kids, in particular, subjecting them to more homework, more standardized tests, and ever-greater competition for entry into good high schools and colleges or even to pass into the next grade. Accountability has trickled down to the preschool level. Some states now require children to pass tests before they enter kindergarten and/or first grade (in the 1998–1999 school year, 5 percent of America's 4 million kindergartners were repeating that grade), and since the fall of 2002, all Head Start preschool programs have been required to test children several times a year in order to qualify for continued federal funding (Fuentes, 2003; Howe and Strauss 2000, 206–10).

Not that this is a peculiarly American problem. A critique of the South Korean educational system complains that it is driven by "examination wars" (Cho 1995). In Japan, over 70 percent of all schoolchildren attend *juku* (cram school) or private tutoring after regular school (Manzo 2002). A 1995 study described children "returning home at midnight to do homework, perhaps play an electronic video game (the epitome of 'efficient, solitary play'), fall asleep around 2 a.m., and awake early to start over again the next day." The author warned that such a regime was "taking its toll on their bodies," noting that Japanese kids are "increasingly subject to 'adult diseases,' such as elevated blood cholesterol levels, ulcers, and high blood pressure" (Stephens 1995a, 25).[2]

In some places, recess is falling victim to the relentless drive for higher academic accomplishment. On the grounds that play is irrelevant to the intellectual and academic development of children and that the time might be better spent under the guidance of adults, a growing number of American school districts are abolishing or limiting recess (Scott 2000). In a study of preschool programs in India that compared public programs targeted at disadvantaged children and private commercially operated nursery schools, it was found that although a nonformal, play-oriented approach was endorsed by experts as best for all children, it had little support in actual practice. Most parents who could afford it opted to send their children to private preschools that reduced playtime but promised an academic head start (Prochner 2002). Play itself may be harnessed for educational purposes. Toy catalogs with titles like "One Step Ahead" and "MindWare—Brainy Toys for Kids" are clearly targeted at parents anxious to give their kids an edge in the educational competition.

Dealing with the Daily Grind

How do kids make sense of the adult world of school? Jackson (1968) concluded that, forced to "acquiesce to the network of rules, regulations, and routine in which he is embedded," the most useful quality a student can acquire is *patience* (36). Other research indicates that students, like other relatively powerless people, have employed a variety of strategies to challenge, circumvent, or undermine the authority of their superiors, including the following:

1. *Withdrawal or detachment:* In a study of high school students, subjects were provided with electronic paging devices that beeped them at random intervals over the period of a week. When signaled, students recorded where they were and with whom, what they were doing, and how they felt (including a rating of their level of concentration). The results showed that levels of boredom were dramatically higher and that levels of concentration were lower in the classroom than in any other setting; on average, students were paying attention less than half the time they were in class (Boocock 1980, 152). A more extreme form of withdrawal is the phenomenon

that Japanese educators have named *school refusal syndrome*. Investigation by the Japanese Ministry of Education revealed that, by 1998, the number of elementary and secondary school students who were absent from school more than thirty days reached nearly 128,000. While some of the absences were due to illness or economic reasons, the greatest increase was in numbers of children who simply refused to go to school (Tsuneyoshi 2001, 106).

2. *Covert resistance*: The version of the "Battle Hymn of the Republic" quoted at the beginning of this chapter offers a kids' perspective on schools and teachers. One of the first sociologists to attempt an inventory of covert strategies for resisting school authority concluded, "Whatever the rules that the teacher lays down, the tendency of the pupils is to empty them of meaning. By mechanization of conformity, by 'laughing off' the teacher or hating him out of existence as a person, by taking refuge in self-initiated activities that are always just beyond the teacher's reach, students attempt to neutralize teacher control" (Waller 1932, 196). In interviews conducted in thirty focus groups drawn from Dutch high schools (some consisting solely of native Dutch students, some entirely nonnative, and some containing both native and nonnative students), students spoke about their teachers in "negative, disrespectful or indifferent terms" and underscored the importance of learning how to "establish a precarious balance between present aims of having fun and a school life that is not too 'stressy' on the one hand, and future aims concerning further education and job perspective on the other." In a group discussion on how to deal with teachers, one student said: "I really suck up to them. . . . You can make fools of them and stuff, you should have a good time, shouldn't you? But at the end of the day, you have to make sure they're your friends" (Du Bois-Reymond et al. 2001, 154–56).

3. *Overt resistance*: In addition to the growing problem of school refusal syndrome, Japanese junior high schools and, more recently, elementary schools have been plagued by breakdowns of classroom discipline. Students refuse to take their seats or follow instructions; fights break out and cannot be brought under control; and teachers are insulted, threatened, and occasionally assaulted by students. It is estimated that at least one class in every large-scale elementary

school is in a state of *gakkyu hokai* (classroom disintegration or chaos); about 10 percent of the teachers surveyed in one region of Japan said they had experienced *gakkyu hokai* in their own classes. In a few cases, the disorder was so extreme that teachers abandoned their classes in the middle of a school year (Tsuneyoshi 2001, 104–5; see also Shotaro 1999). In a different context, after Palestinian youths achieved high peer status through their participation in the intifada (uprising against the Israeli occupation), the intergenerational balance of power shifted in schools, where students began interrupting teachers, taking over classroom discussions, and refusing to do homework assignments and occasionally closed down a school altogether (Yair and Khatab 1995).

Efforts to deal with student resistance in American schools have generally been at one or the other of two extremes. Those at one extreme acknowledge the damaging effects of the competition and stress but take a Band-aid approach to helping children deal with them, for example, by adding instruction in yoga or knitting or ballroom dancing. At the other extreme and currently in the ascendancy is the *zero-tolerance* approach, which relies on suspensions and other get-tough measures to control student behavior and make schools safer. A zero-tolerance policy was introduced in Kentucky in 1997 after a fatal shooting at a high school prayer meeting. The immediate result was a sharp increase in suspensions, rising to 68,523, approximately 10 percent of the entire school population, in the 2000–2001 school year. The impact on school violence was minimal since school crime was already very low and most of the suspensions were not for violent or dangerous behavior but for "defiance of authority," a broad but vaguely defined violation of school rules that included violations of the dress code, talking back to a teacher, and any other behavior that offended an adult (Fuentes 2003).

Some countries have tried a more comprehensive and less punitive approach to discipline problems. For example, Japan is experimenting with publicly funded special classes and in some cases free schools with more flexible curricula, a more relaxed atmosphere, and more rather than less student choice and autonomy (Tsuneyoshi 2001, 106–7). Mainly, however, kids look to each other for relief from the daily grind, creating a world of their own within the physical confines of School 1.

SCHOOL 2: THE KID WORLD

If the adult-controlled school world is a kind of foreign country to many students, something to be endured or resisted, the "real world" of school is the one created and controlled by their peers. As the Dutch student quoted at the beginning of this chapter points out, school is first and foremost the place where kids meet their friends. Smaller families and the loss or reduction of available play space mean that school becomes more and more the center of children's friendship networks. (Note that the current trend toward reducing recess time is at variance with many kids' major incentive for going to school.)

From her interviews with Irish schoolchildren, Devine (2002) concluded that the peer group is "central in helping children cope with the highly evaluative context of schooling, as well as enabling them to regain some measure of autonomy in the face of persistent adult control. . . . In this culture children immersed themselves in a world of games and disputes, free from the adult 'gaze.' Governed by their own series of rules and regulations (related to for example telling tales, being a goody-goody, being popular, best friends), peer relations are a core element to children's experience of connectedness to and participation in school life" (315). A fifty-six-year-old Japanese writer who adopted a least-adult role by attending a fourth-grade class as a pupil several days a month for a year found relief from the daily grind in brief exchanges with like-minded classmates. Glancing around the room during one seemingly endless lesson,

My eyes met those of a girl next to me. Apparently sharing the boredom, she shrugged slightly and grinned, then turned her eyes forward. I followed to find she was not looking at the teacher, but at the clock.

I heard the faint tap of a pencil and looked at her again. She opened her hands, spreading her fingers, as if to say, "Ten minutes to go, Jiro-chan!"

At the break that followed, we played together, feeling as if we had shared a secret. "I always look at the clock feeling happier every minute," she told me. "But at such times, the clock always seems to move so slowly."

I could not help but nod in agreement. Through going out to have a drink of water with our classmates or by playing tag in class, we were energized and regained the ability to endure the next 45 minutes in class. (Jiro 1999, 86–87)

In-Groups and Out-Groups: How Kids Organize Themselves

In both of the schools she studied, Scott discovered that even first graders knew how to create and maintain social groups. Most of the girls she observed and interviewed belonged to two different peer groups: friendship groups and the class club, each with its own rules. A friendship was usually initiated by one girl learning another girl's name (often during a classroom activity) and inviting that girl to play with her during recess. Once established, friendships were maintained by spending recess and lunch time together; sharing snacks, money, and toys; and providing consolation and assistance when a friend was sad or needed help. Membership in the club was obtained by asking the leader's permission to join and maintained by obeying the leader and adhering to club rules. In both schools, almost everyone who sought membership was accepted unless the leader thought the group was too big for her to control or the applicant was considered too "wild." The leader made the rules and could change them at will. The most common rules were to follow the leader no matter what, to discuss club affairs only with other members, and *never* to play with boys—though chasing or teasing the boys was highly approved. Any girl who broke an important club rule could be immediately expelled and could rarely gain readmittance. Favorite club activities, which tended to be somewhat more organized than friendship activities, included climbing and sliding on the jungle gym, jumping rope, chasing the boys, and, in one of the two schools, practicing drill team routines (Scott 2003, 192–95, 198–200).

As children progress through the elementary school years, peer group structure and activities become more complex. The evolution of peer culture among preadolescents is the subject of an ethnographic study, titled *Peer Power*, that focuses on third to sixth graders in a predominantly White middle- to upper-middle-class suburban community. (Note that the community in this study was similar to the middle- to upper-middle-class community studied by Lareau and her associates, though an important difference was that the researchers, Patricia and Peter Adler, were residents of the community and parents of two children who also served as subjects and informants.[3]) Over a period of eight years, the Adlers "observed, casually conversed with, and maintained an acquaintance with literally hundreds of children," and formed closer relationships with a smaller subset with whom they interacted frequently and conducted in-depth, unstructured interviews (Adler and Adler 1998, 6).

A major finding of *Peer Power* is the prime importance of *popularity*, as evidenced by the time children devoted to debating "who is popular, who is unpopular, and why they are popular" (Adler and Adler 1998, 38). In the schools studied by the Adlers, concern about popularity is linked with gender differentiation, and both emerge earlier than has been shown in previous research. Girls derived high status by being physically attractive and well groomed and wearing the right clothes, being from a rich family (which enabled them to enjoy material possessions, elite leisure pursuits like riding or skiing, and vacation travel to fashionable places), going with popular boys, and getting good grades. In contrast, boys were accorded popularity and respect for athletic ability but also for "distancing themselves from deference to authority and investment in academic effort, and for displaying traits such as toughness, troublemaking, domination, coolness, and interpersonal bragging and sparring skills" (55).

A second and related finding was the significance of *cliques* in children's social lives to the extent that "the fabric of their relationships with others, their levels and types of activity, their participation in friendships, and their feelings about themselves are tied to their involvement in, around, or outside the cliques" (Adler and Adler 1998, 56). Cliques are friendship circles, but the Adlers emphasize that they're more than that. Teachers recognized the intensity of peer power represented by the clique structure and their limited ability to defuse or redirect it. A fourth-grade teacher observed, "The popular clique controls everything, classroom climate, so far as who feels comfortable blurting out an answer to a question. They just have a lot of power. So that even the people who are not popular but relatively comfortable will always keep an eye on the popular clique" (76).

The clique structure is highly stratified. Those at the top of the social hierarchy "function as bodies of power within grades, incorporating the most popular individuals, offering the most exciting social lives, and commanding the most interest and attention from classmates" (Adler and Adler 1998, 56). The top cliques themselves have a hierarchical structure dominated by their leaders. Exclusivity is maintained through

careful screening of members and through frequent shifts in membership when leaders eject kids who fail to meet clique standards and replace them with more promising candidates. The tenuous quality of
group membership

> created an atmosphere of competition, setting members against each other
> in their quest to remain accepted and well-regarded. . . . One of the primary
> ways leaders held dominance was by alternately gracing followers with their
> favor and then swinging the other clique members against them. Over time,
> everyone had the opportunity to experience the vicissitudes of this treat-
> ment, with its thrill of popularity and its pain of derogation. . . . Few had the
> courage to defy the leaders and stand up against them when they or their
> friends became the butt of teasing and exclusion. . . . As a result, they
> learned that the price of loyalty was severe, and that it was safer not to stick
> up for their friends but to look out for themselves instead. (79)

Moving down the status hierarchy, the Adlers found that each class
contained three levels, in descending order:

- *Wannabes*, less popular kids who "follow the cool kids around," im-
  itating their clothing, hairstyles, and behavior. Some go as far as to
  "run and fetch things for popular people, carry their messages to
  others, and threaten to beat people up who were out of favor with
  the crowd" (82)
- A *middle rank* composed of diverse subgroups comprised of students who weren't considered popular but who "didn't try to be
  cool or to be accepted by the cool people" (84)
- *Social isolates*, often referred to by other kids as outcasts or losers.
  They were seldom included in their classmates' social activities,
  had few or no friends, and often served the function of scapegoats
  (88–89).

Ironically, the middle-rank students enjoyed greater social security
and more satisfying interpersonal relationships than kids higher up on
the social ladder. Because they weren't in the running for membership
in the top cliques, they worried less about winning or losing favor. Because of the greater support they received from their peers, they had
more positive self-concepts than their higher-status classmates. A

middle-rank fourth grade girl described the interpersonal relationships in her circle as follows:

> There's no one who is mean in our group, who thinks she's better than the
> rest of us, or who lords it over all of us. So we know we can really count
> on each other, like if anyone makes fun of us, we know that our friends
> will always stick up for us. (Adler and Adler 1998, 87)

In contrast, the social isolates who constituted the bottom social stratum
were fair game for mistreatment by anyone else:

> While popular leaders degraded their followers, followers degraded the
> wannabes, and wannabes degraded the middle people, everyone could
> safely offset their own humiliation by passing it on to individuals at the
> lowest stratus. No one came to these individuals' defenses, and everyone
> could unite in feeling superior to them. (89–90)

In sum, peer culture both unified children in the later years of elementary school by providing them with an identity in relation to older
and younger groups in society and at the same time "divided them by
stratifying and setting them against each other" (Adler and Adler 1998,
217). While some kids created small subcommunities based on loyalty,
trust, open expression of feelings, and mutual support, others engaged
in competitive, aggressive, sometimes cruel behavior, and some were
continually victimized by their classmates.

Conflict within and between Groups

The speed with which conflict can escalate in children's groups has
been demonstrated experimentally by Muzafer Sherif, a refugee from
Nazi Germany who devoted his professional life to understanding the
processes by which "normal" people became hostile and sometimes
murderously aggressive and "normal" societies broke down into warring
factions. The series of experiments for which he is best known were carried out in boys' camps created by his research team. Most had two
phases. In the first phase, boys were allowed to interact freely and make
friends while engaging in the sports and games usual to children's summer camps. Left to their own devices, the campers began almost imme-

diately to form smaller groups based on friendship, most of which quickly developed a division of labor, a stratification system, and strong in-group solidarity. In the second phase, the boys were divided into two teams that purposely separated boys who had become buddies during the first phase. The researchers then introduced a series of competitive activities that pitted the two teams against each other. As a result of this experimental manipulation, in-group solidarity and out-group hostility rose, especially the latter. Fights broke out, often between kids who had been best buddies in the first phase, and intergroup conflict escalated to the point that the researchers had to intervene to prevent boys from destroying property and harming each other (Sherif 1956).

These experiments demonstrated how little it took to change pairs of kids from friends to enemies, make groups of kids fiercely competitive and hostile to outsiders, and reduce a small orderly social world to pandemonium. Sherif did *not*, however, consider what happened in the boys' camps unique to children. Like Baumgartner (1992), he believed that conflict was caused as much by social circumstances as by age or developmental level. Boys who had created their own groups commonly developed slogans, rules, and identifying elements of dress to distinguish their group from others, but they seldom resorted to violence unless their environment was manipulated externally.

The subjects of Sherif's experiments were boys, and it has been commonly assumed that conflict and confrontation are absent or rare among girls. Recent research has challenged this assumption. During her extensive fieldwork with working-class African American children, Goodwin (1990) discovered that they invented intricate and highly structured modes of dealing with their not-infrequent disputes. One form of confrontational dialoguing, called *he-said-she-said* (which became the title of Goodwin's book), occurred almost exclusively in groups of girls who regularly interacted with one another. He-said-she-said is employed when

one girl accuses another of a particular breach: having talked about her behind her back. The offended party confronts an alleged offending party because she wants to "get something straight." While some he-said-she-said disputes can be brief and even playful, on other occasions accusations can lead to an extended dispute which the girls treat as quite consequential for the social organization of their group (one he-said-she-said culminated in the ostracism of a girl for several months), as well as an event of high drama within which character and reputations can be gained or lost. (Goodwin 1990, 190)

In the following exchange, Bea accuses Annette of gossiping about her with another girl (Kerry) who is not present. The confrontation also involves another group member (Ruby) who aligns herself with the plaintiff. This particular he-said-she-said ends in a stalemate, though Annette's parting remark implies that it will be resumed at a later time:

> Bea: Kerry said *you* said that I wasn't gonna go around *Poplar* no more.
> Annette: You said you weren't.
> Ruby: She—Kerry—say . . .
> Bea: And Kerry said that um you said that Bea wasn't gonna go around Poplar no more.
> Annette: That's what Kerry said.
> Bea: Well I know what Kerry said that you said. She said—She sat there and looked at you. And Kerry—and she said—And if you have anything to say about *me* you come and say it in front of my face. . . . Cuz every time you go around Poplar you always got something to say.
> Ruby: Kerry said it too.
> Bea: And I'm tellin' Kerry too that she said it.
> Annette: I gotta go somewhere. I'll be back. Okay? (215–16)

While he-said-she-said confrontations do not address "deep-seated concerns and breaches underlying disputes," they provide a means for girls to air complaints about others in the group, to develop their individual identities, and to construct and maintain social order. (They also exemplify the interactionist perspective discussed in chapter 2.) Moreover, the variety and complexity of the linguistic routines observed by Goodwin and the skill with which they were performed refute common stereotypes about lack of structure or logic in the speech of working-class children in general and Black children in particular. Corsaro, who credits Goodwin with documenting the linguistic and social competence of children who tend to be overlooked or marginalized in mainstream social science research, also notes that *intergroup* conflicts among kids may result not from linguistic deficiencies on either side but from lack of familiarity with each other's favored modes of verbal interaction:

when children who have spent most of their time in different sociocultural groups come together for play, they often misunderstand each other's styles. Middle-class white girls, for example, often find the teasing oppositional style of Latina and African-American girls to be threatening, bossy, and mean, while African-American and Latina girls see the mitigated and polite style of middle class white girls as patronizing. (Corsaro 1997, 181)

The Underside of the Kid Sphere: Peer Abuse

Ambert, whose pioneering study of the effects of children on their parents was discussed in chapter 5, is also the author of the first extensive review of sociological research on the prevalence and long-term consequences of what has come to be called *peer abuse*. Though the very notion of peer abuse *"goes against the grain of accepted constructions of children as nonactors,* as passive recipients of adult treatment, as little innocents"* (Ambert 1995b, 193), kids reported far more mistreatment by their peers than by their parents or other adults. The evidence available also indicated that peer abuse has longer-term effects than abuse by adults and, like sexual play, is likely to be concealed from them. A child targeted for abuse is defined as deviant in some respect from the dominant peer culture, though kids *"can be rejected through no fault of their own* but, for instance, simply because they do not belong to the proper race, religion, social class, or, even do not wear 'appropriate' clothing, do not belong to the 'in' groups, and do not share in the values or pastimes of their peers"* (186). Ambert classified the major types of peer abuse as 1) direct physical aggression (assaults with blows or weapons, hazing, and rape), 2) verbal aggression (repeated teasing and ridiculing, threats of physical harm or expulsion from the group, racist or sexist remarks, and circulation of malicious rumors), 3) passive aggression (repeated or prolonged exclusion from group and failure to warn of a danger), and 4) indirect aggression (stealing, hiding, or destroying a victim's money, books, clothing, lunch, or other possessions).

For a number of reasons, peer abuse is greatly underreported. Victims may be too ashamed or embarrassed to report it or fear retaliation if they violate the strong norm against tattle-telling. If they do report the abuse to an adult, they're likely not to be believed. Feeling powerless to do anything about it, many children come to accept it as a normal part of growing up. Lack of adult awareness is a major factor. Not only do adults tend to disbelieve the victim, they often fail to notice abuse that is going on right under their noses. After reading Ambert's paper, a New Jersey middle school teacher who prided himself on his positive relationships with his students asked them to write essays about any peer abuse they had experienced or observed. He was astonished and dismayed by the results. Students had little difficulty recalling recent incidents of bullying, verbal taunts or threats, and various kinds of sexual harassment; most gave multiple examples. When he asked them why *he* had not seen the abuse that occurred in his class, the usual reaction was some variation of, "Duh, you're an adult!" (Tom Thorp, personal communication). Adults may also fail to "see" abuse because, counter to stereotype, peer abusers are not necessarily unhappy or unpopular kids but may, on the contrary, enjoy high self-esteem and high status among their peers. As the Adlers' study showed, the leaders of the most popular clique often used their power to make life miserable for their classmates, including—or especially—other clique members.[4]

James, Jenks, and Prout (1998, 92) note that children's peer cultures may teach racism and sexism as well as the values of loyalty and sharing. These issues will be taken up in greater detail in the next two chapters, but we'll close our discussion of peer abuse with a summary of findings from two empirical studies of sexual harassment by peers, carried out in two different countries, focusing on different age cohorts and utilizing different research methodologies. Both support Ambert's contention that adults' stereotyping of children as incapable of cruel or aggressive behavior may blind them to even the most blatant instances of abuse.

The objective of an ethnographic study of sixth graders in two small-town English primary schools was to "break the silence regarding young children's sexual cultures and 'presumed innocence'" by analyzing "the neglected and underreported area of young children's experiences of different forms of sexual harassment—not as isolated and unconnected incidents, but as part of children's everyday interactive social worlds, peer networks and relationships" (Renold 2002, 429). From a series of informal, open-ended group interviews held throughout the school year, Renold learned that aggression, both physical and verbal, was ubiquitous and multidirectional. Boys insulted girls verbally using terms such as "bitch," "slag," "tart," and "slut"; they punched girls in the breast, pulled their bras, and flipped up their skirts; one boy bragged to his mates about beating up his girlfriends. Girls, many of whom were larger than their male classmates, mocked and derogated boys. One girl hit her boyfriend and stamped on his toes, and another repeatedly slapped her boyfriend hard enough to leave hand marks on his back or face; a group of girls ganged up on an unpopular boy and pulled down his pants. Boys who did not display interest in football, fighting, and girlfriends were accused of being gay and were harassed by boys and girls alike. Girls who were not interested in current fashion, their physical appearance, and the pursuit of boyfriends were subject to ridicule and exclusionary tactics. As Renold predicted, in neither school had any of the incidents the children discussed openly in the small-group interviews been reported to a member of the teaching staff.

Data from a national survey of American eighth to eleventh graders (Lee et al. 1996) showed that 83 percent of girls and 60 percent of boys reported receiving unwanted sexual attention in school, ranging from comments, jokes, gestures, or looks to forced sexual intercourse. Victimization was related to gender but not to race, ethnicity, school performance, or family status. Not only was harassment ubiquitous, but it had serious consequences as well: the more severely students were harassed, the greater the likelihood that they also suffered from psychological problems or academic difficulties—a finding that is congruent with Japanese data showing that many kids who refused to go to school had been persistently bullied by schoolmates (Stephens 1995a, 25).

An unexpected finding was that nearly three-quarters of the American students who had been victims also reported harassing schoolmates and, conversely, that students who harassed others were themselves more likely to be harassed than students who had not harassed others, suggesting that, to say the least, "the line between victims and perpetrators is very fuzzy" (Lee et al. 1996, 395–99). The authors thus reject a "simple perpetrator-victim model" (which would suggest individual therapy as a solution) in favor of the more contextual or culturally based explanation that kids are likely to experience more—and more severe—harassment in schools and communities where it is so embedded in the culture that it is ignored or viewed as normal behavior and where the moral and ethical problems underlying sexual harassment are not acknowledged and openly discussed. In many schools, peer abuse is so widespread that the majority of students have been victims, perpetrators, or both, and much—perhaps most—of the abuse is concealed from adults. Solving the problem requires changes in the social settings in which abuses occur, and students need to be included in this process.

One of the few strategies involving students in applying the cure rather than just receiving it is *peer mediation*, an approach that acknowledges peer power but directs it toward unifying kids rather than pitting them against each other as it did in the schools studied by Patricia and Peter Adler. Although peer mediation is often billed as a recent American invention, conflict resolution techniques are routinely taught in some other societies. For example, Killen and Sueyoshi (1995) observed Japanese preschools in which teachers purposely introduced conflict (e.g., by removing supplies or not distributing enough to allow each child to have his or her own) and then by declining to intervene compelled the children to rely on each other for a solution to the problem. Research by cultural anthropologists reveals that the basic principles underlying peer mediation have long been practiced in a number of traditional societies. Of particular interest are the Semai people of Malaysia (viewed by anthropologists as one of the world's most peaceful cultures), who employ peer mediation practices for adults and children alike. When a dispute or act of aggression occurs in a children's group, the problem is not settled by adults. Rather, a children's *bcaraa*, or parliament, is convened where, seated in a circle, the children discuss what happened and then try to reach agreement on "how to resolve the issue and repair the injured relationship. Everyone thus profits from the dispute by learning the lesson of how to handle frustrations and differences peacefully" (Ury 2002, 42). Note that the he-said-she-said mode of dealing with complaints within girls' friendship groups discussed earlier in this chapter is also a form of peer mediation, in this case one invented by children themselves.

While far from conclusive, the growing and mostly positive body of research on the effectiveness of peer mediation in addressing classroom disorder as well as peer conflicts and abuse (Johnson et al. 1995; Woodhead and Faulkner 2000) suggests that what works in Japanese preschools and small communities in the Malaysian rain forest may apply as well to problems in American schools.

SCHOOL LIFE COMPARED TO HOME LIFE

While an unequal balance of power between kids and adults is common to home and school environments, there are some crucial differences. As Jackson (1968) pointed out, family members share a personal history, and "emotional ties between children and parents are usually stronger and last longer than those between children and teachers" (29). The Irish fifth grader who identified children as the least important people in his school hastened to add, "We are important to our mams" (Devine 2002, 314). Kids can "be themselves" at home in ways that are generally unacceptable at school, a distinction that was vividly demonstrated to Boocock during a period of research in Tokyo, where she sometimes accompanied a colleague to meet her son, a first grader, after school. Reportedly a model of decorum in the classroom, the boy was transformed into a whining, clinging baby when he passed through the school gate and spotted his impressively empathic mom. On more than one occasion, the boy lay down on the road outside the school and had a tantrum. According to his mother, the infantile behavior he frequently displayed at home ceased when he returned to school the next day.

However much schools claim to be concerned with kids' overall development, they are by necessity less holistic than the home in relating to them. Entering School 1, children "find themselves treated as group members rather than as individuals" (Mayall 1994, 124) and have "their first experience with power that has personal consequences for them wielded by a relative stranger" (Jackson 1968, 29). This distinction is underscored in the rather dour observation by Emile Durkheim (1961), one of the founders of the discipline of sociology, in a lecture delivered to students at the University of Paris at the beginning of the twentieth century, that

> the schoolroom society is much closer to the society of adults than it is to that of the family. For, aside from the fact that it is larger, the individuals—teachers and students—who make it up are not brought together by personal feelings or preferences but for altogether general and abstract reasons. [The] rule of the classroom cannot bend or give with the same flexibility as that of the family [nor can it] accommodate itself to given temperaments. . . . It is a first initiation into the austerity of duty. Serious life has now begun. (24)

CONCLUSIONS

When they enter school, children enter a bifurcated world. On one side is the formal educational system designed and controlled by adults, where children learn how to survive the daily grind. On the other side is the (to most of them) far more important sphere created and controlled by and with their peers. While adults continue to debate whether school work is "real" work, kids continue to view school as the place where they meet their friends.

After reconsidering the problems besetting his country's schools from the perspective of the children attending them, the Japanese writer whose experience as a fourth grader was described in this chapter proposed to his fellow adults that they "rid themselves of their self-serving belief that children should always do as the grownups say. It is really thanks to the incredible patience of children that the Japanese education system has somehow survived to this day. Through the decades, schools have taken advantage of that patience to silence the children and keep them in line, when those children actually deserved far better as legitimate beneficiaries of the nation's education system" (Jiro 1999, 85).

The research reviewed in chapter 6 and this chapter indicates that in or out of school, children are neither the naive innocents nor the uncontrolled monsters of adult imaginations. On the one hand, they frequently display creativity and inventiveness, loyalty and generosity, and great skill in organizing groups and group activities. On the other hand, they are capable of aggression and cruelty, racism, and sexism, much of which they learn from each other. As in adult groups, external pressures may precipitate disorder and even violence among kids.

In the next two chapters, we'll examine some of the social characteristics that differentiate children and sometimes divide them from each other.

NOTES

1. More recent research suggests that the daily grind can be found in many preschool programs as well. For example, in six licensed day care centers observed by Leavitt (1991), the adult staff organized children's time according to prescribed schedules, managed their bodies according to "routinized caregiver

practices," and enforced their participation in "procedures" that required waiting, turn taking, and compliance. Thus, "children's daily routines are tightly scheduled, with one activity leading at a prearranged time into the next, the whole sequence of activities being imposed by a system of formal rulings" (95).

2. For more recent evidence in support of Stephens's "early warning" about the health hazards to children of sacrificing leisure time and physical exercise to academics, see Nishino and Larson (2003). Cram schools are now a major export from East Asia to Western nations. The Kumon Educational Institute, whose enrollment of 1.5 Japanese students makes it the nation's largest cram school system, now serves almost as many children overseas (Manzo 2002).

3. Chapter 1 of *Peer Power*, in which the Adlers discuss their parent-as-research roles, makes an interesting companion piece to Lareau's appendix on methodology (see chapter 5, note 1).

4. The Internet makes peer abuse even more difficult to detect, enabling bullies to torment their victims out of sight and at a distance. A *New York Times* investigation reported that "tools like e-mail messages and Web logs enable the harassment to be both less obvious and more publicly humiliating, as gossip, put-downs and embarrassing pictures are circulated among a wide audience of peers with a few clicks" (August 26, 2004).

IV

VARIOUS CHILDHOODS

8

RACE, ETHNICITY, AND SOCIAL STATUS: THE CREATION OF SOCIAL HIERARCHIES IN CHILDHOOD

I had a girlfriend who was Asian, but only in the sense of the way she looked. Her family was fully Americanized, or whatever . . . I considered her to be white, basically, except physically.

—White American male high school senior

You're the same color as the rabbit poop.

—White American girl, age three,
to an African American preschool classmate

Generally speaking, whites and people of color do not occupy the same social space or social status, and this very visible fact of American life does not go unnoticed by children.

—Debra Van Ausdale and Joe R. Feagin

In a chapter titled "One Childhood or Many?," James, Jenks, and Prout (1998) argue that a comparative understanding of children and childhood requires considering both 1) "what it is that all the children in a given society have in common" and 2) "the ways in which childhood is cross-cut by [significant] social divisions," producing, in their words, "plural childhoods" (125). In this chapter and the next, we'll focus on the latter by examining the social *variables* that determine children's life opportunities and experiences—that decide who is favored and who gets shortchanged, who receives a "world-class" education and who receives the kind of "counterfeit" education described in chapter 7 or none at all, and even who lives to a ripe old age and who dies young. Since we cannot cover all the characteristics that differentiate children and affect their lives, we'll limit our discussion to the most powerful predictors, in any society, of children's social position and their opportunities, experiences, and accomplishments:

- Race and ethnicity
- Socioeconomic status and social class
- Gender

In most societies, segregation by race, ethnicity, social status, and gender as well as by age begins early. We noted in chapter 6 that babies recognize and show a marked preference for other babies well before the end of their first year and that kids begin showing a preference for playmates of the same sex between ages two and three and a half and for playmates of the same race between ages three and four—though scholars disagree about the exact ages when these shifts occur. Within each of these categories children are stratified hierarchically so that some are more advantaged than others. We'll also consider how these variables relate to each other and their cumulative impact on children's lives.

RACE AND ETHNICITY: BIOLOGICALLY BASED OR SOCIALLY CONSTRUCTED?

The terms *race* and *ethnicity* have been variously defined, are often confounded, and are the subjects of continuing and often heated debate. In current usage, *race* generally refers to a person's or a group's *physical heritage*, of which skin color, facial features, and other characteristics of *physical appearance* are major indicators. *Ethnicity* generally refers to a person's or a group's *sociocultural heritage*, based on a common or shared national origin, language, religion, dietary and aesthetic preferences, dress and manners, and other traits that denote a common ancestry. In the studies discussed in this section, *race* and *ethnicity* are used variously and sometimes interchangeably, and many specialists in the field concur that "the boundaries between and within racial and ethnic groups are not nearly as sharp and fixed as many people assume. They in fact overlap and, in many ways, are blurred" (McLemore 1994, 11). Research in several disciplines also underscores the *subjective* nature of racial and ethnic definitions and classifications, blurring the boundaries even further.

Recent research in genetics and molecular biology indicates that the standard labels used to distinguish people by race have little or no biological meaning in that human beings, sharing a common ancestry and place of origin (Africa), are all members of the same (human) race. The social implications of this research have been explicated by sociological theorist Walter Wallace (1997) as follows:

> If we could trace Homo sapiens back somewhere between 8,000 and 16,000 generations [or between about 200,000 and 400,000 years ago], we would come to the few Homo sapiens women and men from which every single one of the nearly six billion humans now alive is descended.
>
> All humans, then, are Africans in origin, and except for those of us whose ancestors never migrated outside that original homeland, we all belong to the African diaspora . . . no matter how we identify ourselves ethnically, racially, and nationally now. (17)

Visible differences in skin color, moreover, do not translate into significant biological differences among groups. By contrast to the small number of genes that produce visible external traits including skin color and eye shape, nonvisible ("internal") traits like intelligence, artistic talent, and social skills are likely to be shaped by tens of thousands of genes. And as we saw in chapter 2 (section on biosocial and genetic perspectives), a child's genetic inheritance and the extent to which she is able to realize her biological potential are themselves shaped by environmental influences.

Many of the variations in thought and behavior that are commonly associated with racial or ethnic differences are in fact the result of *culture*. "Overseas kids," children who spend their early childhood outside their native country, do not change skin color, shape of eyes, or other "racial" characteristics, but their behavior—how they speak, eat, dress, and play—will

almost certainly be shaped by the culture of the host society. Many overseas kids become bicultural, fluent in the languages and customs of native
and host societies and adept at using each in appropriate situations. Compared to race and ethnicity, culture is highly *transitory*. Cultural beliefs
about how to raise and educate children shift as rapidly as the products favored by children's peer cultures, and no matter how closely one identifies
with one's race or ethnic roots, adaptation to cultural change is inevitable.

EXPERIENCING RACE AND RACISM

Although most racial *differences* are not strictly biologically based, racial
identity is an important part of children's self-image and their view and
treatment of others. Moreover, research from a number of different societies consistently indicates that children acquire racial awareness earlier than most people believe—or *want* to believe. Some of the clearest
evidence of children's familiarity with their society's racial hierarchy was
gathered from South African children living under the apartheid system
(Foster 1986). By age six, White children shown line drawings of different groups not only differentiated among groups but also assigned positive stereotypes predominantly to Caucasoid-featured faces. Their ethnocentrism increased with age. White Afrikaans-speaking children
appeared to be more prejudiced than White English-speaking children
toward Black children. In early childhood, Black and other non-White
children also identified with and preferred symbols of Whiteness (e.g.,
dolls), and while *misidentification* decreased gradually by age, *preference* for White figures did not. Indian children aged three to six who
were shown a series of pictures and asked to describe the people in
them used words like "lazy," "bad," "stupid," and "dirty" to describe colored and Black figures, whereas White figures were viewed positively
(Foster 1986, 169). Given a choice of racial classification other than
their own, most Black children aged six to fourteen wanted to be White,
and few chose other South African tribal groups—"especially those
groups generally regarded as most similar to their own" (172). Noting
the weak relationship between attitudes and behavior, Foster predicted
that friendship and play patterns would be even more ethnocentric than
stated racial attitudes.

A study comparing the racial orientations of several thousand fourteen- and seventeen-year-old high school students representing all major racial groups, shortly before and after the installation of a popularly elected Black majority government, indicates that this revolutionary political change at the national level has not yet brought about a diminution of racism among South African kids. In fact, scores on two measures of anti-Black African racism rose, particularly among Whites, *after* the election. Among Black participants, both out-group preference for Whites and rejection of other Black groups continued after the end of apartheid. Few colored, Indian, and Black African adolescents displayed positive orientations toward other non-White groups, indicating that "young South Africans who are not White have not integrated a broader openness to other formerly oppressed groups" (Dawes and Finchilescu 2002, 161). These disappointing findings may reflect the short interval between the two surveys and the fact that the new government had had little time to address the vast economic and cultural divisions that fueled interracial hostilities.

Learning Race and Racism in a Preschool

Many readers of *The First R* (Van Ausdale and Feagin 2001) are unprepared for its portrayal of twenty-first-century preschool life. In a highly rated American day care center that many parents chose because of its diversity and its explicitly multicultural curriculum, the authors found a staggering amount of racism in the children's verbal comments and play patterns, nearly always in the direction of minority children being stigmatized or rejected by White children. *The First R* is filled with empirical evidence that belies the common adult misperception that young children have little or no awareness of racial differences and are innocent of racism unless actively taught otherwise (by adults). All the following incidents observed and recorded by Van Ausdale involved three- or four-year-old kids:

- A girl of mixed race preparing for nap time begins to move her cot to the other side of the classroom. Asked by the teacher why she was doing this, the girl, pointing to a Black child on a nearby cot, replied, "Because I can't sleep next to a nigger. . . . Niggers are stinky. I can't sleep next to one" (1).

- Playing in the sandbox, a White girl tells a Black classmate, "You're the same color as the rabbit poop" and "Your skin is shitty. You have to leave. We don't allow shit in the sandbox." On another occasion, the same White girl told the same Black girl not to go in the swimming pool because she would "get the water all dirty" (109–10).
- White girl is pulling two classmates, one White and the other Asian, across the playground in a wagon. This is not an easy task given the heavy load and the loose dirt of the playground, and she eventually drops the handle and stands still breathing heavily. At this point, the Asian girl jumps out of the wagon and picks up the handle. As she begins to pull, the White girl, hands on hips and frowning, admonishes her: "No. No. You can't pull this wagon. Only white Americans can pull this wagon" (104).
- Two White boys, holding the outer corners of their eyes upward and giggling, run up to Van Ausdale and inform her, "We're *different* people. Like Lu" (134; emphasis added). (Lu is a Chinese American classmate.)

Van Ausdale and Feagin summarize the behavioral pattern they find again and again in their data as follows: "We see white children experimenting and learning how to be white and how to handle the privileges, propensities, and behaviors associated with the white position in society. We also see children of color learning how to deal with the reality of being Black, Asian, or Latino in a white-dominated society" (37). As a result of the "glorification of whiteness" that permeates the peer culture even at this "progressive" preschool, "by the age of three [a] Black child has become vigilant for racial language directed at her and reacted strongly to negative remarks about her skin color, especially if those remarks came from white children" (111). At the same time, they believe that the majority of White Americans remain in denial about race and racism, persisting in their belief that young children are ignorant of racial matters. At the meeting of parents and school staff convened by the director to discuss the incident, described previously, in which a mixed-race child refused to nap near an African American classmate, adult denial took two forms: "Initially, the relevant adults seem to be shocked, and they refused to believe that a young child could know much about racial matters, much less use a racist epithet in a meaningful way. Once the fact of the child's behavior is accepted, all adults turn to denying that they are the source of racist behaviors" (she certainly didn't learn that *here* or from *us*). Several of them exculpate themselves by suggesting another person is responsible (e.g., that "redneck" who lives in our neighborhood). Significantly, while the professionals offered to loan the parents some multicultural story-books to read aloud at home and suggested some other methods for teaching their daughter about diversity, *none of the adults paid any attention to "the possible impact of the incident on Black children at the center"* (99–100; emphasis added). Van Ausdale also reports that when she presented her findings to the center staff, they were "baffled and disbelieving of the field data," insisting that "these aren't our kids!" (40). (Scott had similar experiences presenting her observations of African American girls to elementary school teachers and administrators.)

Race and Racism at the Elementary School Level

Adult denial also appeared to explain why a project on the topic "Does Skin Color Make a Difference?," designed by a third-grade girl in Boulder, Colorado, was pulled from her school's science fair. Samples of fifth graders and of adults were asked to rate the prettiness of brown-skinned and white-skinned Barbie dolls, one wearing a purple gown and the other a blue one. Adults preferred whichever doll was wearing the purple gown regardless of skin color, but most kids preferred the White doll regardless of dress color. The project was noteworthy not only for the student researcher's skillful use of experimental methodology but also because it precipitated a furor in the community, with adults divided over whether the findings might be hurtful to children of color, whether such a "controversial" project was appropriate for an elementary student, and whether the student's free speech rights were violated when her project was removed from the fair (*New York Times*, March 4, 2001).

Several recent ethnographic studies provide insights into how elementary school children learn (from adults and from their emerging peer cultures) the meaning of racial categories and locate themselves and others within the racial hierarchy. African American boys are particularly vulnerable to subjective interpretations of race. Both Lewis (2003) and Ferguson (2000) present disturbing examples of school personnel labeling African American boys as criminals in the making, so that their misbehavior "is made to take on a sinister, intentional, fully conscious tone that is stripped of any element of childish naïveté" (Ferguson 2000, 83). Lewis (2003) witnessed the following conversation between an African American fourth grader and one of his former teachers. Asked about his future plans, the boy said that

> he wanted to go to college but first he had to go to prison. When [the teacher] looked horrified and asked him what he was thinking about, he spelled it out for her: "All black men go to prison." He thought it would be more efficient to get his prison term out of the way before he went to college rather than having to do it afterward. (54)

Lewis (2003) found that Latina girls were also stereotyped, in the opposite direction but, she felt, with equally damaging consequences:

> Latinas expressed their alienation from school as silently as African American boys did loudly. In many ways their silence was just as potent and destructive as the negative attention black boys got: these girls' needs still were not recognized or addressed [and their] silence went beyond good behavior to a particular kind of nonparticipation, a pattern that did not receive much attention because the girls were not interrupting or getting in anyone's way. (80)

In an inner-city English school, minority children were stereotyped in ways that affected their peer group position and relations. Girls of South Asian origins were perceived as passive and alien, which rendered them sexually attractive to the boys, while Black girls were positioned to adopt a tomboy identity that limited their ability to acquire a feminine identity and reduced their attractiveness to the boys *as girls* (Connolly 1998). (Scott found a similar propensity to define five- and six-year-old minority girls in sexual terms among American school personnel, though in the schools she studied, African American girls were labeled as sexually precocious.) South Asian boys tended to be perceived as small, helpless, and eager to please, an image that, because of its traditional association with girls, caused them to be excluded from social group activities and to be verbally and sometimes physically assaulted (Connolly 1998). In contrast, Black boys, stereotyped as "walking symbols of masculinity" because of their perceived athleticism and knowledge of popular culture, swear words, girls, and sex, aroused mixed feelings of resentment and respect, and they were often embroiled in conflicts with White boys who felt their masculine identities as well as their play territories threatened (Connolly 1998).

Wilma King's research on southern childhoods before and during the American Civil War documents the complicated history of interpersonal relations between White children and children of color. Even during the most racially divided periods of U.S. history, White and Black kids played together. Indeed, group play was more likely to be divided on gender than on racial lines. Black and White boys played marbles together and engaged in male sports and contests of strength; girls played ring games, jumped rope, and played with dolls, again with little regard for color, although then as now, the quality of toys varied: "White girls sometimes owned porcelain dolls, while their enslaved playmates used rags or corn cobs to represent their babies" (King 1995, 54). Children's fantasy play also reflected the larger society's racial structure. King describes kids using hickory sticks to simulate the flogging of slaves, and White children sometimes used Black playmates as substitutes for Indians in war games. A former slave recalled a game in which "de whites was de soldiers an' me and de rest of de slave boys was de Injuns," who were shot and scalped by White soldiers armed with wooden guns. During the Civil War, southern children played "Harpers Ferry," a reenactment of John Brown's raid, and a number of games pitted White "Federates" against Black "Yankees." Needless to say, the Confederates always won (King 1995).

The psychic costs of belonging to a minority group that is not valued by the larger society have been quantified in a study of children's mental health in which African American children (ages seven to twelve) expressed both more worries and higher levels of anxiety than White or Hispanic children of the same age (LaGreca, Silverman, and Wasserstein 1995).

Race and Racism at the High School Level

The author of an ethnographic study of the top-ranked, competitive-entry high school in a large eastern U. S. city (Lee 1996) found that students, teachers, and administrators alike stereotyped Asian American students as a "model minority" of quiet, polite, hardworking high achievers and African American students as lacking the motivation and abilities of their European American and Asian American classmates (even though *all* students had met the *same* demanding entry requirements). As a result, the mostly White faculty and staff "pit Asian Americans against African Americans and against all students who were outsiders at Academic High School. Although the school played a role in fueling interracial tension between Asian Americans and other students of color, most white teachers and administrators denied the very existence of interracial tension at the school" (70).

In this highly competitive, academically oriented high school, Asian American students, located uneasily somewhere between Black and White, were doubly victimized by racial stereotyping. As members of a "model minority," they were assumed to be a homogeneous group with no problems, which at times led teachers to give them higher grades than they had actually earned but at other times made them quite literally unable to see Asian students who were floundering academically or socially. Most of the Asian students embraced the model minority stereotype and used it to elevate themselves above other racial minorities—Lee (1996) found that Korean American students in particular held "blatantly negative stereotypes about African Americans" as lazy and inferior. They looked up to the White students, believing that "if they dressed and spoke like their white, middle-class peers and otherwise acted like white, middle-class people, they would eventually be accepted." Sadly, their efforts to get closer to their White schoolmates were seldom successful; while some Korean American students claimed to have many White friends, in fact "most of them socialized solely with other Koreans" (101–3).

A very different picture of the model minority is offered by a study of Korean Americans who had dropped out of high school. Like the students in Lee's study, these former students had internalized a view of race as a Black–White continuum, but they situated themselves differently. One respondent said he felt closer to Blacks and Hispanics than to Whites and thought that

> most Koreans are closer to Black culture. It's not that I hate whites, but I
> don't like them either. . . . When I see a white person, the first thing I
> think about is that they are rich and educated, and most Koreans like me
> are not educated and rich. So when I see them, I think they are from another planet. (Lew, in press)

While the elite high school studied by Lee had a racially diverse student body and a few minority teachers, racial segregation continues to be the norm in American public schools. The exposure of minority students to White students has actually declined since 1970. More than fifty years after the U.S. Supreme Court ruled in *Brown v. Board of Education* that segregated schools violated children's constitutional right to an "equal" education, the majority of African American students attend schools with few if any White students (a third are in schools that are 90 to 100 percent minority), Latino students are even more segregated (by language as well as by race and poverty), and Whites are the most segregated of all (only 14 percent attend racially diverse public schools; Cohen 2004; Orfield and Frankenberg 2004).

Language

A number of ethnographic studies have pinpointed language as an important means by which kids construct racial-cultural identities, their own and others'. According to Amanda Lewis (2003), who studied three elementary schools of differing racial composition, "Language is not a neutral mode of communication but a way of telling who people are, where they are from, whether they are in some way collectively different or whether they are 'like us' and therefore people to whom we can easily relate" (132). In a study of two high schools, one predominantly White the other predominantly Black, Pamela Perry (2002) found that in the first school, White students distanced themselves from their African American classmates by referring to them as "cool" but "tough," "gangster," "menacing," and other descriptors borrowed from hip-hop culture and rap music, and Black students were for the most part acquiescent in being thus labeled by the dominant peer culture. In the predominantly Black high school, however, some African American students objected vigorously to Whites' superficial appropriation of their language and culture. As one girl put it, "They'll be listening to rap music and trying to wear clothes that we wear and overdo it. . . . And that's why sometimes we don't like white people because it's, like, you're making me look bad. You're trying to be me, but you're getting only the surface" (126).

Perhaps in reaction to the way they are defined by the dominant culture, some Black kids tend to be more assertive, argumentative, and oppositional in their verbal expression (Corsaro 1997). As the following boy–girl exchange illustrates, they are also likely to be skilled in word-play and extended verbal sparring liberally sprinkled with insults:

> Billy: (laughing)
> Martha: I don't know what you *laughin* at.
> Billy: I know what I'm laughin at. Your *head*.
> Martha: I know I'm laughin at *your* head too.
> Billy: You know you ain't laughin cuz you ain't laughin.
> Martha: Ha ha (mirthless laughter).
> Billy: Ha ha. I got more hair than *you*.
> Martha: You do not. Why you gotta laugh? You *know* you ain't got more hair than me.
> Billy: (taking out shoestrings) Fifty-four inches. (Goodwin 1990, 178)

Joking and teasing between boys and girls were also common among working-class White middle school kids studied by Eder (1995), and Goodwin found that, contrary to stereotype, fifth-grade Puerto Rican and Mexican girls at play hurled commands and insults at each other freely.

Language can be used in various ways to express and maintain group solidarity. As we saw in chapter 6, kids learn early not to talk about sex, toilets, and other taboo topics when they are around adults, and they sometimes create their own vocabulary in order to conceal their knowledge of these interesting subjects. A group of Taiwanese kindergartners strove to achieve a sense of collective identity by engaging in complex word games that involved all members of the group (Hadley 2003). Cantonese-speaking students in an all-English-speaking Canadian high school switched to their home language when conversing with friends outside of class—talking English to a friend was considered pretentious and unnatural (Goldstein 2003). Just as ambitious African American youths engage in linguistic "code switching"—speaking Black English among friends and family but switching to standard English with teachers or representatives of the dominant White culture—so the Cantonese Canadian students learned how to switch back and forth between the language of their families and friends and the language of (White) Canada.

Occasionally, language can be the means for children to cross racial and ethnic barriers. In a dual-language Mandarin-English public elementary school in New York in which the majority of students are children of Chinese immigrants and about 10 percent are African American children who often endure long daily commutes in order to attend a school with a reputation for excellence, there was little racial stereotyping and hostility. Gabrielle, an African American first grader, sees all the children at the school as her friends. On a day when a *New York Times* reporter visited the school, Gabrielle's teacher had assigned her to be a buddy and guide for Linda, a shy new classmate from China's Fujian Province:

> "What do you like to do?" Gabrielle asked earnestly, in Mandarin.
> Linda, who was blushing, shook her head.
> "Do you like food? Do you like toys?" Gabrielle asked, again, in Mandarin.
> Again, Linda simply stared at her.
> Gabrielle looked away, sighed, and concluded, in English, "She doesn't like talking. But I will keep talking to her."
> By the end of the day, Linda still wasn't talking. But she was smiling back at Gabrielle. (*New York Times*, November 2, 2002)

In the preschool where Van Ausdale recorded so many racist incidents, she also observed a budding friendship between two boys who literally did not speak the same language. One of the boys was of Middle Eastern origins and spoke English; the other of Chinese origins spoke only a Chinese dialect. Undeterred by this barrier, the boys created a language of their own that blended elements of English and Chinese. Each boy was able to communicate clearly to adults in his home language, but their invented language was incomprehensible to anyone but themselves. Their parents and teacher failed to see the language for what it was—"an innovative synthesis of two languages formed by young children maintaining a cross-ethnic friendship"—and instead worried that it represented a regression to baby talk, jealousy toward a new sibling, or some kind of developmental disorder. Van Ausdale and Feagin (2001) conclude somewhat sadly that the boys' status as children prevented even the adults who were closest to them from considering an alternative explanation (see also the section "Unknown Inventors" in chapter 6).

RACIAL AND ETHNIC MINORITIES AND MAJORITIES

Among ethnic minorities, children who are members of *outcaste* groups are especially likely to be singled out for discrimination and mistreatment. For example, Gypsy children are stigmatized and discriminated against throughout the world (Buchanan and Sluckin 1994; Okely 1997). In Japan, members of the Buraku minority, although *not* a distinct racial group (differing from mainstream Japanese neither in language nor in skin color or any other visible racial indicator), have suffered from ostracism and severe discrimination since their designation as an outcaste group early in the seventeenth century. Even today, despite the success of Buraku Liberation League activists in promoting legislation prohibiting anti-Buraku discrimination and affirmative action programs to redress past wrongs, Buraku children continue to be more likely than other Japanese children to attend lower-ranked schools, to lag behind their classmates in all academic areas, to have higher absenteeism (twice the national average) and more reported behavior problems, and to drop out of high school.

Although a government-approved uniform curriculum for all Japanese schools is mandated by the Ministry of Education, comparisons of first-grade classes in one large city revealed striking differences in curriculum and modes of teaching and classroom management. In an elementary school in which about a third of the students were Buraku, the first graders spent most of the day being drilled on a few *hiragana* (phonetic characters of the Japanese syllabic alphabet) and a pair of numbers. During one visit, the observer noted that

> the students' role was largely passive—they answered questions when called upon, worked individually in workbooks or handouts from the teacher, and waited for their written work to be checked. Boys frequently broke the class rule against shouting answers without being called upon or got into trouble for fighting or horsing around. The girls were generally silent and ignored by the teacher. The lessons were boring and time dragged. I had a hard time staying awake. (Boocock 2001, 11)

Just a few blocks away, in a second school that enrolled a small number of Buraku children whose identity was not known to many of the school personnel, first graders, singly or in small groups, recited the entire alphabet in the form of a song and were already reading stories (in contrast to the kids in the first school, who had not yet progressed beyond learning to recognize a few two-syllable words). In the first school, considerable class time was spent dealing with misbehavior (nearly always by boys), in the second school, almost none.

Many of the school personnel interviewed for this study explained the academic problems of Buraku students in terms of deficits in their homes and communities. The similarities between the school experiences of these Japanese outcaste children and the African American boys studied by Ferguson (2000) are noteworthy. She too found the low-track classes in which these boys were routinely placed mind-numbingly boring. Students never initiated activities, and the tasks assigned were simplistic and repetitive, encouraging rudimentary levels of thinking and allowing no creative efforts by the students. The teachers' low expectations, negative stereotyping, and disrespectful treatment of these boys set many of them inexorably on the path toward school failure and careers as "bad boys." The silent Buraku girls recalled the passage, quoted earlier in this chapter, from Lewis's observation of Latina girls.

A major impediment to change in children's attitudes and behavior is the tendency of members of majority or dominant groups, such as Americans of western European origins, to view *other people* as having an ethnicity but not *themselves*. Whiteness as an invisible, taken-for-granted identity is manifested in the beliefs and behavior of many White students in predominantly White high schools. The high school student quoted at the beginning of this chapter could see his Asian American girlfriend only in terms of his conception of an American; only when he redefined her as "basically" White could she be considered "fully Americanized." Another White student was incensed by White schoolmates who attempted to copy Black clothing styles and vernacular: "I say, What the hell is your *problem*, man? Can't you dress like *everyone else*? They just look kinda like *freaks*" (Perry 2002, 108–9; emphasis added). Scholars in the new field of White studies have pointed out that Whites who claim to have no ethnicity but assume a universal standard of "people like us" thereby ignore the magnitude of the privileges that come with being White European American and the ethnocentrism of viewing those who are not White European American as "other" (Clark and O'Donnell 1999).

CHILDREN OF MIXED RACE OR ETHNICITY

In a 1996 article titled "Race Is Over," Stanley Crouch argues that because of the explosive worldwide increase in cross-cultural contacts, either face to face through migration and travel or in Cyberspace via the Internet,

> Americans of the future will find themselves surrounded in every direction by people who are part Asian, part Latin, part African, part European, part American Indian. What such people will look like is beyond my imagination, but the sweep of body types, combinations of facial features, hair textures, eye colors and what are now unexpected skin tones will be far more common, primarily because the current paranoia over mixed marriages should by then be largely a superstition of the past. . . . As the density of cross-influences progresses, we will get far beyond the troubles the Census Bureau now has with racial categories. (170–71)

In fact, what people of mixed race or ethnicity will look like does not have to be left to the imagination or the future. A visitor to a public school in almost any part of the United States will find many examples. That the kinds of racial and ethnic combinations Crouch says are beyond his imagination already exist in large numbers is evidenced by the head shots of twenty American children accompanying his article. Included are kids who identified themselves as Pakistani/African American, Filipino/Italian/Russian, Dominican/Russian/Jewish, Hungarian/Japanese, and Chinese/Native American/Filipino/Scottish!

Though increasing in numbers, biracial children, like other minority children, continue to be disproportionately susceptible to stress and stress-related behavior problems. Preliminary findings from a longitudinal study now in progress at University of North Carolina, based on a national sample of American adolescents, indicate that students who identify themselves as mixed race suffer from higher rates of depression, substance abuse, and sleeping problems than other respondents (Udry, Li, and Smith 2003). How it feels to be a biracial adolescent trying to construct a coherent self was eloquently expressed in the memoir of Barack Obama (2004), the newly elected U.S. senator from Illinois who is the son of a White European American mother and a Black African father:

> I learned to slip back and forth between my black and white worlds, understanding that each possessed its own language and customs and structures of meaning, convinced that with a bit of translation on my part the two worlds would eventually cohere. Still the feeling that something

wasn't quite right stayed with me, a warning that sounded whenever a white girl mentioned in the middle of conversation how much she liked Stevie Wonder; or when the school principal told me I was cool. . . . There was a trick there somewhere, although what the trick was, who was doing the tricking, and who was being tricked, eluded my conscious grasp. (82)

SOCIOECONOMIC STATUS AND SOCIAL CLASS: THE BEST PREDICTORS OF KIDS' FUTURES

Of all social variables, the position of parents on the social status ladder is the best single predictor of their children's life chances, from the probability of their surviving infancy and early childhood to the social resources available in their communities and schools to the social positions they attain in adulthood. It also is the most socially constructed of the variables discussed in this chapter. A genetic model that explains persisting status gaps by "natural" *group differences* in capacities has been largely discredited, though social scientists continue to disagree over whether these gaps are primarily the result of social, political, and economic disparities between class, race, ethnic, and gender *groups* or of *individual* differences in effort. On the other hand, epidemiological data document the effects of social status on physical health, in particular, the negative effects of low status in early childhood on life expectancy: "Wherever you stand on the social ladder, your risk of early death is higher than it is for your social betters. . . . The nearer we are to the bottom, the sicker we are likely to be and the younger we are likely to die" (Epstein 1998, 27). Conflict theorists hold the social stratification system responsible for "othering" poor families—blaming *them* for their failure to get ahead and for placing their children "at risk"— and insist that the solution requires changing the institutional structures that create and maintain inequality (Swadener and Lubeck 1995; see also the discussion of conflict theory in chapter 2).

* In sociological analyses, the most frequently used terms for social position are *socioeconomic status* (SES) and *social class*. Like race and ethnicity, SES and social class are variously defined and often used interchangeably. The major components of SES generally include income (earned and unearned), amount and type of education, and occupational

level and prestige. Members of a social class are similar to each other in economic, occupational, and educational characteristics, and, in addition, social class typically designates the power, privilege, and prestige associated with a particular location in the social hierarchy. The variables making up SES or social class are themselves correlated, and some sociologists believe that these correlations have strengthened over time. For example, not only are the level and quality of children's education affected by their family's social status, but

> at the same time, parental education and income have become more highly correlated, owing to the increased payoff to education. Thus students from high-income families are now doubly advantaged in that they tend to have parents with higher levels of education as well. This advantage leads to 5 to 10 percent higher earnings for these youth later in life. (Danziger and Waldfogel 2000, 10)

The transfer of social advantages and disadvantages across generations is a central theme of Lareau's *Unequal Childhoods* (2003). As we saw in chapter 5, Lareau found that class-based differences in child rearing, organization of daily life, and modes of interacting with school and other authorities enabled the higher-status families to accumulate appreciably more of the social capital that would ensure their kids a favorable position in the social hierarchy. However, just as Van Ausdale and Feagin argue that Americans deny the continuing existence of racism, Lareau argues that they deny the power of social class, preferring to attribute getting ahead in life to individual initiative. Surrounded by evidence of the uneven distribution of wealth, good schools, interesting and well-paying jobs, and nice homes in safe neighborhoods, they yet avoid making the connection between differential access to valuable resources and unequal childhoods (Lareau 2003).

Though Lareau's argument relied on qualitative analysis of a small nonrandom sample of families, similar patterns can be found in highly quantitative research (e.g., Duncan and Brooks-Gunn's [1999] statistical analyses of sociodemographic data on the consequences for children's health, well-being, and achievements of growing up poor). Reports on the outcomes of the Scholastic Aptitude Test (SAT) nearly always point out gaps between groups of test takers. Overall, average SAT scores fluctuate over time, though they have been rising in recent years and are currently at their highest average since 1974. However, disparities by status remain large, in particular, the correlation between SAT scores and family income. Recent calculations showed that the total score for students from households with a total income under $10,000 averaged *864*, compared to an average combined score of *1,123* for students from households with incomes totaling $100,000 or more—leading one analyst to comment that this amounted to awarding test takers "an SAT point for every $350 their parents take home" (Berube 2003, 18).

A variety of metaphors and models have been used to characterize and explain the misfortunes of children at the bottom of the status hierarchy. In a collection of studies on some of the most seriously disadvantaged children in the United States—including homeless children, Appalachian children transplanted to northern cities, immigrant children, poor school-aged mothers, and girls placed by court order in an alternative high school where they were routinely abused by older males—the editor characterizes these children as *invisible*, a metaphor used by some of the kids to describe themselves. A nine-year-old boy who had experienced repeated periods of homelessness complained that none of his classmates would play with him: "They think 'cos I haven't got no home that I haven't got nothing inside of me." A recent immigrant from the Philippines said, "When I went to my new school, no one talked to me. It was like I didn't exist" (Books 1998, xix).

In the next chapter, we'll continue the analysis of various childhoods by looking for comparable patterns in the definition and treatment of girls and boys and consider the combined and interactive effects of social background variables. Conclusions for both chapters will be provided at the end of chapter 9.

9

BECOMING GIRLS AND BOYS

I want my girls to be girls and my boys, boys.

—American fourth-grade teacher

As I watch more carefully, what I see surprises me: The girls run more and the boys less than I thought.

—Vivian Paley

GENDER: BIOLOGICALLY BASED OR SOCIALLY CONSTRUCTED?

Like racial and ethnic identities, sexual identity is shaped by a complex combination of physical, psychic, social, and cultural influences. The socially constructed or "sex-specific ways of appearing, acting and feeling can be collectively referred to as *gender*" (Cahill 1986, 165–65). Sandra Bem (1993), a leading theorist on sex and gender, postulates how three assumptions embedded in our cultural beliefs and social institutions lead us to equate or confound gender with sex:

1. *Androcentrism*, or male centeredness, the assumption that males are superior to females and that the male experience is the standard or norm for human beings
2. *Gender polarization*, the assumption that males and females are fundamentally different from each other
3. *Biological essentialism*, the assumption that rationalizes and legitimizes male centeredness and gender polarization by treating them as the natural, inevitable consequences of the intrinsic biological natures of women and men

Like race classification, sex identification is based on learned visual cues. Bem (1993) cites research showing that "fully 50 percent of American three-, four-, and five-year-olds are able to distinguish male from female only when those males and females are clothed and coiffed in a fully gender-polarizing way" (148). Her son learned this on the day he decided to wear barrettes to nursery school:

> Several times that day, another boy insisted that Jeremy must be a girl because "only girls wear barrettes." After repeatedly insisting that "wearing barrettes doesn't matter; being a boy means having a penis and testicles," Jeremy finally pulled down his pants to make his point more convincingly. The other boy was not impressed. He simply said, "Everyone has a penis; only girls wear barrettes." (149)

Like race, ethnicity, and social class, gender is a prime determinant of life chances. Differential attitudes toward and treatment of girls and boys begin at birth or even before. In several Asian countries, most prominently in India and China, the use of prenatal scans for selective abortions of female fetuses as well as infanticide, abandonment, and sale of female babies are producing increasingly skewed sex ratios. Calculations by the Nobel Prize–winning economist Amartya Sen estimated a shortfall of about 100 million females worldwide in the 1990s and no indication of a major reversal of "son preference" (Sen 1990, 2003).

Biologically, female fetuses and infants are hardier than their male counterparts. If not aborted, they are more likely to survive gestation and birth; if not killed at birth, they are more likely to survive infancy. This biological advantage is reversed in early childhood; nature may favor girls, but human society favors boys (Gittins 1998). Reflecting the combined forces of economics, culture, and religion, in "almost every society and culture, boys are preferred and privileged over girls." Gender discrimination "may be subtle, as when boys but not girls are encouraged to pursue advanced education, or when parents expect more work from girls and give boy children more leisure time. It may be pronounced, as when girl children are physically neglected, or given smaller shares of food, health care or other resources" (Seager 1997, 34). In poor homes and poor societies, "it is the girls and women who almost invariably go short or go without" (Gittins 1998, 35).

In prosperous industrialized societies, it is assumed that serious gender discrimination no longer exists and that daughters and sons are equally welcomed and nurtured. Yet two economists at the University of California at Berkeley found indications that even in the twenty-first century, American parents favor boys in ways that have lifelong implications. In every decade since the 1940s, couples with girls divorced more often than those with boys. By the turn of the century, more than 10,000 divorces per year "appear to stem partly from the number of girls in the family." The "divorce gap" was not great for families with a single girl versus families with a single boy but rose with the number of children—the difference between the divorce rates of families with three or four girls versus families with three or four boys was considerable. This phenomenon occurred in every region of the country, though the divorce gap was somewhat greater among Whites than among Blacks and among parents with fewer years of formal education. Parents, especially fathers, invested more money in their family if it included a son (e.g., parents of boys spent on average $600 more a year on housing than parents of all-girl families). Moreover, the effects went beyond mere economics. Among unmarried women who had ultrasound scans, those carrying boys were slightly more likely to marry the father than those with girls. And unmarried fathers were more likely to feed, diaper, and play with sons than daughters. These findings suggest that the favoring of boys is not confined to the past or to developing countries. It may be less widespread and more subtle in the United States than in China or India, but it still gives many boys an important head start (*New York Times*, October 26, 2003).

RAISING GIRLS AND BOYS

Comparing data from two surveys of American fathers, one conducted in 1964, the second in 1982–1983, Alwin (1991) found little change in the socialization of boys and girls, leading him to conclude that "the changes experienced in the social roles of men and women have not yet been felt in changing orientations to children, either because the changes have basically occurred within the framework of more traditional family arrangements and have not affected the deeper structure of relationships, *or* because other changes in the family have mitigated the influences of cultural changes in definitions of gender roles" (219). The research literature is filled with evidence of differential definition and treatment of infants and young children by their parents, caretakers, and teachers. To give just one example, in a study in which parents of newborns were asked to describe them on a checklist of paired adjectives, they "tended to describe daughters as soft and warm while sons were typically described as strong and hardy"—although there were virtually no differences between male and female babies in weight and length or on physicians' ratings of muscle tone, reflexes, and heart and respiratory rates. Cahill (1986) interprets these findings as evidence that once parents "are informed of an infant's anatomically determined sex they view that infant's appearance and behavior as expressing the associated essential nature" (168; see Bem's assumptions 2 and 3). Parents, especially fathers, are still more concerned about sons being girlish than daughters being tomboys. Little girls in jeans climbing trees and swinging baseball bats are generally acceptable, but boys are often forbidden to dress up in their mother's finery, to play with dolls, or to choose girls as playmates by parents who fear this will turn their sons into sissies.

LEARNING AND ENACTING GENDER IN PRESCHOOL

Like racial stereotyping and segregation, gender stereotyping and segregation are so widespread among children of preschool age that they're often viewed as natural phenomena. Paley goes so far as to claim that "kindergarten is a triumph of sexual self-stereotyping." In *Boys and Girls: Superheroes in the Doll Corner* (1984), she provides numerous instances of boys and girls distancing themselves from each other. Girls spent most of their free time with art materials, and boys spent theirs in the block area, using sand, water, and paints only "as an extension of block play— actively, competitively" (30). A boy who approached a group of girls engaged in painting their nails was rejected in no uncertain terms. "Don't come in," he was told. "Only girls are allowed" (10). Paley's reluctant decision to allow girls and boys to conduct their games and running practice in different areas of the gym was greeted with loud cheers (36). On occasion, she asked her child colleagues to clarify these distinctions, as in the following exchange:

> Karen: Girls are nicer than boys.
> Janie: Boys are bad. Some boys are.
> Paul: Not bad. Pretend bad, like bad guys.
> Karen: My brother is really bad.
> Paley: Aren't girls ever bad?
> Paul: I don't think so. Not very much.
> Paley: Why not?
> Paul: Because they like to color so much. That's one thing I know. Boys have to practice running.
> Karen: And they practice being silly. (26–27)

When she observed carefully, Paley discovered that in fact the girls ran around and made as much noise as the boys and were just as messy, and she realized that some of the assumptions she had more or less taken for granted were based less on the children's actual behavior than on her response to it. She admitted that she seldom intervened when yelling girls chased meowing imaginary kittens around the room or argued over a red velvet cape, but

> the boy who runs out of the block area with a Tinker Toy gun in hand is stopped abruptly. He is not noisier than an escaping kitten, but he sounds more violent. He probably has less aggressive intent than the girls grabbing the red cape, but his fantasy makes me uneasy. (35)

Paley also found that the girls had one distinct advantage over male classmates: the range of acceptable behavior is wider for them, and they are less likely to be punished for nonconformity to gender rules.

Just as parents are less likely to accept girlish behavior in sons than tomboyish behavior in daughters, in kindergarten "a boy in a frilly bed-jacket expects to be laughed at, but a superhero cape on a girl creates no stir" (102).

A second preschool study provides greater detail on how gendered behavior may be taught and reinforced by preschool teachers. Through semistructured observations in five preschool classes, Martin (1998) identified a *hidden curriculum* that "turns children who are similar in bodily comportment, movement, and practice into girls and boys" (494). Girls' clothing tended to be less comfortable, more restrictive than boys' clothing, and teachers were "much more likely to manage girls and their clothing . . . rearranging their clothes, tucking in their shirts, fixing a ponytail gone astray" (498–99). They were also more likely to reprimand girls for inappropriate posture and behavior. For example, "girls were told to be quiet or to repeat a request in a quieter, 'nicer' voice about three times more often than were boys" (501–3). At age three, girls were about as likely as boys to engage in rough-and-tumble play, physical fighting, and arguing; by age five, girls were much less likely than boys or younger girls to engage in these behaviors.

Martin (1998) also observed instances of both girls and boys resisting the gender rules—for example, three-year-old boys sometimes dressed up in women's clothing, though five-year-old boys did not; girls were sometimes loud and physically assertive when teachers were not paying attention to them. From such behavior, she concluded that gender differences are neither "natural" nor "easily and straightforwardly acquired" but socially constructed. "Because this gendering occurs at an early age, the seeming naturalness of such differences is further underscored. In preschool, bodies become gendered in ways that are so subtle and taken-for-granted that they come to feel and appear natural" (510; see Bem's assumption 3).

GENDER AND PEER RELATIONS

One of the classics in the sociology of children and childhoods, Barrie Thorne's *Gender Play* (1993) is innovative in conceptualization and methodology and throws new light on the complex world of children's gender beliefs and rituals. Thorne observed more separation and stereo-typing by gender than by race and ethnicity, which were in turn empha-sized more than differences of religion or social class. Gender separation was greater in some locations and situations than others. Especially on the playground, individual identities tend to get submerged as kids hurl gender insults ("sissy boys," "dumb girls"), talk about the other gender as "yuck," and make stereotyped assertions ("girls are crybabies," "boys are frogs"):

> Extensive gender separation and organizing mixed-gender encounters as girls-against-the-boys set off contrastive thinking and feed an assumption of gender as dichotomous and antagonistic difference. These social prac-tices seem to express core truths: that boys and girls are separate and fun-damentally different, as individuals and as groups. (87)

But when, like Paley, she watched more carefully, Thorne discovered that "occasions where gender is less relevant, or contested, are also part of the construction of gender relations" (87). Segregation was rarely total—"even when 80 percent of the playground groups are either all-girl or all-boy, 20 percent of the groups contain both girls and boys" (49). She observed many incidents of heterosexual teasing and taunting (chasing, "cooties" and other pollution rituals, invading each other's turf), but also more cross-gender af-filiation than appears at first glance, especially when you're not looking for it or your assumptions prevent you from seeing it. Thorne learned about girl–boy friendships *outside* of school that went underground *in* school when a male classmate walked by a sixth-grade girl without even glancing at her, after which the girl confided to Thorne, "He's one of my best friends." "But you didn't even nod or say hello to each other," I said. "Oh," she replied, "we're friends in our neighborhood and at church, but at school we pretend not to know each other so we won't get teased" (50).

Thorne's (1993) concept of the *hegemonic view of gender* extends Bem's model and applies, we believe, to all the characteristics discussed in part IV. Thorne identifies the key components of the concept as 1) emphasis on gender as an oppositional dualism and 2) exaggeration of gender differ-ences and disregard for cross-gender commonalities and within-gender variations. If unchecked, gender hegemony can lead to the kinds of sexual harassment documented in the studies by Renold and by Lee and col-leagues (discussed in chapter 7). More generally, when X and Y are defined as opposite sides caught up in rivalry and competition, group (especially out-group) stereotyping and antagonism flourish. We'd postulate that X and Y can represent Black and White, American and non-American, Christian and Muslim, and adult and child, as well as female and male.

GENDER AND ACADEMIC ACHIEVEMENT

Figures from UNICEF (1999) indicate that in developing nations, girls receive less education than boys (about two-thirds of children who do not receive a primary education are girls). In sub-Saharan Africa, the number of girls *not* attending primary school rose from 20 million in 1990 to 24 million in 2002. This trend is disturbing, since researchers have also found that uneducated girls are much more likely to live in poverty as adults, to die in childbirth, to contract HIV, and to raise children who will, in turn, be poor and in ill health (UNICEF 2004). In many parts of Africa and Asia, girls seeking formal education face formidable obstacles, but in countries where religious conservatives who consider education wasted on girls have political power, attending school can be downright hazardous. Even after the post-Taliban government in Afghanistan lifted the ban on education for females over the age of eight, girls and their teachers continue to be threatened, and a number of girls' schools have been damaged or destroyed by rocket attacks, explosive devices detonated in the school buildings, or arson (*New York Times*, October 31, 2002). The highest recorded fatalities occurred at a girls' middle school in Mecca, Saudi Arabia, when a fire started in the kitchen spread to the rest of the building. The only exit was locked, and the only guard with a key could not be found. In the ensuing panic,

> fifteen girls were trampled to death; more than fifty others were injured, some having jumped from the windows. According to eyewitnesses, a number of people had rushed to put out the blaze, but they were turned away by a representative of the Commission for the Promotion of Virtue and the Prevention of Vice—the country's religious police—because the girls were not wearing their [head coverings]. . . . After the fire, the head of the Presidency of Girls' Education announced that it had been "God's will." (L. Wright 2004, 51)

In the industrialized nations of East Asia and the Pacific, the gender gap in primary education is virtually closed, and in North American and western European countries, there is gender parity in enrollment rates at the primary and secondary levels and a growing female advantage at the tertiary level. (In North America, about 90 percent of girls are enrolled in postsecondary educational programs compared to about 75 percent of boys.) Comparisons of student academic performance in industrialized societies continue to show female progress in virtually every area and female advantage in some. In the United States, girls receive a disproportionate share of good grades, high class ranks, and academic prizes, while boys are more likely to repeat a grade, to be put in special education, to be diagnosed with learning disorders, and to be put on behavior-modifying medication like Ritalin. Even in the areas of greatest male advantage, math and science, girls in many countries are catching up, and the male–female gap seems to be explained more by differences in girls' and boys' access to math classes than by differences in their mathematical ability (Baker and Jones 1993). The results of a study conducted by the Educational Testing Service based on a representative national sample of American twelfth graders and comparing outcomes on literally hundreds of different tests and measures showed that

> average performance difference across all subjects is essentially zero. The familiar math and science advantage for males was found to be quite small, significantly smaller than 30 years ago. However, a language advantage for females has remained largely unchanged over that time period. (Cole 1997, 3)

If gender discrimination is so widespread and if, as some critics have claimed, girls are shortchanged or silenced in the classroom, how is the impressive improvement in girls' educational outcomes to be explained? It is probably not coincidental that it was preceded by the "second wave" of feminism that began in the 1970s and that, among other things, called attention to the ways educational systems have failed girls—an important first step toward correcting them. Some of the strategies developed to enhance "girl power" might also benefit their male classmates.

INTERACTIVE EFFECTS OF BACKGROUND VARIABLES

A number of the findings discussed in this chapter and the previous one have indicated that the effects of background variables are not independent of each other. A brief excerpt from Scott's study of African American girls' play patterns describes a school setting in which the interactive effects of race, gender, and socioeconomic status were especially pronounced. In a middle-income elementary school with a racially diverse student population (but in which a majority of the Black girls qualified for free or reduced-price lunch, thereby demarcating their families' low socioeconomic status), first-grade girls frequently engaged in fantasy play about babies and mothers. Through repeated observations, Scott came to realize that assignment to roles was not random, that "mothers" were nearly always African American, and that "babies" were nearly always White. During one episode,

> a White girl crawls onto Tanisha's (a Black girl) lap where she sits until another Black girl picks her up and carries her back to the bench. Tanisha holds out her arms and the White "baby" returns to her lap. Another White girl is also playing "baby," and when Baby #1 is picked up by yet another Black "mother," Baby #2 makes infant gurgling noises and stretches out her arms to Baby #1. . . . When the "mother" carrying Baby #1 moves away, Baby #2 gets up and follows them, extending her hand to be held. (Scott 1999, 89–90)

Occasionally, physically small Black girls played the role of baby, tended by either White or Black "mothers." On one such occasion, a small Black girl being held by a White girl was put down by her "mother" but quickly picked up by a tall Black girl who put the "baby" on her own hip.

Though this is a highly condensed account of a small portion of an extensive long-term study, it contains in microcosm the story of how childhoods can be shaped by the interaction of race, gender, and social status. Despite their shared sex and school grade (first graders in this school were in fact prohibited from mingling with kids in other classes during lunch and recess), the girls divided along race and social status lines in ways that are reminiscent of King's (1995) findings about the play patterns of Black slave children and White children in the antebellum

South. Scott postulates that the girls' play culture mimics society's stratified status system and mirrors its expectations of White and Black females. School personnel interviewed by Scott viewed the African American girls' nurturing of White classmates as natural by-products of their Black femaleness. One adult comment stereotyped the kids of *both* of the school's most numerous minority groups: "Basically it's the Spanish children that will stick in a group by themselves. But not your Black children. They'll reach out, they always do." (This observer did not offer her views on what White children "always" do.)

By various means, messages were conveyed to these girls about what was expected of them. The message to White girls: if you are quiet and docile, you can expect to be cared for, especially by lower-status females of color. The message to Black girls: if you are small, you might be cared for sometimes, but mainly you'll be expected to "reach out" and serve others, especially those of higher status. It's too soon to say what if any effects these messages will have on the girls' future identities and aspirations. What can be said is that even in their first year of elementary school, many are already enacting stereotyped gender, race, and social class roles.

Equally complex is the interaction between effects of race, gender, and biosocial development (see the discussion of genetic and biosocial perspectives in chapter 2). Because of changes in diet and other cultural and economic factors, children's physical development has speeded up in recent decades so that they are reaching puberty at an earlier age (girls even earlier than boys). Though the mass media has issued dire warnings about approaching "epidemics" of preteen pregnancy, obesity, and anorexia, the implications of this radical change in children's bodies have received less scholarly attention. A few recent studies on early onset of puberty in girls suggest that it both affects and is affected by their psychic and social development and by environmental influences as well:

- A study in which age of puberty is the causal variable shows that the early onset of puberty increases the likelihood that girls will engage in deviant or delinquent behavior, including smoking, drinking, truancy, and disorderly conduct, and this relationship holds even when conflict with parents and exposure to peer deviance are taken into account (Haynie 2003).

- A longitudinal study of girls who were eighth or ninth graders at the beginning of the study found that girls who attained menarche before the age of twelve were not only on average taller and heavier than their classmates but also more likely to feel that their bodies were "out of control"(Nichter 2000).
- In a study of White males who were being treated for substance abuse, it was found that fathers' abandonment of their families in their children's first seven years was associated with early onset of puberty and greater incidence of behavioral problems (including early sexual activity) in daughters though not in sons. The researchers offered a genetic explanation of the father absence effect: those fathers who were carrying the AR (androgen receptor) gene, which predisposes humans to impulsive and deviant behavior, were more likely 1) to pass on this to their daughters in whom it is predictive of early puberty and subsequent behavioral problems and 2) to abandon their families (Comings et al. 2002).

Adolescents of both sexes are concerned about body image, but while boys are more likely to immerse themselves in strenuous workout regimes in order to achieve the muscular physique that they hope will gain them acceptance with male peers and the admiration of girls (Eder 1995), girls are more likely to express their concerns verbally. In a study of a multiracial sample of some 300 middle and high school girls, Nichter (2000) discovered that many of the White girls engaged in "fat talk," a verbal exchange that typically opened as follows:

Girl 1: I'm so fat.
Other girls, in chorus: Oh no, you're not.

On further observation, she found that girls who claimed to be "so fat" were seldom above average weight for their age. A fifteen-year-old who refused to engage in fat talk told the researcher,

Most of the people who need to lose weight don't really say it, and most of the people who say it don't really mean it. . . . I'm not going to give them a whole bunch of sympathy for something that they know is not true. (60)

In other words, "fat talk" was not an exchange of information and practical advice on slimming but a social ritual that offered peer support and maintained social solidarity (just as the exchange of snacks and money was a mechanism for initiating and maintaining friendships among the preteen girls studied by Scott).

At the same time, the majority of White and Latina girls in the sample expressed dissatisfaction with their bodies in general or with specific body parts (most often thighs); envied the "perfect" people they saw in magazines, movies, and television; and made hostile comments about other girls who had the desired characteristics of tallness, thinness, and long, flowing (preferably blonde) hair. In contrast, the fifty African American girls in the sample seemed refreshingly free of obsessive concern about their body weight and proportions and were less likely to diet or even talk about dieting. When asked to describe the ideal Black girl,

> their response often began with a list of personality traits rather than physical attributes. The ideal African-American girl was smart, friendly, not conceited, easy to talk to, fun to be with, and had a good sense of humor. . . . When asked about physical attributes, girls tended to respond that ideal girls had it "going on." This referred to making what they had work for them: be it long nails, pretty eyes, big lips, nice thighs, a big butt— whatever. (Nichter 2000, 165–66)

Nichter cautions that forecasts of an epidemic of the eating disorders that make girls dangerously over- or underweight exaggerate the scope of the problem. She estimates the proportion of females suffering from eating disorders at 3 percent or less, though some of the people she questioned about the problem guessed that as many as one in four girls are affected. Though diet talk, like fat talk, was a constant in conversations among girlfriends and some reported experimenting with diet aids or pills (usually stolen from their mothers!), few adhered to any systematic form of dieting for more than a few days.

Still the pervasive perception of dieting as the solution to weight problems is worrisome when linked to findings of other recent studies showing that girls become less and less *physically active* as they pass through childhood and adolescence. A longitudinal study of 1,213 Black girls and 1,166 White girls from age eight or nine until age eighteen or nineteen found a steady and substantial decline in the number of after-school activities involving exercise. The Black girls were more sedentary than the White girls; by the time they were seventeen, almost a third of the White girls but over half the Black girls reported no activity at all (Kimm et al. 2002). The restriction of girls' bodily movement by their preschool teachers described earlier in this chapter suggests, furthermore, that well before they enter elementary school, children receive cultural messages about their bodies that differ according to their race and gender.

FIGHTING BACK: THE BENEFICIAL EFFECTS OF RESISTING RACISM, ETHNOCENTRISM, SEXISM, AND CLASSISM

Considerable evidence now exists, both from experimental research and from evaluations of innovative educational programs, to indicate that *all* students, but *especially* students from disadvantaged groups, benefit from schools in which they are treated respectfully, are expected to perform well, and are set challenging academic tasks that require sustained mental effort and provide the satisfaction of mastering difficult material. (For reviews of strategies and programs that appear to have raised the academic achievement of minority students and reduced the gap between minority and majority students, see Bell 2002/2003; Davis 2003; Fashola 2003; Singham 1998.) Taking a somewhat different approach, some researchers argue that low aspirations and achievement are caused by gender, race, and class *stereotyping*. Two studies using very different research methodologies offer promising prescriptions for raising the academic performance of female, low-income, and minority students by showing them how to overcome the pressures associated with negative stereotypes.

An in-depth study of the handful of low-income African American students in an inner-city high school who had made concrete plans to go on to college and professional occupations showed that unlike their classmates, these "resilient" adolescents had received clear messages about 1) their personal competence; 2) how race, class, and gender operate in American society to constrain the chances of people like themselves; and 3) strategies that would enable them to circumvent or negotiate these constraints. Their mentors included the following:

- An aunt who filed a discrimination suit after being turned down for a job in construction in favor of a less qualified male applicant

- A father who faced down the hostility of White neighbors and threats from the Ku Klux Klan when the family moved into a previously all-White housing complex
- A mother who "raised hell" with local school authorities over racial discrimination in the judging of a school oratory contest
- A history teacher who devoted considerable class time to discussing the struggles and accomplishments of the civil rights movement and who repeatedly warned his students that Blacks would continue be discriminated against unless they continued to fight back (O'Connor 1997).

More than any other indicator of academic performance, *standardized tests* continue to generate race, gender, and social class gaps in achievement. In a series of experiments with college students, Claude Steele and colleagues at Stanford University demonstrated that these gaps are at least partly due to stereotypes that impugn the intellectual abilities of Black, Hispanic, and low-income students and the math abilities of female students. Steele (1997) termed this phenomenon *stereotype threat*. Extending this model to younger students, psychologists at Columbia University and New York University (Good, Aronson, and Inzlicht 2003) have tested methods to help girls and minority and low-income kids overcome the effects of stereotype threat and thereby improve their standardized test scores. In a Texas school serving a low-income student population that was 63 percent Hispanic, 15 percent Black, and 22 percent White, seventh graders were randomly assigned to groups that received different messages about the causes of academic difficulties. Students in group 1 were told that intelligence is not a fixed or finite genetic endowment but can be expanded with mental exercise, group 2 members were told that that it's always difficult to move to a new educational environment but that these difficulties can be overcome, group 3 was given a message combining those given to groups 1 and 2, and students in group 4, a control group, were told how drug use could interfere with academic achievement. When students took statewide standardized tests in math and reading at the end of the year, the poor and minority students in the experimental conditions earned significantly higher reading scores than students in the control condition, and a similar difference in math scores was found between girls in experimental and control groups. Both messages 1 and 2 increased students' test scores, though combining the two messages (in group 3) did not appear to have an additive effect. The only message that had no effect was the one to group 4—being warned about the dire consequences of drug use did not appear to help students raise their test scores! The authors concluded that

> encouraging adolescents to make nonpejorative explanations for diffi-
> culty—that is, to think of intelligence as expandable rather than fixed or
> to attribute difficulties to the novelty of the situation rather than their own
> shortcomings—can meaningfully increase student achievement, *espe-*
> *cially for those students who face negative stereotypes about their abili-*
> *ties.*(658; emphasis added)

Neither of these studies promises that fighting back against disre-spectful treatment by school authorities is easy, nor is success guaran-teed. In one high school, a group of Puerto Rican students organized to provide mutual support and to propose changes in the curriculum. When they asked to meet with teachers and administrators to discuss their recommendations, they were told that those in authority knew best and that "we [students] should just accept the decisions they make for us" (Walsh 2000, 109). However, the research findings we have just re-viewed imply that the act of identifying systemic problems and chal-lenging those who perpetuate them is itself beneficial to marginalized young people and a necessary step toward positive change.

CONCLUSIONS

Each of the social variables discussed in this chapter and the previous one affects children's childhoods in predictable ways. Female children, poor children, and children from discriminated-against racial and ethnic groups are less likely to survive and thrive than male children, children from well-to-do homes, and children of majority or privileged race or ethnicity. When combined, the effects are even more pronounced: "If a baby is not only poor and Black but a girl, her chances of survival dwin-dle still further" (Gittins 1998, 34).

By the time they enter school, most children have become adept at defining themselves and others in terms of their locations in impor-tant social hierarchies. From each other and from observation of their surroundings, kids learn how to operate within the constraints of a racially stratified world. The frequency with which racist acts can be observed even in preschool classrooms is disturbing to adults who assume or hope that young children are not yet cognizant of race matters, yet such acts mirror the racial stereotyping, stratification, and segregation that permeate adult social worlds.

Although sex segregation is so widespread that many believe it is a natural process, models developed by Bem and Thorne and substantiated by considerable empirical research show how socially constructed assumptions about female–male differences prevent us from seeing equally important similarities and the extent of cross-gender relationships and shared activities, not to mention the wide variations *among* children of either sex. Exaggeration of gender differences leads to differential treatment of boys and girls, further dividing them and setting them in opposition to each other.

Though it is the least visible of the social variables discussed in this chapter, social status, as measured by parents' income, education, and occupation and/or by the power and prestige (or lack of them) associated with their social position, is the best predictor of children's opportunities and achievements. Though the pervasiveness of inequalities based on socioeconomic status and social class and the extent to which they determine family lifestyles, modes of child rearing, and children's life chances are well documented, especially in the United States, they tend to be overlooked or denied by those who prefer to believe either that serious inequalities no longer exist or that success or failure in getting ahead is explained by individual or group differences in aptitude or attitude.

Recent experimental and ethnographic research makes a case for the counterargument that inequalities due to social status, race, ethnicity, and gender are neither natural nor inevitable and that they could be significantly reduced by the following:

- Ensuring that *all* students have access to the "world-class" education required for getting ahead in a global society
- Setting *all* students challenging tasks that develop their mental and social capacities to the full and offer the solid satisfactions of accomplishment

- Helping disadvantaged and discriminated-against kids understand the societal forces that constrain them and showing them how the pernicious effects of negative stereotyping can be overcome

In part V, we turn to contextual effects at the societal and global levels, where we'll see how children's lives are affected by the nation and region of the world in which they live and how their childhoods may be transformed by political events and social, economic, and cultural trends that originate far from their homes and communities.

V

KIDS IN THE WORLD

10

THE RAPIDLY CHANGING EXTERNAL CONTEXT OF CHILDHOOD

The child functions as a metaphor for our collective development, progress, and well-being, while simultaneously standing as a metaphor for the failure of society, for its inhumanity, poverty, and ignorance that stunts the lives of so many children.

—John O'Neill

I really do think that at the age of 15 everyone should have a job. . . . I think employment for the young builds character as long as they are not conned out of things by their employer.

—Fifteen-year-old student, Belfast, Ireland

All wars are waged against children.

—Eglantyne Jebb

In chapters 10 and 11, we'll examine the effects on children's lives of political, economic, physical, social and cultural environments beyond their homes and local communities (i.e., in the outer layers of figure 1.1). This external context is multifaceted, encompassing political ideology and policy, economic growth or decline, technological innovations, mass production and marketing of products targeted at children, and popular culture.

It is also multilayered, moving out from children's immediate neighborhoods or communities, where they interact with family, friends, and others face to face, to the surrounding cities, states or provinces, nations, and larger geographical regions (e.g., sub-Saharan Africa, East Asia, western Europe) and, ultimately, to the world as an encompassing environment.

Because many of these contextual layers are far removed from people's immediate surroundings and everyday lives, their impact is not always readily apparent. The importance of children's families, friends, and teachers is more evident than the effects of decisions made in distant offices, sometimes in distant countries, by persons and organizations children may never encounter directly. Not only are there multiple contextual effects, but they are often overlapping, sometimes conflicting. We have not tried to cover them all, choosing instead to focus on how children and childhood are being affected by the transnational flow of commodities, capital, technology, people, and ideas commonly referred to as globalization.

INTERNATIONAL COMPARISONS OF CHILDREN'S HEALTH AND WELFARE

James, Jenks, and Prout (1998) remind us that "there is no absolute distinction between the developing and the developed world; developing countries are not all alike; [moreover,] nations are socially divided and what is true for rich inhabitants is not true for the poor and the poorest" (103–4). It is also important to avoid emphasizing differences between nations or groups of nations to the extent that equally important similarities are overlooked. The terms commonly used to differentiate and compare people and nations are themselves ethnocentric and sometimes inaccurate (Punch 2001). Terms like "developed" versus "developing" or "less developed" emphasize what poorer nations lack (e.g., high per capita income) rather than what they have (e.g., high proportions of children and young people). Though non-Caucasian children in North American and western European nations are commonly referred to as "minority" (and, by implication, as socially and culturally disadvantaged [see chapter 8]), this convention obscures the fact that a majority of the world's children live in the developing nations of Africa, South

America, and South Asia. In 1999, the 189 million persons under age eighteen living in the thirty-one countries classified by UNICEF as industrialized constituted less than 10 percent of the world's total child population (UNICEF 2001, 97). Numerically, it is *these* children who are "minority." Designating children as minority or majority becomes even more complicated as mass migrations have brought large numbers of people from "less developed" but "majority" nations into Euro-American nations where they are classified as "minority."

Acknowledging that all the terms used in international comparisons are biased in some respect, we have, in the interests of clarity and consistency, chosen to use "prosperous" or "industrialized" nations and "poorer" or "developing" nations in the following discussion. (Of course, direct quotations will include other terms as well.)

Given the huge and growing divergence between the technological and financial resources available to rich and poor individuals, groups, and nations, it is not surprising that there are vast disparities between children in the industrialized world and children in the developing world on many indicators of status and welfare, including sheer survival. Compared to their counterparts in most industrialized nations, children in the least developed countries can be characterized as follows, according to statistics compiled by UNICEF:

- They are twelve times more likely to die within a year of birth and sixteen times more likely to die before their fifth birthday. If they survive infancy and early childhood, they have life expectancies about two-thirds that of children in prosperous countries.[1]
- They are more likely to have a low birth weight, to suffer from malnutrition, and to have smaller gains in height and weight throughout childhood.
- They are more likely to lose their mothers to death in childbirth.
- They are less likely to have access to pure drinking water and to health services, including immunizations against communicable diseases.
- They are less likely to complete primary schooling and obtain any kind of secondary schooling.
- They are more likely to live in poverty or near poverty throughout their lives (James et al. 1998, 129–30).

A number of critics contend that the free market economic policies associated with globalization and the austerity measures forced on poor nations with huge indebtedness by international financial institutions have increased the number and proportion of children living in poverty as well as increasing inequalities among children, with serious consequences for their health, welfare, and life chances. The global free market was itself preceded by years of drought and famine and the political turmoil that occurred in many parts of Africa and Latin America during the late and postcolonial period. As a result, average household incomes have fallen, and government programs and services for children and their families have been cut drastically. In sub-Saharan African countries, for example, more of the national budget is spent servicing debt repayment (about $10 billion annually) than on providing education, health, nutrition, and family planning (about $9 billion annually; Bass 2003, 147). The blunt conclusion of an analysis in the *UN Chronicle*: "Children are paying the third world debt with their lives" (United Nations1989, 48).

In addition to the large gap between the industrial world and the developing world on all indicators of children's health and well-being, there are substantial differences both *among* and *within* the rich industrialized countries, in particular, between the Nordic and western European nations that support generous and comprehensive social welfare programs to which all children are entitled and the United States. Two comparative studies of prosperous countries (Kennedy, Whiteford, and Bradshaw, 1996; Smeeding and Torrey 1988)[2] found that there were poor children in each country but that the rates of child poverty varied, from 5 percent in Sweden to almost 20 percent in the United States, the wealthiest of the nations studied. Intergenerational inequalities were also greatest in the United States, with older people getting significantly larger shares of income and other resources, so that while children constitute only about 25 percent of the total U.S. population, nearly 40 percent of the American poor are children (Guzman et al. 2003).

Within the United States, the overall child poverty rate, which peaked at 23 percent in 1993, fell to about 16 percent in 2000 (Moore and Redd 2002); however, the material conditions of children at the lowest end of the income distribution and children who are members of most racial minorities have been deteriorating since the 1980s. According to the 2003 annual report of the Children's Defense Fund, nearly a million

Black children live in "extreme" poverty (defined as a family of three with an annual income of $7,060 or less), the highest level since the government began collecting such figures in 1980. A study of the United Kingdom found that the gap between poor children and more affluent children in life expectancy, health, and welfare is greater now than it has been for fifty years, a phenomenon that is spreading in other prosperous countries as well: "Despite the 'consumer revolution' and the flood of surplus food and inessential goods to the West—often produced by children living in conditions amounting to slavery in the Third World— poverty *within* western countries has escalated in the past few years" (Gittins 1998, 32–33; emphasis added).

WORKING CHILDREN IN A GLOBAL ECONOMY

Current debates about children's work reveal considerable misapprehension and disagreement about what constitutes work, in particular, whether unpaid and/or household work is "real" or "productive" work,[3] and about what (if any) kinds of work and working conditions are appropriate for children. In most countries it is not even known how many children are actually employed and at what kinds of work. (It is noteworthy that UNICEF's annual report, *The State of the World's Children*, does not yet include employment among their routinely computed social indicators.) James et al. (1998) believe that "unofficial figures can vary from official ones by a factor of ten or more" but guess that "the number of children working worldwide greatly exceeds 100 million" (104).

Child Labor in the Past

Historical research leaves little doubt that until well into the twentieth century and in virtually all parts of the world, most children were put to work in some capacity by about age seven. In a fascinating book that incorporates a rich body of primary sources (including journals, interviews, and other first-person accounts), Phillip Hoose (2001) documents the substantial economic, social, and political contributions made by children and youth throughout U.S. history. In the earliest colonial settlements, European American children were employed as apprentices or indentured laborers. The first factory workers in U.S. history were boys and girls, most aged twelve or younger. By 1830, more than a million children worked in the textile mills, and some participated in strikes for more pay and shorter hours—in 1836, 1,500 girls staged a walkout at the Lowell, Massachusetts, mill. Employment of children in factories, sweatshops, coal mines, and the military was routine until well into the twentieth century.[4]

Research conducted for a British television series on childhood (Humphries, Mack, and Perks 1989) presents a similar picture. An investigation into child labor in London estimated that during the early 1900s, around a quarter of all schoolchildren aged five and over and about half of all schoolchildren aged ten and over had paid jobs outside school hours. For girls, the majority of jobs were in domestic service (about one in four of all teenage girls), dressmaking, offices, and factories. Boys were recruited for unskilled or semiskilled work in factories and in heavy industries like shipbuilding and mining, though many more worked in dead-end jobs with high turnover (e.g., errand boys and packers) where "experienced" boys were regularly replaced by younger ones willing to work for less pay. Contrary to popular belief, true apprenticeships were relatively rare. In rural areas, children and adults alike were hired at annual fairs where prospective domestic and farm laborers were inspected by potential employers and "contracts" involved nothing more than a handshake. The authors also note that well before they entered full-time labor outside the home, most children worked for their parents, running errands and helping with domestic chores and child minding. The pervasiveness of child labor in the 1900s was consistent with a general societal perspective that did not differentiate much between children and adults. On the one hand, this "gave children a degree of independence, and some adult privileges [like smoking, drinking, and gambling] which today seem quite surprising." On the other hand, children "were seen as criminally responsible for their actions and so could be punished and placed in prison much the same as adults" (Humphries et al. 1989, 23).

Child Labor in Industrialized Countries

It is commonly believed that, however widespread in the past, child labor has pretty much disappeared in the industrialized nations of the world, where children are loved and protected and childhood is a time for play and learning (see discussion of Zelizer's model of the "economically useless but emotionally priceless" child in chapter 5). In fact, children's employment is more widespread and their contributions to family and national economies are greater than is generally recognized. Surveys in Britain, Holland, Germany, and the United States carried out between the early 1970s and late 1990s showed paid employment rates between one-third and two-thirds of children between the ages of fourteen and eighteen (*Economist* 2000, 8; James et al. 1998, 112–14). The reasons why children work are similar to the reasons why adults work—for income and to help out the family but also to gain independence and opportunities for socializing with age-mates (Mizen, Pole, and Bolton 2001). Although children's work in a family business is often defined as "helping out," in fact they are contributing labor that would otherwise have to be paid for (Song 1996). Criticizing the tendency to overlook the economic value of domestic work, Solberg (1990) argued not only that the cooking and cleaning performed by Norwegian latchkey children contributed to the household economy but also that "self-care" by kids contributed to the public economy by releasing women from child care to engage in paid work. Similarly, caregiving by children, usually of younger siblings or older relatives and usually unrecorded and unremunerated, is economically useful work that would otherwise have to be covered by other family members or by the state (Becker, Dearden, and Aldridge 2001).

What is problematic for kids everywhere is obtaining a *good* job, and even in the richest countries, a substantial portion of children's work is undertaken illegally. Studies in the United Kingdom found that opportunities to use or acquire specific skills were rare; most of the jobs available were for unskilled work around the edges of the formal labor market. A national survey of British ten- to sixteen-year-olds revealed that 44 percent of those working were doing so in violation of laws regarding age, the nature of the work, or hours worked (Mizen et al. 2001; O'Brien 1995). In the United States, investigations by national and state departments of labor have turned up widespread violation of child labor laws:

In New York, it is the garment industry; in California, the fast-food restaurants; in Iowa, the farms; in Maryland, the door-to-door candy sellers. Violations of child-labor laws shot up from 8,877 in 1984 to a record 22,508 [in 1989], as ever younger children worked ever longer hours at jobs no one else would take for the pay . . . many are undocumented immigrants or impoverished members of the urban underclass. (*Time*, March 26, 1990, 18)

Ironically, in the United States and many western European countries, middle-class kids are likely to have more opportunities for paid employment than poor kids, whose local areas offer fewer opportunities for babysitting, mowing lawns, and delivering newspapers and for whom transportation to and from places of employment may be problematic.

Child Labor in Developing Countries

In the nations where the majority of the world's children live, the majority of jobs, for children and adults alike, are in the agricultural sector. The care of animals that are a family's major source of income is often allocated to children. For example, in the herding communities of Outer Mongolia, children from an early age

> know animals intimately. Their work responsibilities are very arduous. They have learnt to be physically very tough, and to withstand hunger and thirst, and extreme heat and cold. They can assess and weigh the balance of all kinds of variations in their environment. (Penn 2001, 93)

A study conducted at about the same time in rural Bolivia (Punch 2001) showed that, as in Mongolia, kids were routinely put to work from age five. It also showed that they became adept at negotiating with their parents and siblings about distribution of household responsibilities, developing strategies to avoid the most onerous tasks and to escape family surveillance in order to meet friends—strategies reminiscent of those invented by schoolchildren to circumvent the demands of their teachers (see chapter 7).

From a two-year participant observation study of open-air urban markets in Senegal, Bass (2003) learned that many children were both economically useful and cost effective. Child labor, though illegal, was "visible and tolerated" (Bass estimated that about a third of Senegalese children aged ten to fourteen were working full time), and (or because) their work "often represents a family strategy for economic survival" (127–28). Kids were employed as sellers in market stalls; as apprentices to carpenters, shoemakers, and tailors; and as beggars (the latter often working for a religious leader in return for training). Bass coined the term *duplicating-dad imitating-mom* to describe a common pattern of child labor, in which kids learn their parents' trade in the expectation that they will eventually replace them. She quotes the owner of a market stall selling school supplies who noted with satisfaction that once his sons had mastered the work, they could take over the business, and "I won't have to work then" (142).

The most rampant exploitation of child laborers occurs in areas of extreme poverty coupled with political and social disorder. In such situations, many children become responsible not only for their own survival but for that of their families as well. The following description of Afghan refugee children at work in a carpet-making factory packed into the refugee quarters of Quetta, Pakistan, is reminiscent of a scene from a Dickens novel:

> Dozens of children between the ages of five and fifteen were stacked up on narrow platforms in front of their looms. Their tiny flexible fingers make them the employees of choice. They work with lightening speed, hooking colored threads on the loom and pounding them into place. They follow complicated patterns hanging on charts from the ceiling and hop up and down from their perches to grab a new colored thread. [Like other] children I met closer to the front lines, they were all coughing. They had respiratory problems from inhaling the wool fibres they were working with. Their nails were broken and infected and their hands bore wounds from being caught in the looms. And for their troubles, they were paid the princely sum of 100 rupees (about 60 cents) when their team of little kids completed a 7 × 7-meter (12 × 25-foot) carpet—about a week's work. It was just enough to keep their families from starving. (Armstrong 2002, 172)

The reviewer of a documentary film on child workers in Bangladesh, himself a former child worker in his native Nepal, points out that the most vocal opponents of child labor are often

> opposed to any serious state measures to tackle poverty that would neutralize the need for child labor for family survival. They are for promoting self-help, personal responsibility, and self-empowerment, but oppose child labor which fundamentally represents all of these three qualities.
> Furthermore, I find it quite amusing that most of these same people are openly supportive of children in America going from door to door to

sell cookies or some other merchandise in the name of fund raising for some school activities. While most of the money these children raise goes to the companies supplying the merchandise the children get paid nothing. That is, these companies openly exploit children with the approval of their own parents and schools. These people also support children working as newspaper deliverers or lawn mowers or babysitters or doing some other jobs for less than minimum pay. (Shrestha 2000, 49)

Shrestha argues that given the realities of the global economy, children's welfare will not be enhanced by forbidding them to work but by ensuring that their work does not prevent them from attending school and that child workers have the same rights as adults to decent wages, a safe working environment, and health and other social welfare benefits.

Work and Schooling

The enactment of child labor laws coincided with enactment of compulsory education laws and the worldwide expansion of national education systems during the past century (Boli-Bennett and Meyer 1978). However, education laws and labor laws may work at cross-purposes. In nations that lack sufficient funds to provide free education, compulsory school attendance is likely to lead to an *increase* in child labor in order to cover school fees, uniforms, and supplies (Boyden 1990, 206). In Senegal and other West African nations, where fewer than half the children of school age are actually attending school, children's work, legal or illegal, not only constitutes an immediate contribution to the household economic but also may be viewed as "a reliable mechanism to train children for future market careers, either through hands-on sales or craftwork training" (Bass 2003, 129). Even in prosperous countries, the "reality facing the majority of children [requires] combining education with employment," though educators tend to ignore this reality and continue to view work as of little if any educational value (McKechnie and Hobbs 2001, 22). Opinions vary among kids themselves. In a study of fifteen-year-olds in Belfast, Ireland, who met in focus groups to discuss the pros and cons of combining school and paid employment, some participants maintained that education should take precedence over work, while others felt that education by itself would not prepare them adequately and that employment experience while at school would enhance their chances of finding good jobs later on. What they did agree on was their right to be treated as equals in the workplace, with union representation and wages equal to older workers doing the same job (Leonard 2004).

Globalism may have exacerbated the discontinuity between work and schooling. Under pressure from reformists, multinational corporations with factories in developing nations have developed guidelines that prohibit the use of children under the compulsory school age (usually fourteen). Yet when child workers were dismissed from the Bangladesh garment industry in the early 1990s, most of them continued to work but for lower wages under far more risky conditions. None went back to school, as they could no longer afford the fees. In a petition to the press, the children advocated combining light factory work with part-time school attendance (James et al. 1998).

For the Mongolian child herders, combining work and school has become more rather than less difficult. Under the former Soviet regime, formal education was actively promoted for the first time, and Penn (2001) found that most herder kids attended regularly even if it meant living away from home, boarding with relatives or at the school. Since the fall of communism and the adoption of free market economics, increased competition and the need to pay for services that were formerly provided by the state have forced many families to build up their herds, precipitating a rise in school dropout rates as more children are needed at home to care for the extra animals.

TRANSNATIONAL COMMERCE IN CHILDREN

The widening gaps in wealth and birthrates between prosperous and poor countries and the huge and growing number of poor children have fueled an international market in children, in particular, to provide 1) babies and young children for adoption and 2) cheap, often involuntary, labor. A researcher who assessed this market at the end of the 1980s described the dynamics of the system as follows: "At the heart of the trade is a simple economic equation: the First World is rich but has a low birthrate. In Third World countries the position is exactly the opposite" (Tate 1990, 144).

Transnational Adoptions

In the April 2000 issue of *National Geographic*, a full-page ad for Holt International Children's Services offered its readers adoptive children from China, Ecuador, Guatemala, Hong Kong, India, Korea, the Philippines, Romania, Thailand, and Vietnam. The number of international adoptions officially recorded rose from 5,315 in 1978 to over 20,000 in 2001, but the number *not* officially recorded is thought to be much greater. Though domestic adoptions still outnumber international ones, that margin appears to be closing (Corbett 2002).

There are strong disagreements between proponents of international adoption, who view it as "a humanitarian enterprise that results in providing homes and families to children who would otherwise languish in orphanages" (Tessler, Gamache, and Liu 1999, 8), and opponents, who view it as a corrupt system that robs a nation of some of its most precious assets—children—without addressing the basic problem of widespread child poverty and abuse. Because empirical evidence is scarce and often of questionable quality, it is difficult to assess the competing claims. Most research on the outcomes for the children involved are based on small nonrandom samples from a single "donor" country, without control or comparison groups. Obtaining reliable data on the processes by which children are procured and made available is even more difficult because of poor (or no) record keeping and widespread corruption in many if not all foreign adoption systems.

On the positive side, studies of Korean children adopted by U.S. parents in the 1950s and 1960s show that most of the parents and children expressed high levels of satisfaction with their lives and the impact of the adoption on the family (Kim 1977; the sample of Korean adoptees was obtained through the Holt agency mentioned previously). More recent studies of children adopted from orphanages in Romania and the former Soviet Union show that most soon caught up with other kids in the host country in terms of physical development. On measures of emotional and cognitive development, children adopted in early infancy fared better than those adopted later; the longer the orphanage experience and the older the children, the greater the likelihood of delayed development. In particular, kids who spent their earliest months or years warehoused in inadequately staffed and supplied institutions had often suffered from such severe malnutrition and neglect that they had difficulty forming attachments to their new families, and some had health, developmental, and behavior problems that defied accurate diagnosis and appropriate treatment (Groza 1997; Small 2001). Indeed, one scholar has suggested that such experiences constitute "diabolically perfect" natural experiments on the effects of severe early sensory deprivation, experiments that would be impossible to perform in societies where scientists cannot, for ethical reasons, "take a population of newborns and confine them to cribs in a gloomy, ill-heated orphanage with a small, rotating staff of caretakers who might spend an average of 10 minutes a day talking to them or holding them" (Talbot 1998, 26; see the discussion of experimental methodology in chapter 3).

What little data are available on the adoption systems in donor countries suggests that questionable practices abound. An investigation of the Cambodian system (Corbett 2002) found that the "moneymaking potential in foreign adoptions is so great that it has inspired a network of unofficial 'recruiters' who scour neighborhoods in search of young children, often plying birth mothers with lies or false promises in addition to cash," sometimes stealing babies outright. Local officials may be bribed to assist in the creation of false paperwork so that a child is "in effect, laundered—moved into an orphanage with no true record or his or her birthplace or parents, rendering the child untraceable" (45). In such cases, neither researchers nor adoptive parents can obtain reliable information about the children being offered for adoption or the people and processes involved in making them available.

Some donor countries are attempting to address the most serious abuses. In Indonesia, laws have been passed requiring foreign couples to be resident there for seven years before becoming eligible to adopt; in India, some reformers have initiated a campaign to stop foreign adoptions altogether. Given the demand for adoptive children and the profits to be made in providing them, the extent to which the market can be regulated remains to be seen.

Involuntary Labor

Though growing in number, adoptions account for but a small fraction of international transactions. By the 1990s, an estimated worldwide total of about 200 million children between the ages of five and fifteen engaged in domestic, agricultural, or industrial work under conditions that fit the UNICEF definition of slave labor (Backman 1991; Springer 1997, 29).

The largest concentration of involuntary child workers can be found in the sex business. UNICEF estimates that in the twenty-first century, at least 1 million persons under age eighteen are recruited, often forcibly, into prostitution every year. The great majority of child prostitutes are recruited, bought, or kidnapped in the world's poorer countries (UNESCO statistics indicate especially high figures from Colombia, Brazil, Benin, Thailand, and the Philippines). Trafficking between prosperous and poorer countries operates in both directions. Children from poor countries are smuggled into brothels in the industrialized nations of Europe, North America, and East Asia, while sex tourism brings clients from rich countries to poorer ones (for a case study of a village in the Philippines given over to child prostitution, see Forbes 1990). According to an investigation by the Bernard van Leer Foundation (1996), child sex tourism is a highly organized international industry, linking governments seeking to raise national income through tourism to charter airlines, travel agents, and other commercial establishments and to local service providers such as massage parlors and escort services, reinforced in some instances by superstition (e.g., the belief that sex with young girls enhances men's potency or extends their life expectancy or that young children are free of the virus that causes AIDS).

There is no doubt that the international trade in children raises some serious ethical questions. Tate's (1990) investigation uncovered some truly appalling findings, for example, on links between child traffickers and drug traffickers (who sometimes used the same couriers and the same routes for delivery of drugs and babies) and on the procurement of children to be "harvested" for body parts for transplant surgery. In the absence of more systematic data collection and analysis, it is hard to tell whether such practices are sporadic or institutionalized, but it seems fair to conclude that while many children do end up in comfortable homes with loving adoptive families, many others do not, and some end up in situations that can be described only as deplorable. And the number of children remaining in donor countries but living in extreme poverty continues to grow.

LIVING BETWEEN WORLDS[5]

Like earlier mass movements of people, recent migration has been mainly from poorer countries to more prosperous ones and from rural areas to urban centers as large numbers of people seek to make a better living or to escape from wars or oppressive political regimes. As a result, most of the world's industrialized nations are rapidly becoming more heterogeneous ethnically and culturally. Increasing numbers of children do not fit easily into national molds. Since migrants tend on the average to be younger than the general population, they may also cause changes in the age composition of the societies they leave and the ones they enter.

From a child's perspective, migration inevitably means becoming, however temporarily, an outsider and having to learn the rules of a new culture. However, children's experiences of migration vary depending on 1) whether the migration was voluntary or involuntary and 2) whether they accompany their families or other persons responsible for their welfare or are on their own.

Voluntary Migration

Voluntary migration with family members is generally the least stressful. Still, a study of immigrant children in France found that many felt "apart" from mainstream French society and were painfully aware that they were viewed and treated as backward or inferior. In turn, many of them felt superior to and expressed stereotyped views of *other* immigrant peoples. Children from the Maghreb countries of North Africa discriminated against immigrants from other parts of Africa as well as against those from China and Vietnam. The following comment by a Tunisian girl combined bigotry against a group viewed as lower on the status ladder with feelings of inferiority vis-à-vis "real" French people:

> I take a bus to school. When it goes along the Rue Barbes and I see the Africans, still wearing the clothes they wear in Africa, I want to lean out of the bus window and say: "Why don't you dress like the French? Why don't you at least pretend to be like them? Then you'll fit in better." They look absurd. In front of them I feel French. But as the bus moves on, to

another street full of ordinary French people in ordinary clothes, then I lose my sense of identity. (Chisholm and Moorehead 1990, 173)

A similar finding is reported in a study of native-born and immigrant children between the ages of eight and twelve living in Germany:

Lumping everyone together seems to be more common among the various groups of immigrants than among the German children. Polish and Turkish children often dislike Russian children, and Russian children often dislike Polish and Turkish children. Sometimes, this leads to German children who are friends with immigrants or asylum seekers adopting their aversions. (Hengst 1997, 55)

Among the native-born German children interviewed by Hengst, stereotyping had not disappeared, though it was often subtle (describing Turkish kids as *almost* the same as we are") rather than blatant (describing Turkish kids as "always looking for a fight"). Most knew children of other nationalities and ethnic groups, and some had brought them home to play or visited in their homes. Hengst is hopeful that increased contact between children from different societies and societal subgroups will produce "a generational shift in the dominant ways identity and difference are conceptualized—away from nationally framed differences between 'us' and 'them'" and from automatic attribution of "otherness" to foreigners or to immigrants, guest workers, or political asylum seekers in their own society.

Nonvoluntary Migration

Whatever the difficulties of voluntary migration, forced migration, whether caused by natural disasters, wars, or hostile government actions (e.g., ethnic cleansing, relocation, or imprisonment in a concentration camp), is much more likely to expose children to danger and substandard living conditions. Many refugees are not able to migrate far from the conditions that caused their plight and may spend weeks, months, or even years in crowded refugee camps, dependent on the generosity of their host governments or international benefactors.

It is hardly surprising that the greatest concentration of refugees has occurred in the poorest countries. In Somalia, a nation with some of the worst global statistics for income, maternal and child mortality, life expectancy, literacy, and public services, about one-eighth of the population are refugees. In the late 1980s, this included 300,000 kids in forty-three camps. Ironically, in many cases kids were better off in refugee camps than in their "home" villages since the camps were more likely to offer primary education and health services (Shaw 1990). A journalist who visited refugee camps in Pakistan where Afghan families had come to escape the Taliban, a prolonged drought that destroyed their crops, or the post-9/11 American bombing of Afghanistan found that nearly all the children were undernourished, underweight, and suffering from respiratory illnesses and diarrhea, exacerbated by inadequate shelter (even sick children often had to sleep on the bare ground). Death rates among children were extremely high, though specific causes of death were often difficult to identify; one frustrated doctor said, "They just died. I don't know why." Many kids injured in bomb blasts died because they couldn't get to a medical center or could not get to one soon enough; many who did survive had amputated limbs or permanent burn scars (Armstrong 2002). The poor physical condition of Afghan refugee children laboring in carpet-making factories established in refugee camps was described earlier in this chapter.

Refugee children generally fare better if familiar social networks can be maintained even in hostile surroundings. Studies of Palestinian refugee camps in Lebanon have found that camp policies that prevented families from being split up benefited children, a finding that is consistent with studies of London children during World War II showing that evacuation to the countryside or to North America "proved to have more damaging long-term effects on children than did the most punishing of German air raids" (Randal and Boustany 1990, 74).

Influences outside the family may be even stronger. A study of Palestinian children in a Jordanian refugee camp found that their perceptions of the situation and their aspirations for the future were shaped both by the peer culture and by the international mass media (despite the cramped and generally substandard housing in the camp, most kids had access to television and the Internet) and were not always congruent with their parents' values and aspirations. A twelve-year-old girl whose parents were not very religious was attracted to the Islamist movement that was active in the camp and began praying regularly and urging other girls in her class to do likewise. She did not, however, go along with the religious leaders' "comprehensive rejection of western cultural influences and rigid separation of males and females. Even as she adopted the headscarf and more conservative style of dress, [she] continued to enjoy television and pop music [and] to imagine a future career for herself outside the role of wife and mother promoted in Islamist rhetoric" (Hart 2002, 44).

Kids defined as different or deviant may be targeted for peer abuse as readily in refugee and concentration camps as in any other communities. The daughter of an American father and a Japanese mother who was incarcerated in a prison camp for Americans of Japanese descent when she was ten years old experienced disturbing shifts in peer status. After the bombing of Pearl Harbor, she was called a "Jap" by schoolmates who had formerly befriended her; in the camp, she was rejected by other kids because of her mixed race and remembers doing a lot of fighting. She never succeeded in making friends with girls in the camp, though she discovered that "if you can beat a boy, he becomes your friend" (Hoose 2001, 207).

Kids' feelings about the homes they left behind range from nostalgia to ambivalence to indifference. Essays written by Croatian children forced to flee their homes in the 1990s tended to draw a line between an idealized past in which they lived "a beautiful life in their home towns and villages, with their families, friends, and pets, in big houses and beautiful natural surroundings," and the bleak present brought about by a war that they viewed as unjustified but temporary (Povrzanovic 1997, 88). In contrast, many of the children in the Somalia refugee camps had been there so long that they were described in one report as "a generation of children for whom any other home is no more than a vague memory of a parent's sad story, for whom a temporary resting place has become a place of exile, a place of endless waiting to return where some have never been" (Shaw 1990, 210). Even among children who were voluntary migrants with opportunities to visit their former homes, there was a range of feeling. Some of the immigrant children living in France had happy memories of their earlier years and looked forward to and enjoyed visits to their home countries; others found that their experiences in France had made them strangers in the country of their birth (Chisholm and Moorehead 1990).

Children of Migrant Workers

In many societies, itinerant laborers constitute a sizable migrant group. Though some, like Mongolian, Lapp, Bedouin, and other no-madic herders, are romanticized in the popular imagination, all are mar-ginalized and many—Gypsies in particular—are universally mistreated. Though substantial in number, migrant workers are less visible than many disadvantaged people because the work available to them is mainly in rural areas and because they are constantly on the move, of-ten ranging over wide geographical areas in the course of a year.

The children of American migrant agricultural workers were the sub-ject of one of Robert Coles' studies in the series titled Children of Cri-sis (for which he twice was awarded a Pulitzer Prize). Coles rejected quantitative modes of data gathering and made no attempt to be de-tached and objective, relying instead on informal and unhurried con-versations with children and their parents and extensive collections of children's drawings interpreted for him by the artists.

Whether a U.S. citizen or a legal or an illegal immigrant, a migrant worker's child was likely to be born without medical attention and to learn "right off that he has no particular possessions of his own, no place that is his to use for rest and sleep, no objects that are his to look at and touch and move about and come to recognize as familiar" (Coles 1967, 51). Coles found these children a study in contradictions: "both active and fearful, full of initiative and desperately forlorn, driven to a wide range of ingenious and resourceful deeds and terribly paralyzed by all sorts of things." On the one hand, he observed children

> take care of one another, pick crops fast, go fetch water and food at the age of two or three *and* know what size coins or how many dollar bills must be brought back home, talk about the police, listen to a car engine and comment on its strengths or weaknesses, discuss the advantages and disadvantages of harvesting various crops, speak about the way property owners profit from the high rents they charge for their cabins. (63)

On the other hand, he heard the same children complain about how tired they were and how difficult it was to make sense of their lives.

In a given year, migrant children may pass through several schools but spend little time in any. The kids Coles studied averaged about eight days a month. A few like going to school because it's comfortable and safe there, and they enjoy the snacks and the few teachers and kids who are friendly. But like the immigrant children in France, most feel "apart" from the life of the school and are aware that they are not really welcome there. They also learn early that employers and sheriffs are much more powerful than their parents, who can be hassled or even arrested just for stopping beside the road to rest or eat.

Using the crayons, paints, and paper Coles supplied, the children drew themselves and their families, the fields where they worked, and the roads they traveled from one job to another. Their physical surroundings were rarely presented as attractive, comfortable, or safe places. Some of the most poignant pictures were of things the artist yearned for. A boy who did not have a birth certificate (which often prevented or delayed his enrolling in school) drew one that he could show school personnel to prove that he had a right to be there. A girl drew a suitcase to hold

> a few things that are mine—the comb, the rabbit's tail my daddy gave me before he died, the lipstick and the fan. . . . I've already lost a lot of things. I had a luck bracelet and I left it someplace, and I had a scarf, a real pretty one, and it got lost, and a mirror, too. That's why if I could have a place to put my things, then I'd have them and if we went all the way across the country and back, I'd still have them. (Coles 1967, 100–101)

Coles does not hesitate to give vent to his anger at how "unspeakably devastating a migrant life can be for children." Lacking roots, or a sense of *belonging anyplace*, they are, he says, permanent refugees in their own country (109). A similarly bleak picture is presented in Jones's (1993) ethnographic study of children living in a hostel for migrant workers in South Africa. Children's diaries are a major source of data in this study.

Kids on Their Own

Children become "unaccompanied" migrants for a variety of reasons. According to UNICEF (2001) estimates, "In the last decade of the 20th century, over a million children were orphaned or separated from their families because of armed conflict" (36), a large number, though nowhere near the estimated 13 million such children at the end of World War II (Shaw 1990). Others strike out on their own in order to escape from impoverished or abusive homes or societies. During the Great Depression of the 1930s, thousands of American children and teenagers left home to hitchhike and ride freight trains around the country (Hoose 2001). At present, an estimated 10,000 unaccompanied child refugees from North Korea are temporary residents in China while trying to obtain political asylum in South Korea (Paterniti 2003).

A Cambodian boy who escaped from enforced military service to the Khmer Rouge and spent six months alone in the jungle before reaching a refugee camp in Thailand from which he was adopted by an American couple experienced both involuntary and voluntary migration. After being so long on his own, he found adjustment to a "normal" life in a small New Hampshire town difficult:

> I had terrible nightmares almost every night. I didn't know where my family was, or if they were even alive. I slept on my bedroom floor because I couldn't get used to a bed. I still didn't feel safe. It was very hard for me to believe that I no longer had to hunt for food. At night I would steal down to the refrigerator almost every hour and take food back to my room. I would put bananas under my pillow so I could eat in the safety of the night. . . .
>
> School was terrible. Even though I couldn't speak English, they put me in ninth grade. I had never been to school before, except for a little time at a Buddhist monastery when I was very young. . . . For two years I failed every course in high school, but they let me and the two other Cambodian boys stay in school because we were so good at soccer. We took our anger out on the field. (Hoose 2001, 238)

Street Children   Probably the largest groups of unaccompanied children are street children, sometimes referred to as runaways or throwaways (suggesting that it is not always clear whether their migration is voluntary or involuntary). Found in growing numbers in the urban areas of almost all developing nations and many industrialized nations as well, children enter street life for many reasons. Some are there just to work, going elsewhere to eat and sleep; others work and sleep on the streets or in various temporary squats. Some spend periods of time back home; others have cut all family ties. Some earn money in relatively conventional ways (e.g., shining shoes or selling newspapers); others survive by begging, stealing, or prostitution. Whatever the variations in their life circumstances, what virtually all street children share is extreme poverty (Burr 2002; Glauser 1990; Mickelson 2000).

Street children are not a new phenomenon. In seventeenth-century England, the hordes of runaway children living in the streets of rapidly growing cities exceeded the resources of city officials charged with responsibility for orphans and abandoned children, leading to the transport of thousands to the American colonies as indentured laborers (Hoose 2001). In the industrialized cities of the post–Civil War United States, the swarms of unattended, often homeless children roaming the streets were viewed as a threat to social order and stimulated reformers to create agencies and institutions for their "protection" (Boocock 1975). In some cases, stray and destitute city kids were forcibly relocated. The Orphan Trains operated by the New York Children's Aid Society between 1854 and the 1930s transported thousands of kids from the slums of New York to farms and small towns in the Midwest and West where there was a severe labor shortage. Though billed as an effective and humane method of "saving" poor children, it was not lost on its promoters that transporting kids by the trainload, at discounted group rates and with minimal staff supervision, was considerably more cost effective than placing each child individually; it also provided rural homes and businesses with cheap manual labor. Programs modeled on the Orphan Trains were set up in England, Germany, Norway, and Sweden (O'Connor 2001).

As the number of street children continues to grow, so does the number of programs designed to help them. Most such projects continue to be based on perceptions of individual street children as deviant, isolated, and undersocialized and street children en masse as a social problem to be solved. Many attempt to enroll them in literacy and vocational education programs and ultimately to get them off the streets. A study of Calcutta boys enrolled in a government-sponsored vocational education program that provided meals and shelter but no payment found that few boys completed the training. Most were bored by the routine and resented the limits on their freedom and the lack of tangible rewards or future prospects. One boy saw no point in "going to a school to learn a job that needs you to work only with your hands? I can learn this on my own by working with someone as an assistant and moreover I will earn a regular income while learning" (Balagopalan 2002, 25). From a similar study of boys in Hanoi, Vietnam, Burr (2002) concluded that however well intentioned, legislation and interventions by external agencies that do not take into account the economic realities of the children's lives are likely to have little impact.

Indeed, the presence of street children may be as threatening to mainstream adult values as to the actual welfare of the children concerned, making it difficult to "hear what street children are saying because their [very presence] challenges adult notions of what constitutes an acceptable childhood" (Burr 2002, 52). Recently, ethnographic studies in which children have been allowed to tell their side of the story have been carried out in a number of nations, including India, South Africa, Vietnam, and Canada. In some respects, the motivations and experiences of street kids appear to be similar worldwide. Studies in Cape Town, South Africa (Scharf, Powell, and Thomas 1986), and in Toronto, Canada (Visano 1990), showed that in both places, runaway children initially viewed the street as the solution to personal troubles at home or school and the means of achieving freedom. Challenging the conventional view of street children as unsocialized or undersocialized, Visano traced the complex processes by which the Canadian kids established street contacts; learned how to acquire money, food, and shelter; and experimented with new identities—again similar to the experiences of the South African kids. However, an important difference in the careers of street kids in prosperous and poor countries is suggested by Visano's finding that over time, many of the Canadian kids became frustrated with the hazards and limitations of street life and estranged from their peers and, with no intervention by adult authorities, began a process of disengagement that propelled them back into mainstream society—seldom an option for poor kids in poor countries.

WARS AND OTHER POLITICAL STRUGGLES

Political leaders are wont to proclaim that the wars they wage are for the sake of their country's children. An analysis of childhood during the Cold War era found that American children were widely depicted "as the vulnerable core of American society, whose protection from foreign enemies required the construction of a vast and powerful nuclear defense system" (Stephens 1997, 103). Opponents of this justification for war, like

Eglantype Jebb, the early twentieth-century British social reformer quoted at the beginning of this chapter, argue that on the contrary, children are war's victims, not its beneficiaries (Moorehead 1990, 5). A report released by the United Nations Children's Fund just as we were completing this chapter indicates that almost a century later, the evidence continues to favor Jebb's position: nearly half the estimated total of 3.6 million people killed in wars since 1990 were children (UNICEF 2004).

The Persian Gulf War of 1991 and the Iraq War of 2003 are cases in point. Estimates of civilian deaths resulting from the 1991 war vary greatly, but all studies indicate that the majority of the dead were children. A conservative estimate is at least 200,000 child deaths from the bombing raids and, during the following year, from illness and disease brought on by malnutrition, air and water pollution, and lack of medical care. Infant and child mortality tripled and in some areas quadrupled. An international medical research group visiting Iraq in the summer of 1991 concluded that a million children were malnourished, with 120,000 suffering severe or acute malnutrition. All these conditions were worsened by the imposition of economic sanctions against the Iraqi government in 1992. This "silent war," as one scholar has put it, caused an average of 300 child deaths *per day* during the following decade. The death toll since military operations resumed in 2003 is now estimated at over 100,000 and rising, with children accounting for a disproportionate number of the civilian casualties (Clark 2002; Mamdani 2004; Morizumi 2002).[6]

The Israeli–Palestinian conflict provides a rich body of data on the many ways in which children and childhood are affected by political violence. According to Amnesty International figures, in the two-year period between September 2000 and September 2002, 250 Palestinian children were killed and 7,000 wounded, while seventy-two Israeli children were killed and "hundreds" wounded. Most of the Palestinian child casualties were from shooting or aerial bombardments by the Israeli military; most of the Israeli child casualties were from Palestinian suicide bombings. Preliminary findings from a survey, conducted by Johns Hopkins University, of 1,000 households in the West Bank and the Gaza Strip indicate that half the children are now suffering from chronic or acute malnutrition, compared with about 10 percent two years ago. Another consequence of this conflict for children is disruption of schooling. Curfews imposed by the Israeli army in many Palestinian communities have forced school closures, though residents in some areas have organized informal classes in homes or shops, and a few schools have reopened in defiance of the curfew. Although most Israeli schools have remained open throughout the conflict, more and more school time is given over to civil defense instruction, including how to respond to a poison gas attack and how to identify a potential suicide bomber (Grossman 2003, 188; *New York Times*, July 26 and September 24, 2002, January 3, 2003).

In the world's industrialized nations, children are generally excluded from military planning and operations and kept far from combat zones. However, even in the richest countries, huge military budgets may result in reduced public investments in services and programs that benefit children directly.

Child Soldiers

In many wars, children are more than bystanders or "collateral damage." Human Rights Watch (2004) estimates that at least 300,000 kids under age eighteen are fighting in armed conflicts in approximately forty countries, some voluntarily, other drafted by force. Rosen (2005) emphasizes that child soldiers are not a new phenomenon. Children have been serving in armies for centuries, although they have not always been identified as such. In the American Civil War, about 20 percent of the soldiers on both sides were under age eighteen. What *is* a new phenomenon are the current efforts to exclude children from the military and to highlight situations where child soldiers are abused and exploited (David M. Rosen, personal communication, August 24, 2004). Ironically, the number of child combatants appears to be increasing at the same time that initiatives by the United Nations and some national governments have raised the age at which soldiers may be recruited and criminalized the use of child soldiers—though so far the international community has not been able to enforce the new laws (Boothby and Knudsen 2000).

Casualties among child soldiers can be high. During the Iran–Iraq conflict of the 1980s, when boys as young as ten received instruction in martyrdom and marched into battle armed only with the keys their teachers told them would ensure their entrance into heaven, some 2,500 boy soldiers died in a single engagement in the spring of 1982 (Moorehead 1990). In the fighting between Cambodians and Vietnamese in the early 1980s, a fifth of wounded soldiers were between the ages of ten and fourteen (Boothby and Knudsen 2000). There is also considerable evidence, belying the stereotype of childhood innocence, that child soldiers can become as ruthless and inured to violence as their adult counterparts. A Cambodian boy who was enslaved by the Khmer Rouge when he was eight years old, handed a machine gun, and forced to fight for a year before he succeeded in deserting described his experience as a warrior:

> In a war you have to shoot or be shot. Sometimes I didn't know whether I was shooting at a Vietnamese or a Cambodian. I just shot. We were so deep in the jungle we could barely see each other. When I found out I had killed someone I didn't want to think about what I had done. I would say, "No, that couldn't have been my bullet." (Hoose 2001, 237)

In Cambodia, El Salvador, Liberia, and Uganda, initiation of child soldiers often required them to kill captives and sometimes to commit atrocities in their own villages, including murdering members of their own families (Boothby and Knudsen 2000; Rubin 1998). The commander of the UN peacekeeping force in Rwanda in 1994 reported that during a period known as the "hundred days of genocide," over 300,000 children were slain, *most of them by other children* (*New York Times*, July 15, 2001). The worldwide availability of inexpensive automatic weapons has narrowed the generation gap in soldiering, enabling children and adults alike to become effective killers at limited expense and with little or no training.

Child Political Activists

Though most adults do not tend to think of children as political actors, many kids have voluntarily participated in national and ethnic struggles, sometimes initiating and leading such actions. Striking examples can be found in the following countries:

- *South Africa*: The Soweto Uprising in the spring of 1976, which signaled the beginning of the end of the apartheid system in South Africa, began with a school boycott of Black elementary and middle school students—joined only later by parents and other adults who initially opposed the boycott as too risky—to protest the inferior and bigoted "Bantu Education" provided for them. In June

1976, some 500 students participating in a peaceful demonstration were killed by South African police. By the end of 1985, more than 2,000 child activists under age sixteen had been detained, a number sentenced to long prison terms, and several executed (Chikane 1986; Gobodo-Madizizela 2003; McLachlan 1986). Pamela Reynolds (1990), an anthropologist who did extensive fieldwork in Black South African communities, was not surprised by the extraordinary maturity and courage displayed by children during this period, pointing out that, for them, "childhood is not a time of protection and nourishment, either physical or psychological." Faced with the oppressive power wielded by the state, many kids "have taken it upon themselves, or had it forced on them to become warriors standing against that power" (114, 123).

- *Afghanistan*: During the Russian, Northern Alliance, and Taliban occupations of Afghanistan, thousands of schoolgirls participated in public demonstrations and underground resistance activities in support of national independence and freedom from the rule of religious fundamentalists. The Revolutionary Association of Women of Afghanistan (RAWA), a human rights organization founded by a female university student, trained girls to chant poetry when confronted by armed soldiers and police or mobs of religious fundamentalists. The total number of girls who were killed, tortured, or imprisoned for their political activities is unknown (Benard 2002; Brodsky 2003; RAWA website: www.rawa.org).

- *Palestinian Occupied Territories*: Evidence from a study of the first (1987–1992) intifada (uprising) indicates that it was initiated and led mainly by young people. As a consequence, the status of kids was greatly enhanced with a concomitant erosion of the status traditionally accorded to adults and elders: "By defying their parents, they resisted the occupation. By defying Israel, they undermined the authority of the older generation and the values it represented" (Yair and Khatab 1995, 103). As we saw in chapter 7, students also challenged the authority of teachers to control assignments and classroom discipline. Consistent with the tendency for subordinate groups to wish to free themselves from the stigma attached to children and childhood, noted in chapter 2, young Palestinian activists insisted on being called *asbaal* (lion cubs) rather than *awlaad* (children).

- *United States*: African American children and adolescents played active roles throughout the civil rights movement of the 1960s. Their participation was particularly notable in the May 1963 marches in Birmingham, Alabama, then the most racially segregated U.S. city. On some days, kid volunteers outnumbered their adult counterparts. In his memoir *Walking with the Wind*, John Lewis (1998), a leader of the movement and now a U.S. congressman from Georgia, recalls

> hundreds and hundreds of teenaged and even younger children, stepping out from the Sixteenth Street Baptist Church, singing and clapping, striding together toward the center of the city, where Bull Connor's officers stopped them and steered them into waiting paddy wagons and patrol cars. By the end of that first day, nearly a thousand of Birmingham's black children were in jail. (197)

When children continued to march the next day, Connor ordered a more forceful police counterattack. That night, television screens around the world showed

> snarling German shepherds loosed on teenaged boys and girls, the animals' teeth tearing at slacks and skirts. Jet streams of water strong enough to peel the bark off a tree, aimed at twelve-year-old kids, sending their bodies hurtling down the street like rag dolls in a windstorm. . . . It looked like battle footage from a war. (197)

Carolyn McKinstry, who participated in the Birmingham demonstrations when she was fourteen, remembers the training she and other children received at her church:

> They told us if we were knocked down we should stay down. They told us not to resist the dogs. Just stand there. Don't run from them. Before we went out they passed around big wastebaskets and told us to put in anything that could be seen as a weapon. A fingernail file, even a sharp pencil. We were not to give the police any reason to say, "We knocked that child down because she pointed a fingernail file at me." (Hoose 2001, 222)

McKinstry participated in the second day's march with hundreds of other students from her school, when the police turned giant water hoses on the children. She recalls,

It felt like the side of my face was being slapped really hard. It hurt so bad I tried to hold on to a building so it wouldn't push me down the sidewalk, and it just flattened me against the building. It seemed like it was on me forever. When they finally turned it off I scooted around the side of the building and felt for my sweater. They had blasted a hole right through it. And then for some reason I reached up and touched my hair. It was gone, on the right side of my head. . . . Why did they have to do *that*? (222–23)

A few months later, four girls, all friends of McKinstry, were killed, and twenty other children were injured when Whites bombed their church.

Effects of Political Struggles on Children

There was considerable disagreement among parents and adult leaders of the American civil rights movement about whether children should be exposed to such dangers. When Carolyn McKinstry's father got home the day she lost half her hair, he "hit the ceiling" and told her she was grounded. Her reaction: "I barely heard him. Nothing he was saying meant as much as what had happened to me" (Hoose 2001, 223). Congressman Lewis, himself a young adult at the time, considered the involvement of children and adolescents "natural and necessary. . . . We weren't far from being teenagers ourselves, and we shared many of the same basic feelings of adolescence: unbounded idealism, courage unclouded by 'practical' concerns, faith and optimism untrammeled by the 'realities' of the adult world, [and willingness] to risk everything for something noble and deserving, for the cause" (2001, 196–97).

From an adult ideological perspective, children are innocent and helpless victims of political violence who will inevitably suffer psychic as well as physical damage and will need the help of adult professionals in order to recover. Opponents of this view point out that it contains an *ageist* bias parallel to the *sexist* bias that women are kinder, more compassionate, and *weaker* than men and thus in need of male protection. Though much of the research on children and war is inconclusive (e.g., a review of multiple studies on the effects of the civil war in Lebanon [Randal and Boustany 1990] showed differing results regarding children's subsequent adjustment), the evidence in support of the adult ideological view is not compelling. Robert Coles's clinical evaluations of African American children who participated in civil rights demonstrations and braved hostile mobs in order to enter racially desegregated public schools reveal no consistent patterns of emotional damage and considerable evidence that many child activists developed impressive reserves of psychic strength. One Black male student in a White school said to Coles, "It's sweet pain this time, because however they try to hurt me, I know that just by sticking it out I'm going to help end the whole system of segregation; and that can make you go through anything" (*Time*, February 14, 1972, 39). Some studies carried out in Northern Ireland, South Africa, and Israel indicate that children's involvement in political protest strengthened family bonds, group spirit, or moral values (Boothby and Knudsen 2000; Cairns and Dawes 1996). Research conducted by the Palestinian Center for the Study of Nonviolence found that drug and alcohol abuse, until then a serious problem in the occupied territories, virtually disappeared among Palestinian youth who were active in the early phases of the first intifada (1987–1992), when the preferred tactics (selective boycotts and shutdowns) were based on Gandhian principles of nonviolence. No such change was found in a comparable group of youth who lived in areas where there were no opportunities to participate in nonviolent resistance; in these communities, "drugs and alcohol continued their destructive course" (Nagler 2001, 148).

In contrast to the children who participated actively in the civil rights movement, the negative effects on American children of the September 11, 2001, bombing of the World Trade Center, when their role was mainly as passive television viewers, seem to be more long lasting. A study conducted several months after the event for the New York City Board of Education concluded that because of lingering effects of the trauma, "roughly 200,000 of the 712,000 public school children in grades 4 through 12 were candidates for some sort of mental health intervention" (*New York Times*, May 14, 2002). Participation in meaningful, even dangerous, social action may be no more damaging to kids' physical and emotional health than remaining helpless if blameless victims.

Perhaps the most serious and prolonged trauma is suffered by children who live in violent communities and feel helpless to do anything about their situation. James Garbarino, president of the Erikson Institute, who has studied children in dangerous settings around the world, observed that "at least in a war zone you know the battle will end and peace may come. But with community violence in America, the war never ends and peace never comes" (*New York Times*, December 6, 1992). By the end of the twentieth century, more children and teens in the United States died in gun-related violence than from HIV/AIDS, cancer, pneumonia, asthma, and influenza combined (Children's Defense Fund 2002). A study of fourth and fifth graders and their mothers living in impoverished inner-city neighborhoods found that high scores on a measure of twenty-five types of community violence (from regularly hearing the sound of gunfire to being beaten up or attacked with a knife or gun or witnessing others being attacked or killed) were statistically associated with high levels of posttraumatic stress disorder. It is noteworthy that the researchers found discrepancies between children's and mothers' reports, with mothers consistently *underestimating* both their children's exposure to violence and the extent of their psychological distress (Ceballo et al. 2001).

A major negative outcome of national and transnational armed conflicts is a tendency for the two sides to polarize, with each side "otherizing" its opponents. As a foreign correspondent who has covered many wars put it, "When we venerate and mourn our own dead we are curiously indifferent about those we kill. . . . Our dead matter, theirs do not." Thus, "many Israelis defend the killing of Palestinian children whose only crime was to throw rocks at armored patrols, while many Palestinians applaud the murder of Israeli children by suicide bombers" (Hedges 2002, 13–14). In a statement on the mounting civilian casualties in the Israeli–Palestinian conflict, the Israeli justice minister drew a distinction between Israeli children who were "really murdered" or "murdered on purpose" and Palestinian children who were "accidental casualties" or "not hurt deliberately" (*New York Times*, October 5, 2002). In a speech delivered on May 1, 2003, proclaiming the U.S. military victory over Iraq, President Bush referred to "the cold murder of children" on September 11, 2001 (an estimated total of eight children),[7] but made no mention of the hundreds of thousands of Afghan and Iraqi children killed or seriously wounded by American military action. An interesting comparison is provided by the global death rate of about *40,000 children per day* from hunger and hunger-related diseases. A specialist in world hunger has noted "that's as if 100 jumbo jets with 400 children on each were to crash today, killing all aboard" (Sam Harris, quoted in Tynes 1991, 29).

In times of national crisis, distinctions between insiders and outsiders are also drawn within societies. Stephens (1997) noted that certain American children were not sheltered under the protective umbrella of Cold War policy: Native American or Mormon children living downwind of Nevada weapons testing sites, indigenous children in the Pacific Islands nuclear testing zones, and children diagnosed as retarded who were used as subjects of government-sponsored radiation experiences. Defined as outsiders, these kids "could legitimately be put at risk in the interests of safeguarding 'normal' children at the heart of Cold War visions of American society" (105).

CONCLUSIONS

In this chapter, we have touched on only a few of the political, economic, and social trends of the late 1900s and early 2000s that have transformed children's lives. Still we believe that several generalizations can be made about the effects of external environments.

First, inequalities in the distribution of wealth and other resources among and within the nations of the world are so great that children's life chances—indeed their chances of surviving long enough to *have* a life—continue to depend on *where* in the world they are born and grow up. In the twenty-first century, the number of children living in extreme poverty continues to increase, as does the number of families who lack the resources to overcome the harmful effects of severely disadvantaged or dangerous environments.

Second, a cost–benefit analysis at the societal level indicates that children continue to have economic as well as emotional value, as evidenced by the huge and lucrative international market in children for adoption and for labor. Despite labor market vicissitudes and efforts to limit or eliminate child labor, in many societies and societal subgroups, childhood is a time for work as well as for play and school, and children remain major contributors to their families, communities, and societies.

Third, the findings reviewed in this chapter warn us that we ignore global trends at our peril. A critique of World Bank policies and programs (Penn 2002) concludes that because such policies and programs are based on false premises, they often exacerbate the very problems they seek to cure. A much-lauded program in Medellin, Colombia, that provided low-cost early childhood care and education staffed mainly by female child minders who lacked training, job security, and a living wage offered little defense against the misery wrought on children's lives by the anarchy, civil war, and displacement of people precipitated by the drug trade. World Bank programs for overcoming malnutrition among African children gave token acknowledgment of societal problems such as indebtedness, war, and HIV/AIDS but concluded that faulty child-rearing practices were the fundamental cause of the problem. Similarly, explanations of the sharp increase in numbers of abandoned children in eastern European countries recently freed from Soviet control have tended to focus more on shortcomings of individuals or families than on the extent to which individual and family livelihoods have been undermined by current societal conditions far beyond their control (Demenet 2000).

Fourth, many of these findings challenge adult-centered ways of thinking about children's problems, especially their concentration on the differences between adults and children. While few would disagree with the claim that armed conflicts "put children into situations of enormous physical danger, psychological trauma and social instability" (Stephens, 1997, 10), don't they put *everyone* at risk? While few would disagree with the claim that child workers need to be protected from the worst forms of abuse and exploitation, shouldn't *all* workers be so protected? Are children of school age really incapable of judging what is in their own or their family's or their society's best interests and of taking risks in order to improve their lives and the lives of those around them? In resisting laws or systems of government that they considered unjust, many children have made momentous, life-and-death moral decisions and acted on them. "Society is, in consequence, challenged to re-think the notion of childhood in terms of children's vulnerability, responsibility and accountability" (Reynolds 1990, 114).

As a result of migration and travel, more children are, as Khalaf (2004) has put it, "positioned on the crossroads between cultures" (65), where they are likely to encounter kids and adults whose cultural backgrounds and lifestyles differ from theirs. At the same time, the rapid transfer of information and popular culture via mass media and electronic modes of communication means that children everywhere are becoming familiar with the same music, videos, games, and styles in clothing. In the next chapter, we'll examine what some sociologists view as an emerging global children's culture.

NOTES

1. Gittens (1998) reminds us that the effects of *historical time* are equally significant. While it is true that "a child born in Cameroon has a life expectancy of 50 years, less than two-thirds of an American child," it is also true that "in the Middle Ages, the life expectancy of a peasant child at birth would have been about half that of a child born in Cameroon today" (32).

2. The six countries in the Smeeding and Torrey study were Australia, Canada, West Germany, Sweden, the United Kingdom, and the United States; the ten countries in the Kennedy et al. study were Australia, Canada, France, Germany, Italy, Luxembourg, Netherlands, Sweden, the United Kingdom, and the United States. Both studies used children rather than households as the unit of analysis, as recommended by Qvortrup (see chapter 3).

3. The debate over children's work mirrors earlier debates over whether housework, caretaking, and other tasks traditionally carried out by women qualified as *real* work, worthy of serious scholarly attention and inclusion in official labor market or economic productivity statistics.

4. For photo evidence of American children's engagement in a variety of waged and domestic labor, see the catalog for the exhibit titled *Priceless Children* at New York University (Dimock 2002) and the collection assembled by the Children's Aid Society of New York (1978).

5. This title is borrowed from an essay of the same name by Roseanne Saad Khalaf (2004), in which the author reflects on her own experiences and those of her students during and after the seventeen-year civil war in Lebanon.

6. The pros and cons of the economic sanctions policy and the U.S. invasion have been heatedly debated, and we will not enter that debate. The relevant point here is that whatever the merits of these actions, Iraqi *children* clearly have not benefited from them.

7. Of the approximately 3,000 recorded 9/11 fatalities, eight have been identified as children between the ages of eight and eleven, three of them passengers on United Airlines flight 175 that crashed into the World Trade Center and five aboard American Airlines flight 77 that crashed into the Pentagon. A listing of casualties by age can be found at www.cnn.com/Specials/2001/memorial.

①

KID CONSUMERS IN
A GLOBAL ECONOMY

Parents and grown-ups ask us how we know about all this stuff. But how can we not? It's all around us.

—Fourteen-year-old girl living in Utah, United States

We are all human beings, who share the same lifestyle; we all play with the computer or watch TV in our free time.

—Eleven-year-old boy of Turkish–Cypriot origins
living in Manchester, England

For once in our civilization, children are educating older people.

—Fifteen-year-old boy living in Alberta, Canada

Despite the great inequalities among children examined in the previous chapters, their consumer power has been enhanced by the ever-greater amounts of money at their disposal and their ever-greater access to the electronic media that have facilitated worldwide dissemination of products and culture. How these trends are judged depends on perspective. From the perspective of many parents and social critics, the worldwide marketing of products targeted at kids represents an erosion of traditional values and promotes more passive, less imaginative modes of play. From the perspective of advertisers and the marketing staff of multinational corporations, kids represent both: "an influential market with growing power to influence parental choices" and "a market segment of primary users with increasing disposable income and the power to purchase particular goods" (Kline 1995, 115). From the perspective of kids, the global market offers opportunities to learn about and obtain products that enhance their enjoyment of leisure time and their status with peers. As children throughout the world are becoming familiar with the same foods, clothing styles, toys and games, computer software, music, and films, they are, some have claimed, creating the first global children's culture.

FOOD AND EATING HABITS

From his investigation of the American fast-food industry, Eric Schlosser learned that more than 90 percent of the children in the United States eat at McDonald's at least once a month and that close to 100 percent could identify Ronald McDonald. (The only fictional character with a higher degree of recognition was Santa Claus.)[1] From its beginning, McDonald's founder, Ray Kroc, envisioned children as McDonald's "target customers." As he saw it, "A child who loves our TV commercials and brings her grandparents to a McDonald's gives us two more customers." As a further inducement to their kid customers, the fast-food industry has forged promotional links with toy manufacturers, giving away small toys with children's meals and selling more elaborate ones at a discount. Sales of McDonald's Happy Meals soared after a Teenie Beanie Baby was included with each meal. McDonald's also operates some 8,000 playgrounds at its restaurants, more than any other nonpublic institution in the United States. Finally, given that the average employee preparing meals at a McDonald's restaurant is a teenager, one might say that "this is an industry that both feeds and feeds off the young" (Schlosser 2002, 9).

The change in children's eating habits exemplified by McDonald's coincided with a huge expansion in children's advertising. During the 1980s, most major ad agencies established children's divisions, and new marketing firms focusing solely on kids were opened. Compared to much scholarly research on children, market research is well funded and technically sophisticated. Television ads beamed at kids run on most channels and around the clock; efforts to ban or restrict ads aimed at young children have been successfully blocked by industry groups (Schlosser 2002). Moreover, fast-food chains are now gaining access to the last advertising-free outposts of American life: schools. Hundreds of public school districts across the U.S. have entered corporate "partnerships" in which they receive "prize" money from fast-food vendors in return for allowing the companies to sell their products in school cafeterias and to advertise them in school newspapers, on the walls of school corridors, and over the public address systems in schools and school stadiums. Not surprisingly, the financial gain is many times greater to the companies than to the schools.

Recently, corporate attention has turned to the People's Republic of China, the world's largest and fastest-growing kid market. Anthropological studies conducted in China during the 1990s (Jing 2000) trace the processes by which the introduction of snack foods and fast-food franchising has not only changed the food preferences of Chinese children but also increased their influence on family diet and eating habits. One explanation for the increased consumer power of kids is the combination of a stronger national economy and the government-imposed one-child-per-married-couple policy, leading to what the Chinese call the "4-2-1 syndrome"—families composed of four grandparents and two parents all concentrating their attention and resources on one child. Frequent reference to kids born in this era as "little emperors" reflects their privileged position in their families and their society. "In 1995, the average couple in urban China spent as much as 40 to 50 percent of their combined incomes on their child. Also in that year, children in Chinese cities received an aggregated yearly income of US$5 billion in the form of weekly allowances and birthday and holiday gifts from their parents and grandparents—a sum roughly equivalent to Mongolia's gross domestic product" (Jing 2000, 304).[2]

Hoping to tap into this huge market, Kentucky Fried Chicken (KFC) equipped its Beijing restaurants with child-sized furniture, play areas, and space for birthday parties—the latter a recent import to China that, Jing (2000) believes, reflects a profound shift in generational power, replacing "rituals of longevity" with "celebrations of youth" (204). When market research indicated that Colonel Sanders did not appeal to child customers, he was replaced by Chicky Chicken, a child-friendly mascot dressed in oversize red sneakers, striped pants, a red vest marked with the KFC logo, and a blue baseball cap worn pulled to one side hip-hop style. Winking and dancing around with cap askew, Chicky symbolizes the fun and excitement to be enjoyed at a KFC restaurant, though in deference to Chinese values, he also gives out back-to-school pencil cases to child customers, exhorting them to "study hard, play hard" (119).

Demonstrating familiarity with popular new food products is also an important element of contemporary peer culture in China, where, as in the New Jersey schools studied by Scott (1999, 2003), children create and maintain friendships through eating together and sharing food (see chapter 7). Being an informed kid consumer is not without costs: "Peer group pressure to consume trendy foods became so intense at one Beijing primary school that one student, according to his father, told his friends that he had eaten Wall's ice cream, while in fact he never had. . . . The boy felt he had to lie to avoid losing face" (Jing 2000, 108–9).

BEING IN FASHION

Baseball caps, jeans, and mobile phones have been described as the international uniform of twenty-first-century kids, a phenomenon that reflects the global dissemination of clothing fashions as well as wider acceptance of the idea that kids are entitled to pick out their own clothes. However, variations in children's clothing design still reflect ambivalence about how they should be dressed. An observer at an international trade show classified the children's fashions displayed as either Victorian style or miniature adult style. The former was "aimed at parents who were intent on creating for their children a sheltered place apart from the front-page news," who not only wanted "to make their sons' and daughters' childhoods a more nearly perfect version of their own" but also to "bar the door to adulthood and all its responsibilities, insisting on childhood as a totally different state of being." In contrast, the miniature adult style was targeted at parents who wanted "to dress their children as miniature versions of themselves as they look today, when their clothes testify to the kinds of people they've become." Examples included "kid-sized tuxedos, fur coats (rabbit dyed to look like lynx or cheetah or chinchilla), leather bomber jackets, and Burberry trench-coats" (Brubach 1990, 126–28).

Brubach noted that this bifurcation reflected conflicting *adult* views of children and childhood and that neither style took into account how kids themselves want to dress. Exactly when clothing designers and manufacturers began paying more attention to the latter is a matter of debate,[3] but "child power" is now viewed as a major influence on the fashion industry. An American importer of high-fashion European children's clothing told a *New York Times* reporter that "starting at about age 7, but sometimes as young as 3 or 4, children start making the fashion choices. They come in with their parents, their minds already made up. And if the parents make the selection, they often end up returning it because the kids refused to wear it" (*New York Times*, August 16, 1998).

The author of a new sociological study of child and youth marketing (Schor 2004) counterargues that encouraging little girls to buy designer clothing more suitable for adult women represents not "child power" but exploitation of kids by the fashion industry comparable to that by the fast-food industry. One of the hottest marketing tactics, according to Schor, is *age compression*, or the practice of pushing products originally designed for adults or adolescents at younger children, thus the aggressive promotion of cosmetics and elaborate hairstyling as well as high-heeled shoes, low-rise jeans, miniskirts and other provocative clothing for "tweens" (girls between the ages of five and ten). The Girls Intelligence Agency, a marketing company that opened in 2002, claims to have 40,000 "agents" between the ages of eight and eighteen who are paid in product samples and encouraged to host slumber parties for the purpose of learning what other girls have and want to have and reporting their findings to the company (Schor 2004).

These data on marketing trends would be of little more than passing interest were it not for empirical research findings showing that the surfeit of designer clothes and other consumer goods that are supposed to enrich children's lives may on the contrary be detrimental to their health and well-being. From her own survey of 300 children between the ages of ten and thirteen living in the Boston area, Schor (2004) found that kids who had high scores on an eighteen-item Consumer Involvement Scale[4] were also most likely to score high on measures of depression, anxiety, and several psychosomatic complaints and low on measures of self-esteem, leading her to conclude that "less involvement in consumer culture leads to healthier kids, and more involvement leads kids' psychological well-being to deteriorate" (167).

A few girls are exerting child power by rejecting the messages beamed at them on television and in teen magazines (now also marketed to tweens). This small countermovement is exemplified by GirlCaught, an organization founded by a fourteen-year-old girl and whose members analyze advertisements targeted at girls and organize boycotts of products whose ads portray them in demeaning or stereotypical ways (Bridges et al. 2003/2004, 53). However, comparison of the resources at the disposal of GirlCaught versus those available to the Girls Intelligence Agency serves as a crude indicator of the difficulties of "decommercializing" childhood.

BARBIE AND G.I. JOE

Among the products introduced by American toy makers in the 1960s and 1970s, none were more successful than Barbie and G.I. Joe. Now the world's most popular doll, Barbie was launched with a massive television advertising campaign that was designed to "stimulate little girls' fantasies about teen life" and promote the broadest possible demand for the doll among American girls. "Mattel has continually built on this initial product concept, by expanding the range of Barbie accoutrements to include first couturier clothing, and later a massive array of lifestyle clothes and accessories including home furnishings and cars"—and, of course, Barbie's companion Ken (Kline 1995, 116).

Having achieved market saturation in the United States, where between 90 and 95 percent of all girls ages three to eleven own at least one Barbie and many have three or more, Mattel attempted to replicate its success globally. Its first efforts were only moderately successful because of insufficient attention to cultural differences in standards of attractiveness (e.g., bright blond hair, big blue eyes, and white toothy smiles did not appeal to Japanese girls, who found them "scary") and regulations restricting children's television advertising in many European countries. With the opening up of commercial television worldwide, "Mattel renewed its merchandising efforts and re-positioned Barbie in a more culturally diverse world with explicit international themes"—for example, adding a UNICEF Barbie doll and sponsoring a "Barbie Summit" in 1990, for which girls from twenty-eight countries were flown to the Waldorf Astoria Hotel in New York to discuss world peace (Kline 1995, 123–24). Mattel also acknowledged a more diverse United States with the addition of an African American Barbie.

Though a tremendous commercial success, the doll has from the beginning generated fierce controversy. Feelings about Barbie divide little girls, most of whom love her, from their mothers and female teachers, who are at best ambivalent. Even many of the businesspeople who profit from the sale of Barbies disapprove of her sexiness. Barbies are a favorite medium for girls' fantasy play, including communication of secret sexual lore. From informal interviews and observations of kids playing with Barbie and Ken, Lord (1994) concluded that they "don't cut their creativity to fit the fashions of Mattel. One girl who wanted to be a doctor didn't demand a toy hospital; she turned Barbie's hot pink kitchen into an operating room." A brother and sister enacted "a fairy tale that fractured gender conventions. While hiking in the mountains, a group of ineffectual Kens was abducted by an evil dragon who ate all but one of them, who remained trapped until a posse of half-naked Barbies— knights in shining spandex—swaggered across the lawn and bludgeoned the dragon to death with their hairbrushes" (80–81). In a Mattel market research laboratory, Lord watched three girls playing happily until "Barbie decided to go for a drive with Ken, and two of the girls placed Barbie behind the wheel of her car. This enraged the third girl, who yanked Barbie out of the driver's seat and inserted Ken. 'My mommy says men are supposed to drive!' she shouted"—leading Lord to speculate that mothers may "blame Barbie for negative messages that they themselves convey, and that involve their own ambivalent feelings about femininity" (84). (For a teacher's perspective on Barbie, see Paley 1984, 10–12.)

Two competitors for Barbie's market share illustrate the divide between girl and adult perspectives. The Bratz series, introduced in the summer of 2001, features even more "anatomically advanced" bodies, faintly glazed facial expressions, and urban chic wardrobes containing tight sweaters, minute miniskirts, shredded jeans, and platform boots. Though many mothers object to the doll's trampy look, many preteen girls are replacing their Barbies with Bratz. The adult perspective is represented by the dolls featured in American Girl stores and catalogs, sold in their own stores located in upscale neighborhoods and malls. American Girl dolls resemble well-heeled schoolgirls in tasteful rich-girl outfits (matching items of clothing for the dolls' owners are sold in American

Girl stores, where dolls and owners can also host birthday parties). Both series offer dolls of color, though the Bratz model is a hip young African American or Latino *woman*, while American Girl dolls are *girls* about the age of the girls who buy them and tend to have similar, European American facial features regardless of skin color (*New York Times*, October 26, 2003; May 16, 2004).

A boy interviewed by Lord (1994) while dismembering several Barbies and Kens commented that "more boys would buy Barbies if you could put them together yourself" (81). G.I. Joe "action figures" (*never* to be referred to as *dolls!*) gave boys a chance to do that. By now, several generations of boys have subjected their G.I. Joes to freezing, melting, being thrown from bedroom windows or over cliffs, and other ingenious torments. Joe's identity has shifted over time. When opposition to the Vietnam War rose, he was repackaged as a civilian "adventurer," with big fuzzy hair and beard that would not have been allowed in any branch of the U.S. military. The current line includes Native American, Asian American, Latino, and African American Joes (a Colin L. Powell figure was top G.I. Joe in 1998). G.I. Joes and Barbies are also sought by adult collectors willing to pay high prices for vintage models, a value-added feature not lost on a nine-year-old boy who explained to a *New York Times* reporter, "You can play with your G.I. Joes, save them and someday they'll be worth a lot of money" (*New York Times*, June 30, 2003).

The history of G.I. Joe is also a story about the close relationship between a segment of the toy industry and the U.S. military. An article in the *New York Times* business section reported that Hasbro was preparing for the Christmas market a "Special Forces: Showdown with Iraq" collection modeled on clothing and equipment used by American troops and based on information obtained directly from Army research and development centers and military contractors as well as from mass-media coverage of the war. A Pentagon spokesman acknowledged without embarrassment that the army's M-16 rifle "is based on something Mattel did" and that the military is continually looking over the latest products of toy and game manufacturers for "ideas that can be developed effectively and inexpensively as battlefield tools" (*New York Times*, March 30, 2003).

Cross promotions have also strengthened relationships between the toy and film industries, leading to joint distributions of films and toys, games, and clothing based on film characters, all promoted via television ads. For example, the Disney Company's *Aladdin*, which achieved ticket sales of about $200 million during the first six months of its North American release, earned an additional $250 million from videocassettes and licensing of products ranging from dolls to pajamas to Nintendo video games, plus $250 million from worldwide seat and product sales (Kline 1995, 110). (For a scathing critique of the Disney Company for "attaching children's desires and needs to commodities," promoting stereotypical views about national identity, race, and gender and distributing their products through companies that routinely exploit child workers in developing nations, see Giroux 1999.) Like fast-food companies, the manufacturers of electronic toys and games have been far ahead of most sociologists in taking children's interests and expertise seriously. Hasbro hired "alpha pups," boys between the ages of eight and thirteen who were identified by their peers as "the coolest kid you know," to try out a new electronic game, then gave them additional games to hand out to their friends, who would, it was hoped, pitch the game to more kids and so on—a marketing strategy borrowed from medical research on the course of epidemics (Tierney 2001).

KIDS AND COMPUTERS

In a best-selling book published in 1982 titled *The Disappearance of Childhood*, Neil Postman argued that childhood is more strongly affected by technological breakthroughs than by any other contextual factors because technological change precipitates change in all other social institutions. By making books available to a mass audience, the printing press encouraged the spread of literacy, which in turn led to the social institution of the school. In contrast, television requires little instruction beyond learning how to turn on the set, a skill easily mastered by babies. Postman blamed television for the disappearance of childhood for three reasons: "first, because it requires no instruction to grasp its form; second, because it does not make complex demands on either mind or behavior; and third, because it does not segregate its audience. [It] provides everyone, simultaneously, with the same information" (80). Since it's hard to hide the television set or place it out of the reach of children, they are likely to watch the same programs as adults (on any given night, millions of American preschoolers watch late-night television) and thus gain access to the same information about sex, violence, and the pleasures and perils of consumerism.

Although *The Disappearance of Childhood* was published before personal computers had become widely available and affordable, Postman mentions them briefly at the end of the book, noting that they require a high degree of literacy, though of a different sort from reading, and that computer hardware and software change more rapidly than the technology of book production. Sherry Turkle, a sociologist on the faculty of the Massachusetts Institute of Technology (MIT) and pioneer in research on children and computers, postulates that kids who have had extensive exposure to computers from early childhood think differently than do adults or children who have not had such experience. Preschoolers who play with interactive computer toys and games are more comfortable than their elders with the idea that humans are not the only beings that possess awareness and intelligence, that "smart" machines may be as alive as people. The main difference between computers and people is that only people have "feelings" (Turkle 1984, chap. 1). Turkle predicted that the way kids with extensive experience of computers thought prefigured changes in adult modes of thinking so that "to a certain extent, we can look to children to see what we are starting to think ourselves" (Turkle 1995, 77).

Turkle also found striking cohort and cross-cultural differences in children's responses to computers depending on their personal experience and the pervasiveness of computers in their environments. American children interviewed in the mid-1990s responded differently than did children of the same age a decade earlier. Similarly, the reactions of Russian and English children who had little experience with computers and computer toys were more similar to those of their American counterparts of a decade earlier than to those of American contemporaries, evidence, Turkle believes, that cognitive development—at least with regard to computers—is not just a matter of chronological age but is also affected by children's "interactions with the human and material world" (Turkle 1995, 82–83; see chapter 2 for a discussion of psychological and biosocial perspectives).

As we saw in chapter 5, the majority of western European and North American children now have their own bedrooms, which are likely to contain their own television set, video recorder, video games, personal computer, and telephone or telephone extension, and this new "media-rich bedroom culture" has changed children's use of time and their relations with parents and peers. American survey data indicate that during the past two decades, the amount of time kids spent watching television, listening to the radio, and reading newspapers or reading for pleasure has declined, as has the proportion of kids who engaged in these activities. Only computer use has been rising (Howe and Strauss 2000).

Don Tapscott (1998), who gathered data via e-mail and computer conferencing from several hundred children on six continents, asked his respondents what they did with computers. A seventeen-year-old boy from Minnesota replied, "I run my own business and I create a lot of form letters and whatnot to be sent out to clients. I do a little graphic design—I even got published in the June issue of *MacWorld* magazine for the graphical tip I sent in." Other respondents mentioned using computers to:

> manage their personal finances; organize protest movements; check facts to prove a teacher wrong; discuss zits; check the scores of their favorite team and chat online with its superstars; organize to save the rain forest; make C-friends (cyber friends) or get a C-boyfriend; cast votes; learn more about the illness of their little sister; go to a virtual birthday party; get video clips from a soon-to be-released movie. (4–5)

Overall, the major uses were for entertainment; school work; communicating with family, friends, and chat groups; and shopping.

Are Video Games Good or Bad for Kids?

As in earlier debates over comic books, popular music, movies, and television, adults worry that computers and video games will make children disrespectful, disobedient, unsociable, and aggressive. Though some applaud projects in which computer-savvy kids take the role of teacher, others are anxious about the erosion of parental authority and lack of adult supervision, as illustrated by the editors' introduction to a journal issue devoted to research on children and computer technology:

> Excessive, unmonitored use of computers, especially when combined with use of other screen technologies, such as television, can place children at risk for harmful effects on their physical, social, and psychological development. Children need physical activity, social interaction, and the love

and guidance of caring adults to be healthy, happy, and productive. . . . To ensure healthy and appropriate use of computers both at school and at home, children's computer time must be limited and their exposure to different types of content must be supervised. (Shields and Behrman 2000, 6)

Like the results of research on other media, that on computer and video games is vast but inconclusive. On the positive side, there is evidence that most video games provide enjoyment and some have educational or therapeutic value—for example, improving hand–eye coordination, teaching players how to decode the rules or principles underlying game structures, or allowing vicarious release of tensions and aggressive feelings. The most commonly reported harmful effect is an increase in aggressive behavior, generally short term but sometimes longer lasting in younger children. Some research findings deliver a mixed message. In a recent article published in a prestigious science journal, the authors reported on a series of experiments comparing subjects who played violent action video games, including ones that rewarded players for killing simulated figures, with control groups of nonplayers. In almost all cases, subjects with game experience scored higher than nonplayers on measures of concentration and visual skills, including the ability to apprehend and keep track of many items simultaneously in a rapidly changing visual environment (Green and Bavelier 2003). Such findings leave many questions unanswered, such as whether the lessons taught in experimental or commercial games are fundamentally different from or more desirable than the more explicit instruction in combat skills built into the games developed by the military and targeted at teenage males. America's Army, a war game designed by the U.S. Army as a form of "outreach" (some might call it recruitment) and offered free on the Internet, has been downloaded by more than 10 million people, most of them boys and male youth. In a poll taken by a marketing research firm, some 30 percent of youth with a favorable view of the military said they had developed that view from playing America's Army (Thompson 2004). Indeed, one might say that today's troops received some of their basic training as children. A journalist who spent several months in Iraq with U.S. Marines, many of whom had only recently crossed the boundary from childhood to adulthood, was told by some of these young men that they entered battle feeling as though they were living one of their favorite video games—though it should be added that this feeling that was quickly dispelled by real-life combat (E. Wright 2004).

While he does not dismiss these concerns, Tapscott (1998) reminds his readers that children have always played violent games, from simulated battles with tin soldiers early in the twentieth century to cowboys and Indians or cops and robbers in mid-century to space wars today, and that kids whose parents refuse to buy them toy guns often prove resourceful at creating them from whatever materials are at hand. Moreover, he maintains that the effects of even the most violent games are slight compared to the effects of violent families, neighborhoods, and nations.[5]

Perhaps the most radical effect of computers is the blurring—some would say reversal—of traditional adult–child relations and generational distributions of knowledge and expertise. Tapscott's (1998) assertion that "for the first time in history, children are more comfortable, knowledgeable and literate than their parents about an innovation central to society" is echoed in the statement by the Canadian boy quoted at the beginning of this chapter and illustrated by the experience of an eleven-year-old Canadian girl who told Tapscott that "neither of my parents knew how to make a home page, so I did it by myself and then I taught my sister" (4). While acknowledging the effects of computers and the Internet on their lives, some kids insist that the influences are reciprocal. An eleven-year-old boy who said he "grew up with the computer" and "definitely wouldn't be the person I am without the Net" also claimed that by creating his own Web page, he also *changed the Internet*. A fifteen-year-old boy argued that "kids are one of the driving forces of the Internet, because of our incredible abilities to adapt" (77–78).

Access to the Internet has blurred the boundaries between public and private space as well as those between childhood and adulthood. The new peer culture does not require face-to-face interaction. Not only can kids order products from around the world without leaving their bedrooms, they can also communicate with other kids across local and even national boundaries. An example of the latter is Nation One, a global network of kids whose objective is to help people in poor countries gain access to the Internet. For one project, members in Australia, Canada, Greece, Madagascar, Mexico, and the United States raised funds via e-mail to equip a computer lab for a school in Senegal (Hoose 2001). Of course, the Internet can be used for less benign purposes. As we saw in chapter 7 (note 4), the Internet makes it easier for kids to torment other kids with less risk of detection for the tormenter and more public humiliation for the victim.

Inequalities in Computer Access and Use

For the time being, computers seem to be increasing the gaps between advantaged and disadvantaged groups, both between and within societies and between boys and girls. At the end of the twentieth century, about 95 percent of the households connected to the Internet were in North America, Europe, or the Asian Pacific. In the United States, households with earned annual income more than $75,000 were ten times more likely to be connected than households with earned annual income less than $30,000, European American and Asian American families were more likely than African American or Latino families to have computers in their homes, and schools in wealthy districts had more and newer computers than schools in poorer districts.

However, Roberts and Foehr's (2004) survey of American kids revealed an important change in the pattern of computer access when the unit of analysis was *children* rather than *households* (see discussion of "child-specific" statistics in chapter 3). While both higher household income and higher level of parents' education increased the likelihood that the kids in their sample "live in a home equipped with a computer and that the computer has an Internet connection" (33), the parental education and income effects were weaker or disappeared altogether with regard to children's *personal computer ownership*. That is, kids in higher- and lower-income homes were about equally likely to have their own computer, and the effect of parents' education did not disappear but was no longer statistically significant at all levels of household income—suggesting that at least in some parts of the world, the dissemination of computer technology has been swifter and more equitable in the child population than in the total population.

A host of studies show that boys spend more time on computers at home and at school and are more likely to participate in computer clubs or attend computer camps; indeed, girls "may not simply avoid computers but actually experience stress when using them, even in educational situations" (Cassell and Jenkins 2000, 11). One of the most comprehensive surveys found that even kindergartners viewed video games as more appropriate for boys (Subrahmanyam and Greenfield 2000). Since a large majority of these games offer ample violence but few representations of strong females, they are understandably more appealing to boys than to girls. Robert and Foehr's (2004) analysis showed, however, that "most of the time differential in computer use associated with gender can be accounted for by time devoted to games—boys play a lot, girls don't" (97). When time on games is taken into account, the gender difference in computer use disappears.

The editors of a collection of essays and studies on gender and computer games (Cassell and Jenkins 2000) point out that there are different ways to define and achieve gender equity: "equity through separate but equal computer games, equity through equal access to the same computer games, equity through games that encourage new visions of equity itself" (5). Equity of the first type calls for designing games that will be appealing to girls. Many "entail play situations that have traditionally been associated with girls such as those involving dolls, horoscopes, clothing and make-up" (301). Examples of this type are the hugely popular Barbie Interactive and Barbie Fashion Designer. The question raised by Barbie games is whether they are enhancing gender equity or simply creating a "girl ghetto." After wandering the aisles of a toy store for an hour, a frustrated eight-year-old girl complained that all the games were "either too boyish or too girlish. Why don't they have something in the middle?" (Subrahmanyam and Greenfield 2000, 66).

Tapscott's (1998) claim that the Internet has equalized girls' use of computers is based on the type 1 model of equity. He cites an eleven-year-old girl who had no interest in computers until her parents got a modem and online service that enabled her to join online clubs, which, she claimed, changed her life. After several of her favorite clubs failed, she created her own, whose members shared her interest in reading books from the Babysitters' Club series and who are, she says, "more than just kids who are in my club, they're my friends." Tapscott acknowledges that few boys participate in online social clubs and "just don't seem to have the same affinity as girls for building communities in cyberspace" (168–69).

Type 2 equity is most often exemplified by games in which female characters fight male characters or other females. This approach is justified on the grounds that girls "need to learn how to explore 'unsafe' and 'unfriendly' spaces, and to experience the 'complete freedom of move-ment' promised by boys' games [in order to] develop the self-confidence and competitiveness demanded of professional women. . . . Girls need to be able to play games where Barbie gets to kick some butt" (Jenkins 2000, 291). In Sissy Fight 2000, a Web-based multiplayer game (www .sissyfight.com), female characters with names like Big Patty, Sky Witch, and Blah to You fight for dominance on the playground, using offensive moves like scratching, grabbing, and teasing as well as more defensive or "feminine" moves like cowering and tattling. The question might be raised whether games like Sissy Fight enhance gender equity or simply reinforce the *androcentric* assumption that male behavior is the normal way of doing things (see discussion of Bem's gender theory in chapter 9).

Games based on type 3 equity generally attempt a fusion of boys' and girls' game genres. One such game, Nights into Dreams, retains some of the dangerous and risky elements associated with boys' games but also simulates such experiences as "floating through clouds" and "free-wheeling through colorful landscapes." The protagonists, in androgy-nous garb, confront serpents and monsters (though no armed conflict ensues) and try to reach a destination before an alarm clock awakens them from their dreams and they turn back into boys and girls. The em-phasis is not on winning—"the fun is in the journey rather than the des-tination" (Jenkins 2000, 292–94).

Games that encourage kids to think about gender in unconventional ways are probably the most difficult to conceptualize and construct. Members of a research and design group at a center for children and technology have been grappling with the dilemma of how to introduce the feminine perspectives that are "glaringly absent in technological de-sign without colluding in stereotypical understandings of femininity." A major technological difficulty is that it's far easier "to simulate shooting somebody dead" than "to simulate persuading somebody" (Brunner, Bennett, and Honey 2000, 73, 83). Finally, there's the question of how parents and teachers will react to games that sanction gender-bending—how many, for example, would feel comfortable with a game in which "children are given a choice of identifying themselves as a hermaphro-dite, transvestite, or transsexual?" (Cassell and Jenkins 2000, 220).

In one of the few well documented projects in which children were given the skills and opportunities to create their own games (Kafai 2000), fourth graders in an ethnically diverse inner-city elementary school in Boston, in cooperation with the MIT Media Laboratory, spent six months learning programming, game design, and alternative learning strategies, culminating in the creation of video games to teach third graders about the solar system. Analysis of the games showed that those designed by boys, most of whom had played a lot of video games, were likely to be structured as a contest between good and evil and to incorporate the kinds of violence found in commercial "adventure" games. Players who gave incorrect responses to questions about the solar system saw their game characters "kicked to the moon," "turned into an ice cube," or "sent frying to the underworld." Girls favored nonviolent feedback options, such as "sending the player back to another planet," "not receiving a piece of the map," or having to start again. Only one girl chose to end her game with a helicopter crash if the player gave a wrong answer. At the same time, boys displayed more variability in game designs, including a willingness to adopt features ordinarily found in games designed for or by females. In sum, the results showed considerable consistency in gender differences but also suggested that boys' preferences are more flexible than has been assumed and that girls' involvement in game design and play can be stimulated when they are offered topics and technology that resonate with their interests and learning styles.

Closing the computer gap between advantaged and disadvantaged kids, communities, and nations presents even greater difficulties. A few projects designed explicitly to increase socioeconomic equity—for example, training students to build computers for schools that cannot afford to buy them and to troubleshoot technical problems in classrooms and computer labs—have shown impressive results. The projects initiated by Nation One, mentioned earlier in this chapter, represent child-initiated efforts to promote more equitable access to computer technology at the international level. Wider dissemination of online instruction is undoubtedly more cost effective than the training or retraining of teachers that would be required to raise the educational levels of the most impoverished nations. Yet even the generally upbeat *Economist Survey on the Young* acknowledges that while computer access is spreading, the "gap between the rich world and the poor one is still at its most glaring in the young" (*Economist* 2000, 15). We're still a long way from the world envisioned by the Turkish–Cypriot boy quoted at the beginning of this chapter—where all kids have the free time and the means to watch TV, play with computers, and "share the same lifestyle."

CONCLUSIONS

Is there a globalization of childhood? Many social scientists believe that there is, though this trend may be viewed from two quite different perspectives, one essentially negative, the other more positive. The first, which might be called the *Euro-American export model*, views the dissemination of technology and mass culture as essentially an "export of modern Euro-American notions of children, childhood, nations and nationalisms around the globe" (Stephens 1997, 11). Childhood is largely defined by *play* and *learning*, neither of which is recognized as equivalent to productive work. Indeed, the Euro-American export model "problematizes" children's work since it disturbs comfortable if complacent adult views about children's limited competence and need for protection. A slightly different but equally negative version of the model is represented by (mainly North American) critics who blame multinational corporations like Disney, Mattel, Hasbro, Coca-Cola, and McDonald's for disseminating a worldwide *"kinderculture"* that is turning kids into uncritical consumers indistinguishable from one another (Giroux 1999; Steinberg and Kincheloe 1997). The corporate perspective is exemplified by the claim made by the marketing director for Coca-Cola International, apparently without irony, that "the same kid you see at the Ginza in Tokyo is in Piccadilly Square, in London, in Pushkin Square, at Notre Dame" (Kline 1995, 109).

The second perspective, which might be called the *children's international culture model*, is more optimistic, focusing on the creative and empowering aspects of globalization. Kids are not simply passive victims of international marketers. On the contrary, they're likely to be among the first to understand and to *adapt* as well as *adopt* new technologies and consumer goods, and the effects of kid culture and corporate culture are reciprocal. Like peer cultures in general, children's international culture assumes "a general community of interest and mentality with other children" that they do not share with adults, exemplified by a German boy who explained that "children are always more like each other than like adults of their own or other nationalities" (Hengst 1997, 57). In the children's international culture, the Internet may be a more important source of information than families and schools, and kids imbued with an international perspective may be ahead of their elders in rejecting stereotyped definitions of insiders and outsiders and in moving beyond nationalisms based on racial and cultural purity and toward more inclusive definitions of themselves and their countries.

Though often equated with Americanization, the children's international culture is not a single, homogenized phenomenon. To be sure, children around the world are familiar with American films and TV series. "Yet, the American entertainments that have spread around the world have themselves been shaped by artistic practices from diverse parts of the globe, as one mass culture meets another" (Tignor et al. 2002, 439). Kids who watch Disney films are also likely to play Nintendo games, practice martial arts originating in various Asian cultures, and listen to music from many nations and societal subgroups. Multinational corporations that successfully enter new markets—as Kentucky Fried Chicken did in Beijing—do so by using what Kline (1995) calls a glo-local marketing strategy: designing and presenting products that promise connection with an exciting global culture while deferring to traditional values and local customs.

Perhaps the most important implication of the research presented in chapter 10 and this chapter is that in the absence of understanding social change at the national and international levels, efforts to improve children's lives are not only misplaced but also doomed to failure. In the next chapter, we turn to an assessment of some of the more promising efforts to create a world fit for children.

NOTES

1. Similarly, a 1991 study published in the *Journal of the American Medical Association* found that "nearly all of America's six-year-olds could identify Joe Camel, who was just as familiar to them as Mickey Mouse. Another study found that one third of the cigarettes illegally sold to minors were Camels" (Schlosser 2002, 43).

2. A similar phenomenon is reported in Japan, where newborns are often referred to as "five pocket children," who will need this many pockets to hold the money they receive from parents, grandparents, aunts and uncles, and

neighbors—though in this case the precipitous drop in the national birthrate has occurred despite government efforts to encourage women to have *more* babies (Creighton 1994).

3. In a historical analysis of children as consumers, Cook (2004) argues that during the 1930s children's views about "goods, spaces, and social relations of consumption" were first accorded serious attention; while parents' views were not ignored, they were now examined primarily in relation to children's. During this period, marketing experts also began to justify their efforts to attract children's business as a means of developing their educational, psychological, and/or social literacy.

4. Items on the Consumer Involvement Scale include the following: I like shopping and going to stores; I care a lot about my games, toys, and other possessions; I like clothes with popular labels; being cool is important to me; I feel like other kids have more stuff than I do; I wish my parents gave me more money to spend (Schor 2004).

5. Tapscott's argument is supported by evidence that a child is much more likely to injure or be injured, even killed, by a gun in her home than by playing any kind of video game. See also the discussions of the effects of neighborhood violence in chapters 5 and 10.

VI

APPLYING RESEARCH: STRATEGIES FOR IMPROVING KIDS' STATUS AND WELL-BEING

12

TOWARD A WORLD
FIT FOR CHILDREN

On May 8, 2002, thirteen-year-old Gabriela Azurdy Arrieta addressed the United Nations General Assembly, a noteworthy (though little noted) occasion because the speaker represented the last group of people to be invited to present their views in the world's principal international political forum (see the discussion of children as a minority group in chapter 2). Reading from a statement drafted by the 300-member children's delegation to a UN Special Session on Children, Azurdy Arrieta, a resident of Bolivia, challenged the all-adult membership of the General Assembly to create a world fit for children, among whom she explicitly included street children and child victims of war and HIV/AIDS (*New York Times*, May 9, 2002).

The General Assembly had, in November 1989, adopted the UN Convention on the Rights of the Child. Signed by enough member nations to enter into force in 1990 and by all nations except Somalia and the United States by 1996, the convention is the first comprehensive international statement of law regarding children's rights and also the most widely and speedily ratified human rights treaty in history. A few critics have faulted the convention's designers for failing to follow up with the necessary laws and procedures to ensure its implementation, for failing to take account of conditions (wars, extreme material deprivation, nonvoluntary migration, genocide, and other forms of cultural or ethnic suppression) likely to override concern for children's rights, and for setting global standards "based on Western and, in particular, Christian notions of children's interests which simply may not be transferable to other cultures" (Smart, Neale and Wade 2001, 188; see also American Sociological Association 1998; Bernard van Leer Foundation 1996). What most critics failed to note was that this important statement of children's rights was prepared without input from children.

If children are our most precious commodity, as adults are wont to proclaim, why are people having fewer of them, and why are there still so many poor, abused, and neglected children even in the most affluent societies? What are the practical implications of the research reviewed in the preceding chapters? In this final chapter, we'll try to respond to Azurdy Arrieta's plea by assessing some of the strategies that have been proposed and, to varying degrees, tested for raising children's status and improving their well-being. Following the order of the preceding chapters, our discussion will move from strategies aimed at strengthening children's families, to those aimed at changing schools and schooling, to those designed to improve children's status in the larger society, national and global. We'll conclude with a few noteworthy efforts to offer children better childhoods by creating new societies or communities.

STRATEGY 1: STRENGTHENING FAMILIES

As we learned in chapter 4, perceptions of a "good" family differ, and proposals for strengthening families are likely to fit the preconceptions of those who draft the proposals. Borrowing from the terminology developed by Jan Pryor and Bryan Rodgers (2001) to characterize alternative perspectives on family structure and functioning, we'll describe three explanations for current family difficulties and strategies for resolving them. From a *conservative perspective*, weak families are viewed as the result of the individualistic, hedonistic consumer culture of modern societies in which people's sense of obligation to their families and communities is overpowered by their self-interest and desire for material goods. From this perspective, the solution lies in revitalizing family values and promoting good parenting practices, and this is best accomplished in traditional married-parents-with-children families with clear gender and generational distinctions. From a *liberal perspective*, weak families result from the rapid change, relentless competition, and social inequities endemic to a world ruled by free market economics. In such a world, the solution lies in increased public and private investment in children and their families and fairer distribution of the financial and other costs of child rearing between households with and without children and between the family and other social institutions. From an *emergent perspective*, family diversity is inevitable but not inevitably harmful to children. The solution lies in providing nonintrusive social services that will help family members manage the changes in their personal lives and social surroundings. This is the only perspective that explicitly advocates taking account of children's views on family matters.

Solutions Based on the Conservative Perspective: Marriage and Better Parenting

In the welfare reauthorization bill brought before the U.S. Congress in 2003, states receiving federal funding are required to establish services to encourage the formation maintenance of "healthy" two-parent married families. One of the projects funded under this program, a series of workshops on how to get and stay married, was offered in a public housing project in Oklahoma. In a case study of one of the Oklahoma workshops, the author (Boo 2003) noted that the turnout for most sessions seldom totaled more than five (all African American women, one of whom had been married but had divorced her physically abusive husband) and that the curriculum, developed a quarter century earlier for engaged or married couples, included videos of middle-class couples resolving conflicts over the husband hogging the home computer or not helping clean the guest bedroom, situations not likely to arise among impoverished families living in decrepit, crime-ridden housing projects. Nor did the program motto, "Two parents means two paychecks," jibe with the personal experience of most of the women who were recruited for the workshops. (At the time, only about half the African American men in Oklahoma were employed and almost ten percent were incarcerated.) The workshops have yet to produce a wedding.

Of course, it is unfair to judge an entire policy on the basis of a single ill-conceived and poorly funded project. More substantial doubts about the "marriage cure" model are raised by the Fragile Families Project, an important ongoing longitudinal study that is tracing some 3,700 couples in sixteen U.S. cities who had a child in the late 1990s. The participants, mostly low-income and unmarried, were interviewed shortly after the birth and again when the children were approximately twelve, thirty-six, and sixty months old. The last two interviews included in-home assessments of the parents' relationship and the children's development (McLanahan et al. 2003). From the data gathered so far, the researchers have learned that few of their subjects needed convincing about the desirability of marriage: most of the unmarried couples interviewed *wanted* to marry, were committed to each other and to their children at the time of the birth, and had "high hopes for their future together." A year later, however, only 9 percent of the couples who hoped to marry had actually done so, and almost half were no longer in a "romantic relationship" with each other (Bendheim-Thoman Center 2003b).

Why this discrepancy between attitudes and behavior? The major impediment was not, as had originally been assumed, the parents' lack of motivation but rather their severe shortage of social capital. Few were equipped to support themselves let alone a family. Annual earnings of the unwed fathers in the sample averaged just over $16,000, and few had the educational or employment credentials that would enable them to better their financial situation. For unwed mothers, making ends meet was a constant balancing act. Regardless of the status of their relationship with the baby's father, a majority of the mothers relied on some form of public assistance during the year following the child's birth. Comparison of the married and unmarried couples in the sample revealed, moreover, that the incidence of substance abuse, domestic violence, and mental health problems was substantially higher among the latter and that unmarried fathers were much more likely than married fathers to have been incarcerated for a violent crime. In the long run, the researchers conclude, any viable strategy for increasing the number of stable, healthy families "will need to do more than just get parents to sign a marriage contract." They estimate (Bendheim-Thoman Center 2002, 2003a, 2003b) that even if current programs were expanded to address parents' financial, employment, and mental health problems as well as strengthening their relationship skills, only about a third of the couples in their sample *might* benefit from them.

Better Parenting The assumptions underlying marriage-promotion workshops have also been applied to programs to improve parenting skills. Generally targeted at disadvantaged or "at-risk" families, these programs, often termed *interventions*, have included home visits to observe and offer advice on children's physical and emotional development and enrichment programs that teach mothers how to play with their babies or young children so as to provide "the right experiences at the right developmental stages" (Danziger and Waldfogel 2000, 6–7). In recent years, the importance of fathers has been underscored in programs like Responsible Fatherhood (RF), whose objective is to help fathers become "(a) more capable of financially supporting their children; (b) more compliant with Child Support Enforcement, and (c) more involved in their children's lives as positive role models and nurturers." In one of the few RF programs studied by outside observers (Anderson, Kohler, and Letiecq 2002), the participants, all low income and most African American, received services such as life skills training and vocational and mental health counseling and in addition met for six months of focus group discussions. From their perspective, the major benefit was the emotional support of their peers: "Being able to voice my opinion about how I feel about certain things and knowing that someone is listening and understandin' where I'm comin' from." On the other hand, few of these men felt that their most pressing financial and employment concerns were being addressed. Many were working two or more jobs of physically demanding work for low wages, and none of the job placements available through the program would raise their income substantially or match the financial rewards offered by the illegal underground economy. As one father put it, "If you can make $1,500 a day dealing drugs on the street, why would you choose to work for minimum wage?" (151). There was little evidence that the program was meeting its stated objectives of increasing fathers' financial support or involvement in their children's lives—perhaps because men who were behind in their child support were reluctant to join a program that was associated with the agency responsible for collecting it or perhaps because most of these low-income fathers, like the men in the Fragile Families sample, were already involved in their children's lives and had contributed financially and in other ways during and after the pregnancy (Bendheim-Thoman Center 2003b).

Responsible Fatherhood has been criticized for reinforcing traditional gender hierarchies and defining fathers primarily as financial providers. Anderson and colleagues (2002) also point out that more systematic evaluation of RF programs would be required in order to identify the most (and least) effective program practices. Evaluations of home visiting and enrichment programs have shown generally positive outcomes, though only if the benefits are rather narrowly defined. Interventions may reduce the rates and severity of a particular problem, but as Ambert (1997), points out, most of the available programs are too costly to reach most of the parents who need them, and many of the families for whom they are intended are too dysfunctional to benefit from them. Nor, we might add, are these programs likely to give disadvantaged families access to better schools, safer neighborhoods, and more dependable public services or enable them to climb up many rungs of the social ladder. (Interventions are seldom targeted at wealthy and powerful people, no matter how serious their family problems.)

Solutions Based on the Liberal Perspective: Greater Investment in Children

We saw in chapter 5 that becoming a mother raised women's risk of poverty, that men's financial status may also be negatively affected, and that the income gap between parents and nonparents is growing. Understandably, many adults, especially middle-class adults, are having fewer kids or none at all. The problem is that what may be economically rational for individuals, who bear the costs of raising children, is economically disastrous for society as a whole, which reaps the benefits of child rearing. The solution, often referred to as the "kids-as-capital" model, is for societies to assume more of the costs of child rearing. This strategy is based on the premise that investments in children not only improve their health, welfare, and academic performance but also have value for their parents and societies. Such investments facilitate parents' employment, thus enabling them to contribute both to their families and to the economy. They also ensure a continuing supply of skilled workers who will support the older generations as well as maintain the nation's international competitiveness (Hernandez 1995; Pong, Dronkers, and Hampden-Thompson 2003; Seccombe 2002).

Arguably the most highly developed, comprehensive, and forward looking in this regard are the social welfare systems in the Nordic countries and France, all of which have substantially higher tax rates than the United States. In Denmark, Finland, Norway, and Sweden, parents of infants and young children are entitled to paid leaves with job security, and all children are entitled to a broad range of health, child care, and educational benefits. Such a system depends on a highly educated and productive adult population, "a large public sector, a strong state-managed social security system, and a comparatively high degree of equality between social groups" (Dencik 1995, 107). A substantial body of research shows that in these countries, extensive preschool experience is positively associated with children's social and psychic development and later academic success. The French system includes universal prenatal care, children's allowances, and medical insurance; free all-day preschool programs from age three; and subsidized day care for younger children. Preschool teachers have postgraduate training (at state expense), civil service status, and salaries comparable to those of primary and secondary school teachers. Though preschool attendance is not compulsory, close to 100 percent of all French three- to five-year-olds and a growing number of two-year-olds attend *ecole maternelle*, or nursery school. National surveys conducted during the 1980s and 1990s indicated that each year of preschool reduced the likelihood of school failure, especially for disadvantaged children; it also reduced slightly the achievement gap between children from high- and low-income families (Boocock 1998).

In the twenty-first century, the United States is almost alone among industrialized nations in not providing a publicly financed social safety net for all children and their families, but it is doubtful whether any system that involves an extensive redistribution of wealth would be acceptable to most Americans, who tend to view any government interference with family life with suspicion. Some look to the private sector for solutions, pointing to the Bill and Melinda Gates Foundation as a model. Founded in 1999 and now the largest U.S. foundation, the Gates Foundation has pledged $3.2 billion, to be paid out over the next two or three years, to support development and distribution of vaccines and immunization against AIDS, tuberculosis, malaria, and other diseases that now cause the deaths of about 3 million children per year (*New York Times*, July 13, 2003). To place the Gates donation in context, in the same month that

America's wealthiest private foundation pledged a total of $3.2 billion to be shared by all nations over a two- to three-year period, U.S. government estimates of expenditures for the war and postwar occupation of Iraq were $3.9 billion per month. It is difficult to see how private investments could replace public investments without an overall loss of support for programs and services benefiting children and their families.

Among poorer nations for which reliable data are available, probably the most impressive improvements in children's welfare were achieved in Cuba after the dictatorship of Fulgencio Baptista was replaced in December 1958 by a socialist government led by Fidel Castro. As a result of policies that substantially reduced the huge gap between rich and poor and created Cuba's first coherent government-supported social welfare system, the following had taken place by the early to mid-1990s:

- Child malnutrition had been virtually eliminated.
- The child survival rate (the proportion of children born who lived at least to age five) rose to equal that of the United States.
- Almost 100 percent of all one-year-olds were immunized for tuberculosis, diphtheria–pertussis–tetanus, polio, and measles (U.S. rates during the same years ranged from 84 to 94 percent).
- School attendance and literacy rates were the highest among Latin American nations.
- Availability and quality of medical services for children, day nursery, and kindergarten programs were comparable to those in some of the world's wealthiest countries (Ennew and Milne 1990; UNICEF 1999, 2001).

A more recent but equally ambitious effort to increase investment in children and their families has been launched in Brazil, another Latin American country with vast income disparity between rich and poor. At his inauguration in 2002, President Lula da Silva, who himself grew up in extreme poverty, announced a national war on hunger and proposed a series of cash transfer programs. Under Family Grant, the first program to be implemented, poor families receive small monthly stipends on the condition that their children attend school regularly and have periodic medical checkups. Although the objective of the stipend is to motivate parents to put their children in school rather than putting them to work, kids are allowed to have jobs outside school hours, and most do. For deeply impoverished families, the government grant, averaging $30 to $35 a month, is their biggest source of income, and if it hasn't lifted them out of poverty, it has enabled them to be better fed and healthier. The goal of Family Grant is to reach 11.4 million families, about a quarter of Brazil's population, by 2006 (Bearak 2004).

The weakness of the kids-as-capital model is that it requires levels of financial and political commitment that are difficult to achieve and maintain in the current global economy, where the prevailing tendency is toward *less* investment—some call it *disinvestment*—in children. The weak performance of the Brazilian economy and the cost of servicing the huge national debt have already forced President da Silva to cut back on spending for his welfare and income redistribution programs. Though European social welfare systems continue to be supported by the voters and have so far remained basically intact, governments are under pressure to reduce public support and relax standards for children's programs in order to remain competitive in the global free market and to pay for the full range of services required by the growing numbers of retired and aging citizens.

Solutions Based on the Emergent Perspective: Accommodating Diversity, Listening to Children

The emergent perspective offers a framework for viewing family transitions that incorporates the concept of children as social actors that connects much of the research discussed in this book. Pryor and Rodgers's (2001) studies of children's adaptation to parental separation (discussed in chapter 4) led them to conclude that the quality of family relationships is more important to children's well-being than the composition of households and parents' marital status and that poverty, financial insecurity, and societal instability are far greater threats than unconventional family lifestyles. Most of the children they interviewed were quite resilient in adapting to family change but resentful "when they are not told what is happening, and when adults do not take their feelings and views into account." The challenge for policymakers and counselors then is to "identify ways of enhancing quality and stability of relationships in families, regardless of their structure," and to strike "a balance between [children's] rights to be informed and heard, and burdening them with undue responsibility for decisions made" (258–59, 275).

Both conservative and liberal programs are faulted for imposing "top-down" solutions and subjecting children to unsolicited counseling and other interventions that diminish their privacy and sense of control over what is happening to them. The alternative proposed is to keep family problems in the family whenever possible, a position that coincides with the preference of many child informants. When this is not possible, informal sources of support, such as extended family members or friends, should be explored before ceding authority to lawyers, professional counselors, and other strangers. The studies by Smart and colleagues (2001) of British children, also based on data collected directly from kids (discussed in chapter 4), found that "peer support schemes, internet chat rooms and counseling services like Childline [a telephone hotline], which offer independent access and confidentiality (as well as anonymity), are highly valued by children as a first step in taking a problem outside the family" (160–61).

A similar line of argument using somewhat different terminology can be found in critiques of the equation of family change and diversity with *moral decline*. In one such analysis, Gerson (2000) argues that the problems besetting families today can be solved neither by injections of family values nor by maligning family arrangements that deviate from the model. In her opinion, idealization of the breadwinner-homemaker family that was the predominant family structure for a few decades in the mid-twentieth century "masked its many limitations and was commonly used to chastise and stigmatize those who could not or would not conform" (180). Gerson proposes that we cease trying to impose *any* "one best family" model on everyone and focus instead on the following

- Identifying and controlling the social institutions and arrangements that make child rearing difficult, for example, the excessive demands of the "greedy" workplace, which is responsible for the "cultural devaluation of caretaking that makes it costly to devote time to children, discourages involved parenting (especially among men), and exacts heavy penalties from those who would choose to put their families first" (184).
- Reversing the current decline in social resources for children, both by creating new institutions, such as high-quality, community-based child

care, and by "reinvigorating traditional child-rearing institutions, such as public schools, local community centers and playgrounds" (185).

As the name implies, policies and programs based on the emergent perspective are still relatively few in number and small in scale, with little or no systematic evaluation of their outcomes and cost-effectiveness. This undoubtedly reflects not only the scarcity of research-based knowledge about children's views on family life but also the resilience of the adult ideological perspective, which leaves many adults ambivalent about children's roles and rights but resistant to their becoming full partners even in decisions directly concerning them. The solutions described here overlap to some degree with those based on the liberal perspective in that both call for greater investments in programs that benefit children directly. The underlying rationales are, however, quite different. While the ultimate objective of kids-as-capital investments is to enhance children's *value* to their families and societies, the emergent perspective views stable and happy family life as an *end in itself* and the most direct way to enhance children's well-being.

STRATEGY 2: IMPROVING SCHOOLS AND SCHOOLING

Like strategies for strengthening families, proposals for educational reform tend to represent opposing views of children and childhood. From the conservative perspective, schools should focus on the mastery of basic skills, especially reading and mathematics, and should be held accountable for the results through frequent assessments of student, teacher, and school performance. Liberals believe that substantially greater investments in quality schools will be required to raise academic achievement, reduce inequities, and prepare all kids to succeed in the real world. A third perspective, one that we'll call *alternative*, posits that schools are so fundamentally flawed that, failing a radical overhaul, children should have the option of receiving their schooling outside the formal educational system.

Solutions Based on the Conservative Perspective: Back to Basics

Educational reform in the United States has tended to fluctuate between conservative and liberal solutions to educational problems. The former is currently in the ascendancy. Federal law now mandates that all fourth graders pass standardized reading and math proficiency tests. Standardized tests have even been introduced in Head Start programs, the most extensive testing of such young children in the nation's history. In many districts, schools are required to add extra English and math classes, retain weaker students in the third grade, or require them to attend remedial summer classes. The new curriculum leaves little room for electives. Art and music classes are usually the first to go, but reductions in foreign language, social studies, and science instruction are also common. Pressure to raise test scores has also led many schools to adopt the reduced- or no-recess policies and zero-tolerance discipline policies described in chapter 7.

The most systematic comparisons of national school systems can be found in the cross-national surveys conducted periodically over the past thirty years by the International Association for the Evaluation of Educational Achievement (IEA). Review of IEA survey results over time shows both considerable fluctuations in national standings and considerable variation in the paths to academic excellence. The nation that achieved the highest scores in literacy and near-the-top scores in math and science in the most recent (2003) survey was Finland, whose educational system differs in almost every important respect from the back-to-basics model. In the day care and preschool programs that most Finnish children enter by age one, almost no time is spent on "pre-academic" activities, such as learning numbers and letters or reading-readiness exercises. Cross-national observations of preschool classrooms conducted as part of the IEA Preprimary Project showed that Finnish children spent *less* time in teacher-directed group work and *more* time in activities of their own choice either alone or with another child than did preschoolers in fourteen other countries. People unfamiliar with the Finnish system are surprised to learn that compulsory education does not begin until age seven. Not surprisingly, Finnish kids initially lag behind their peers in other countries, but the IEA data show that they quickly catch up and soon surpass them. Moreover, high reading, math, and science scores are not accomplished by neglecting other subjects or sacrificing recess time. All students are required to learn two foreign languages, and arts and crafts, music, and physical education are also compulsory. After every forty-five-minute lesson period, kids are allowed fifteen minutes to let off steam in noisy outdoor play or by banging on pianos, drums, or electric guitars indoors. Finally, the Finnish educational system is impressive not only for the richness of the curriculum and the high level of academic achievement but also for its cost-effectiveness. The per-pupil annual expenditure, about $5,000, is lower than all but the poorest school districts in the United States and one of the lowest among all industrialized nations (Dickson and Cummings 1996; Elley 1994; Keeves 1995; Mullis et al. 2003, 2004; Weikart, Olmsted, and Montie 2003).

From their inception, the IEA surveys have been subjected to minute examination and rancorous criticism on everything from the sample design to the choice of questions to the mode of computing national rankings. Debate over the validity and fairness of IEA ratings has been particularly heated in the United States, which has never placed at or even near the top regardless of the prevailing educational ideology at the time of the survey. Whatever their shortcomings, the IEA studies indicate that there's more than one way for a nation to improve its standing in the international academic competition but that a nose-to-the-grindstone approach to learning with a narrow focus on basic skills is probably among the less effective ways to accomplish this.

Solutions Based on the Liberal Perspective: Investing in Quality Education for Disadvantaged Kids

During the past two decades, a number of highly publicized philanthropic projects in the United States have been designed for the purpose of enabling at least a few kids from the poorest families and neighborhoods to "beat the odds." One strategy, of which the I Have a Dream project is the prototype, is to obtain pledges from foundations or wealthy donors to cover college tuition for students who succeed in graduating from high school. This strategy has generally proven to be costly with, at best, modest results. One such program, in which 112 West Philadelphia sixth graders were promised college tuition, yielded twenty college graduates and the same number of prison inmates. The donor, a wealthy Connecticut businessman, has recently pledged $20 million and is seeking to raise $30 million more in order to "promise" 400 Harlem kindergartners a college education (*New York Times*, September 30, 2004). A second strategy, exemplified by A Better Chance

(ABC) programs, is to place a few talented youngsters in the private boarding schools that prepare students for entry into elite colleges and universities. Longitudinal follow-up studies of ABC participants indicate that the experience has enabled a handful of African Americans to enter the "White establishment," though most have been prevented by the glass ceiling from reaching the top positions in the corporate and professional world (Zweigenhaft and Domhoff 1991).

We'll examine here two large-scale ongoing educational experiments whose objective is not just to help a few poor kids beat the odds but also to *change the odds,* more specifically, to raise the academic performance of *all* the children in an impoverished neighborhood or school district.

Harlem Children's Zone   Geoffrey Canada, who had the kind of childhood he's trying to change and who succeeded in beating the odds by winning a scholarship to Bowdoin College and going on from there to earn a degree from the Harvard Graduate School of Education, advocates a different approach. In an ambitious educational experiment, begun in the mid-1990s in a predominantly African American neighborhood of New York City, he is attempting to prove that "poor children, and especially poor black children, can succeed—that is, achieve good reading scores, good grades, and good graduation rates—and not just the smartest or the most motivated or the ones with the most attentive parents, but all of them, in big numbers." Beginning with a twenty-four-block area of central Harlem—which Canada named the Harlem Children's Zone (HCZ)—the project

> combines educational, social and medical services. It starts at birth and follows children to college. It meshes those services into an interlocking web, and then it drops that web over an entire neighborhood. It operates on the principle that each child will do better if all the children around him are doing better. . . . The objective is to create a safety net woven so tightly that children in the neighborhood just can't slip through. (Tough 2004, 46)

Concentrating on the most immediate obstacles to success in school, HCZ offers programs to prevent or treat childhood diseases; programs where preschool children can learn phonics via computers; after-school centers where kids can get one-on-one tutoring, write autobiographies and read them to each other, or join an investment club where Wall Street executives explain the Dow Jones and the Nasdaq; and family support centers and home visiting programs to help parents help their kids succeed. Eighty-eight percent of the roughly 3,400 children under eighteen in this core neighborhood are now served by at least one program, and Canada is extending the HCZ to encompass a sixty-block area.

The centerpiece of the project is the promise of better schools in the HCZ. Finding the public school system inadequate to meet the needs of HCZ kids, Canada is seeking to opt out of it by establishing and/or converting public schools into charter schools. At least some of the staff will be nonunion teachers who will be paid more than public school teachers, will also work longer days and for twelve months a year, and can be fired for poor performance. This is probably the most controversial element of the project and has understandably earned Canada the hostility of the teachers' union. The response of parents has been more enthusiastic. Applications to enroll in the first charter school so exceeded the places available that admission was determined by a lottery, and there is a long waiting list—belying the stereotypical view of poor parents as indifferent about their children's education and unable to assess its quality or lack of it (Tough 2004).

The HCZ does not offer solutions to all the problems besetting the children's families, and what is *not* included in the social safety net is revealing of Canada's philosophy of educational reform as well as the hard choices he has had to make. One such problem is the poverty endemic to the neighborhood. To a hypothetical under- or unemployed parent whose child is doing poorly in school and has no place to go after school, Canada replies that HCZ can provide services that directly affect the child's school performance but cannot "solve the problem of you being unemployed. That's not going to go away." Nor does the HCZ project attempt to reduce the high incidence of single mothers. Like the researchers conducting the Fragile Families project discussed earlier in this chapter, Canada acknowledges that of course it would be better if the kids' parents were married but doubts whether the HCZ programs can do much to induce impoverished parents to marry and, moreover, that "if we tried to do that, we'd spend all our time just doing that" (Tough 2004, 48).

Abbott Districts   Another large-scale effort to raise the chances of academic success for disadvantaged children is being implemented in the neighboring state of New Jersey. In 1998 and after years of litigation, New Jersey's Supreme Court mandated that all three- and four-year-old

children in the state's thirty districts with the highest rates of poverty—
to become known as Abbott districts, after the family in whose name suit
was brought against the state for gross inequalities in its educational
system—receive a high-quality preschool education that would prepare
them "to enter kindergarten with skills and abilities comparable to those
of their wealthier suburban peers." School districts were assigned primary responsibility for ensuring that all programs met quality standards
related to teacher certification, class size, curriculum, facilities, meal
service, and family support services (Barnett et al. 2003).

Following further court action to counter efforts by state officials to delay funding and implementing the program, Abbott classes began operating on a full-day schedule in the fall of 2001. The number of children enrolled has risen rapidly, from 19,000 in the first year to over 43,000 in
2004–2005. In addition, the state now funds half-day programs for four-
year-olds in the approximately one hundred districts with the next-to-
highest levels of poverty. At present, the Abbott program is one of only
three state programs in the United States that meet nine out of ten research-based indicators of quality and has been rated among the best in the
nation in terms of the number of children it serves and the resources committed to it by the state as well as its level of quality (Barnett et al. 2003;
Frede et al. 2004). Even more heartening is the evidence of significant improvements in children's learning outcomes. Data collected by the Early
Learning Improvement Consortium (ELIC), a partnership between the
New Jersey Department of Education, academic experts at several state
colleges and universities, and other professionals, headed by Ellen Frede,
provide strong and consistent evidence that even as the number of children enrolled has increased, classroom quality and teaching practices have
improved (on a number of well-validated measuring instruments), and
more children are entering school prepared to succeed. Improvements in
children's language skills were statistically significant, and math skills have
begun to show comparable gains. The authors of the most recent ELIC
report note with some satisfaction that the Latin axiom, "A rising tide raises
all boats," may be applicable to the education of young children as well,
that "when quality increases in preschool classrooms, children learn more,
and this enhances the progress of all children" (Frede et al. 2004, 1).

Universal versus Targeted Programs: Which Are More Effective?
Both the Harlem Children's Zone and the Abbott District programs in-

volve large sums of money, and comprehensive evaluation of their cost-effectiveness is not yet possible. Canada estimates that the services provided by HCZ will cost about $1,400 a year per student, on top of current public funding, but admits that it's too soon to say "what the real price tag is for poor children to succeed" (Tough 2004, 49). In the meantime, HCZ depends heavily on Canada's success in obtaining financial support from foundations, private donors, and various government sources.

The National Institute of Early Education Research (NIEER) estimates that high-quality preschools for all American three- and four-year-olds would require roughly $30 billion in additional public funding, in particular to pay qualified teachers salaries commensurate with their skills and the value of their work (Barnett, Brown, and Shore 2004). Steven Barnett, NIEER's director and a leading authority on the long-term outcomes and cost-effectiveness of early education programs, points out that this is only 1 percent of total U.S. government spending (and, we might add, less than one month's expenditures for U.S. military operations in Iraq), and his longitudinal research on a number of model child care and early education programs has repeatedly shown that programs that boost the academic achievement and social skills of disadvantaged kids result in fewer placements in special education classes, higher high school graduation rates, and lower crime and delinquency rates. The bottom line: considerable savings for taxpayers (Barnett and Hustedt 2003).

Although he has also been one of the moving forces behind the Abbott Districts project, Barnett is quick to point out that there may be more cost-effective ways to change the odds for disadvantaged kids. His own research at NIEER indicates that *targeted* programs, that is, programs restricted to those children who are "at greatest risk of poor achievement, based on economic disadvantage, disabilities or other special needs"—which includes Head Start as well as the HCZ and the Abbott District programs—are generally less successful than *universal* programs that are free or affordable and available to all children of a given age. Targeted programs may seem more economical because they have lower start-up costs, but this initial advantage is offset by the "hidden costs" of establishing and monitoring eligibility for large numbers of children, expenditures not incurred by universal programs. Counter to what one might predict, universal programs are likely to reach and benefit more disadvantaged children than targeted programs, mainly because the latter are seldom fully funded. For example, after three decades and generally positive re-views, Head Start programs are still available to only a fraction of the children who are eligible and rarely deliver all the services as designed. Universal programs also reach children from middle-income families who do not qualify for targeted programs but who tend to lag behind wealthier children in social and cognitive skills. And because everyone's kids have access to universal programs, they "are likely to receive greater public support so that they are both of higher quality and reach more children than targeted programs" (Barnett 2004; Barnett et al. 2004). The highly regarded *ecoles maternelles* attended by virtually all French children, discussed earlier in this chapter, are a strong case in point.

In sum, the Abbot preschools provide evidence that *targeted* programs can prepare children living in poor communities to succeed in school *if* these programs are of uniformly high quality. The French preschools for children of the same age provide evidence that high-quality *universal* programs may do this and more while receiving more generous and willing support from the taxpayers.

Alternative Forms of Schooling

As we saw in a previous section, the overall improvement in the health and welfare of Cuban children in the late twentieth century, unparalleled among developing nations, was accomplished through an extensive system of universal entitlements. Extension of educational opportunities in Cuba during this period was equally impressive, achieving virtually 100 percent enrollment at the primary level and about 80 percent at the secondary level and a 96 percent adult literacy rate. (Later in this chapter, we'll describe the ingenious method used to achieve almost universal adult literacy within a few years.) At the 2004 World Congress of Comparative Education Conference, held in Havana, Cuban officials and scholars insisted, however, that providing free education for all is not enough. The next phase of educational reform calls for greater attention to the quality of classroom life and the happiness of children—priorities very similar to the approach to strengthening families based on the *emergent perspective*. In order for students to develop fully, according to the minister of education, educators must learn how to create classroom environments in which teachers "can concentrate on getting to know each pupil as an individual, meet their family, and discover what their worries, dream, and prospects are" (Guitierrez 2004, 7). As Cuban scholar Franklin Martinez put it, a child "cannot be intelligent if he is unhappy, so first supply the needs of the child and then educate him" (personal communication).

In almost every era, a few exemplary schools capture the attention of parents and professionals alike, generate extensive scholarly debate, and are widely imitated. In the early twentieth century, the pedagogical principles encapsulated in John Dewey's laboratory schools at the University of Chicago and Marie Montessori's preschools designed for Roman slum children were exported to many parts of the globe and remain influential today. Since the later twentieth century, Vivian Paley's nursery and kindergarten classes (discussed in chapter 6), also at the University of Chicago, and the community preschools of the prosperous northern Italian town of Reggio Emilia have had similarly broad appeal.

Though differing in many details, these and other exemplary schools are distinguished by their adherence to *Corsaro's Rule* (see chapter 3). Indeed, the dictum of Loris Malaguzzi, the Reggio Emilia system's founder, that "things about children and for children are only learned from children" is a statement of the rule in slightly different words, and its principle is manifested in the organization and curriculum of the town's schools. Classroom activities are organized around students' interest rather than a preestablished, adult-designed curriculum. Their purpose is to cultivate the full range of children's intellectual, aesthetic, emotional, social, and moral faculties in "a beautiful, healthy, love-filled setting." Long-term group projects that encourage kids to assimilate knowledge from multiple sources and develop multiple skills are favored over repetitive drill on a limited set of basic skills (Edwards, Gandini, and Forman 1993). The basic elements of life in a Reggio Emilia school correspond closely to those of Paley's kindergarten, Dewey's lab school, or a Montessori preschool but bear little resemblance to the daily grind of mainstream classroom life described in chapter 7.

Appealing as they are in their original form, exemplary schools are difficult to replicate in large numbers (only Montessori has been successful in this regard), and few kids have the opportunity to attend them. In recent years, dissatisfaction with public education and the alternatives available has led a growing number of parents to become their children's teachers. Home schooling is, of course, not a new idea. Before the development of publicly funded compulsory education systems during the past century, most education was conducted in the home. The current home-schooling movement in North America was initially dominated by conservative Christians but has been joined by individuals and organizations that hold diverse political and religious beliefs but share a commitment to breaking the state's monopoly on education and protecting their children from overbureaucratized school systems that embody the ills of modern societies (Zinnecker 2001).

As a result of intense political activity, a coalition of organizations in the United States have won the legal right to homeschool, though standards vary from one state to another. In the mid-1990s, an estimated 350,000 children were being taught at home; by 2003, the number had risen to 850,000. This option is, however, limited to those who can afford the time and have the qualifications to essentially operate a one-room school. The home-schooled child requires a tremendous amount of time and attention from at least one grown-up—and that person usually is mom. Besides being impractical for most families, the home-schooling model is at variance with feminist concerns about freeing women from traditional motherhood. It is not surprising that in the United States, the vast majority of home-schooled children come from White, middle class, two-parent/one-earner families with three or more children (*New York Times*, November 10, 2003; Stevens 2001).

Computer technology offers students another way to escape the formal school system via *virtual* schooling. A typical virtual school has no physical plant but instead provides students with a computer, an online curriculum, and an online attendance and grading program. Communication with teachers is generally via e-mail, sometimes by phone, or occasionally in person. Virtual schools have been started by commercial companies and by not-for-profit companies; some are operated by state education officials, and a few are charter schools. For students who chafe under the restraints of conventional schooling, virtual education offers a respite from being treated as children by their teachers or being bullied or shunned by their peers (see the discussions of the daily grind and peer abuse in chapter 7). For parents, it offers a way to homeschool their children without having to do all the teaching themselves. From the school's perspective, it offers a convenient way to get rid of pregnant, disruptive, and other problem students. In 2002, there were about 50,000 American students enrolled in virtual courses, and this number is likely to increase with increasing discontent with conventional schools and increasing acceptance of distance learning (White 2003).

Like home schooling, virtual education is now a viable option only for the relatively privileged; wider dissemination depends on extending access to computer technology and proficiency to lower-income communities and societies. Whether it can be a satisfactory substitute for human teachers remains to be seen. As we saw in chapter 9 (see the section on the effects of resisting racism, ethnocentrism, sexism, and classism), for kids from impoverished and marginalized groups, having adult mentors who help them understand the societal forces that constrain them, show them how to resist and overcome the pernicious effects of negative stereotyping, and challenge them to develop their confidence and capacities to the full appears to be more important than whether their schooling takes place in the formal education system or in an alternative educational program.

STRATEGY 3. EXTENDING CHILDREN'S LEGAL RIGHTS

Until recently, few children in any society had rights of any sort. Basically, they were owned by their parents, and the law supported strong parental control—in some American colonies, disobedience of their parents by children was a capital offense (Stafford 1995). Paralleling the changes in perceptions of children and childhood we have traced in earlier chapters has been a gradual and often sporadic expansion of their legal rights.

Protection Rights versus Civil Rights

Debates over children's rights reflect an "inherent tension between a view of children on the one hand, as dependent on adult protection and incapable of taking responsibility for their own decision-making, and on the other, as people with basic civil rights including the right to participate full in decisions that affect their lives" (Lansdown 1994, 36). They also reflect disagreements over the appropriate balance of rights and obligations between children and nonchildren.

Protection rights recognize that children are legally entitled to be safe from harm and abuse. Many countries, including the United States, have passed laws prohibiting sexual abuse and exploitation of children. Separate juvenile justice systems, an early twentieth-century invention, are based on the premise that persons under age eighteen are not capable of making mature judgments and deserve consideration appropriate to their age. A protective perspective is also exemplified in the growing concern over fast foods and other products that are harmful to children's health and safety and the powerful role of television advertising in pitching these products to kids. In the early 1990s, Sweden outlawed food advertising aimed at children, and some Americans advocate similar legislation. Proposals to ban unhealthy snack foods and beverages from school cafeterias and vending machines also reflect a protective view of children's rights.

Civil rights, sometimes called participation, autonomy, or citizenship rights, essentially grant children the same choices and freedoms as other citizens. A series of federal court decisions have clarified and extended American students' freedom of expression in school, including the following:

- *Board of Education v. Barnette* (1943), in which the Supreme Court ruled that public school students may refuse to salute the flag if this violates their religious beliefs.
- *Tinker v. Des Moines School District* (1969), in which the Court ruled that expelling three students from their high school for wearing black armbands to protest the Vietnam War violated their First Amendment right to free expression of their views.
- *American Civil Liberties Union v. Klein Independent School District* (2003), in which the district agreed to allow a high school junior to form a Gay-Straight Alliance to promote tolerance of gays in her school. In the suit filed on her behalf, the American Civil Liberties Union charged that in repeatedly denying or delaying permission for the Gay-Straight Alliance, the school had violated federal law barring discrimination against clubs based on the content of their speech.

Some propose using the movement for women's civil rights as a model for extending children's rights. Women too were traditionally defined as weak, vulnerable, and in need of protection. Only when they won the rights to vote and own property, to privacy, to physical integrity, and to freedom from assault did traditional views of femininity begin to erode. Lansdown (1994) believes that "if we are to enhance children's status in society, it will be necessary to achieve a comparable change with that achieved for women" (35).

Many issues relating to children's legal status pit proponents of protection rights against proponents of civil rights. The following examples illustrate the difficulty of achieving a balance between the two.

Right to Information   An issue that seems to have been resolved in most industrialized countries but remains controversial in the United States is kids' access to information about sexuality and birth control. Since the 1990s, cross-cultural studies have consistently documented the ubiquity of teenage sex throughout western Europe and North America, with little difference between countries in the proportion of sexually active teenagers or the average age of first intercourse. Research also indicates that while the experience is traumatic for some girls, most have sex by choice and without suffering abuse or distress (Levine 2002; Selman and Glendinning 1996).

There are, however, marked differences between the United States and other industrialized nations in 1) access to information and birth control technology and 2) unwanted outcomes. Throughout western Europe, where access to reliable means of contraception is virtually universal, rates of unwanted pregnancy, abortion, and AIDS are a fraction of those in the United States. In most schools the sex education curriculum does not give disproportionate attention to abstinence but rather "begins with the assumption that young people will carry on a number of sexual relationships during their teen years and initiate sex play short of intercourse long before that (which they do) and that sexual expression is a healthy and happy part of growing up" (Levine 2002, xxxii).

Though the majority of European and American teenagers are sexually active, the latter are much more likely to get pregnant and to have abortions. According to the Alan Guttmacher Institute, funding for and access to family-planning clinics has been reduced in the past two decades, legislation has been passed or proposed in many jurisdictions requiring parental permission or notification before a girl younger than eighteen can obtain an abortion or any kind of birth control services, and public school sex education programs that receive federal funding are required to teach abstinence as the sole option until marriage (birth control and condoms may be mentioned only in terms of their failure rates in preventing pregnancy or disease). Two empirical studies suggest that the strategy of withholding information may backfire. A study of 950 sexually active girls surveyed at several Planned Parenthood clinics in Wisconsin found that a majority claimed they would stop going to the clinic to obtain contraceptives or to be tested for pregnancy and sexually transmitted diseases if their parents had to be notified, though only 1 percent of the girls who said they would stop using clinic services also said that they would discontinue or limit sexual intercourse (Reddy, Fleming, and Swain 2002). A study carried out in Washington, D.C., documented a growing trend for teenagers to avoid pregnancy by engaging in oral sex rather than intercourse. What most do not realize is that "outer-course" will not protect them from sexually transmitted infection and disease (Stepp 1999).

Though still higher than European rates, the U.S. teenage birthrate declined 30 percent during the 1990s, reaching a record low in 2000, along with a comparable decline in abortions. Analysis of national survey data by researchers at Child Trends (Terry and Manlove 2001) indicates that declines occurred in all age and racial/ethnic groups and in all parts of the country. The analysis also indicates that the declines can be credited both to increased use of contraception and to increased abstinence among teens, though the relative contribution of each remains a matter of debate. An assessment of the effects of social policies on teenage pregnancy in the United States and several European countries concludes that fluctuations in teenage pregnancy and abortion rates are also affected by socioeconomic and socioemotional factors. High rates of teen pregnancy and disease are associated not only with lack of access to birth control but also with poverty, lack of educational and employment opportunities, low self-esteem, and low expectations for the future. Young people who have high hopes for their own futures are more likely to protect themselves from disease and unplanned pregnancy (Selman and Glendinning 1996).

Right to Be Consulted and to Exercise Choice   The authors of a recent review of laws pertaining to parental rights observe that changing family demographics in the United States have created new contexts for those assuming responsibility for childrearing. Growing numbers of adoptive, stepparent, grandparent-led, heterosexual cohabiting, gay and lesbian-headed families, and families formed through new reproductive technologies call into question assumptions regarding who has the right and responsibility to parent children. (Skinner and Kohler 2002, 293)

Yet family law still 1) "gives biological parents fundamental rights as an entitlement of procreation" and 2) "establishes parenthood as an exclusive status [recognizing] only one set of parents for a child at any one time" (293). Nontraditional parents still face many legal obstacles to adopting children or gaining custody or visitation rights.

Until recently, most legal conflicts between the family and the state have been over the extent of *parental* rights, most frequently in connection with their children's education (e.g., whether they can opt their children out of compulsory sex education classes or homeschool them with or without government supervision) or medical treatment (e.g., whether they can prohibit their children from being vaccinated or from obtaining contraceptives). Since the 1990s, a number of cases, most involving disputes over adoption or custody, have challenged traditional parent–child relationships by allowing children to be represented by their own lawyer and to have their preferences regarding living arrangements and visiting rights taken into account. In 2002, a judge gave a thirteen-year-old boy the right to decide whether to live with his biological father or with his deceased mother's male companion, both of whom sought custody (*New York Times*, August 21, 2002). Those who favor protection rights fear that making such emotionally charged decisions puts too much pressure on children before they are capable of understanding what's in their best interests. They also warn that allowing children to "divorce" their biological parents undermines the social institution of the family. Those who favor civil rights argue that in some situations a dysfunctional family just can't be fixed and that children should not be held hostage to unresolved adult problems. Skinner and Kohler (2002) conclude that at present "the legal system simultaneously reflects and reinforces society's ambivalence about family structure" (298).

The tension between protection rights and participation rights is especially evident in decisions about the appropriate treatment of children with serious illnesses or disabilities. Studies of children with cancer indicate a growing consensus that child patients and their families should be informed about the disease and its treatment, though less agreement about how the final decision about a child's treatment should be made (Alderson 1994). In a study of children facing orthopedic surgery, interviews were conducted in several London and Liverpool hospitals with 120 kids between the ages of eight and fifteen, and their views were compared with their parents' and the opinions of seventy medical professionals. Some of the children wanted to participate in the decision making, while others did not. A few debated the pros and cons of a treatment with their parents, though it was rare for a child to take a stand in opposition to adults' advice. One who did, a twelve-year-old girl who opposed an experimental growth hormone treatment, against her mother's wishes and her physician's recommendation, did so on the grounds that the prognosis was uncertain and that "I'd rather stay like me. I don't want false bones and all that stuff." Four years later, she still defended her action, saying,

> I felt I was responsible enough to make my own decisions and also my own mistakes if necessary. Children with any type of health problem to overcome grow up very quickly and more credit should be given to them. Society should accept people of all types, and respect everyone's right to make their own decisions once they have all the facts, be they adults or children. If parents and professionals listen to children they will know when they are ready to make decisions for themselves, whether they are 7 or 17. (Alderson 1994, 55–56)

Myra Bluebond-Langner, a pioneer of research on children with life-shortening or terminal illness, believes that certain values need to be respected in deciding on the child's treatment:

> One is that it should be conducted without deceit. Second, that participants should be free from coercion. Finally, children, like any other patients, have a right to know about the procedures that they undergo. The challenge in creating a role for children in decision making is to balance their values with the social fabric of family life and the rights which are accorded to parents in light of their responsibilities for their children. (Bluebond-Langner, DeCicco, and Belasco, in press)

The authors conclude with a scenario of how their model might be implemented in one hypothetical case, though they acknowledge that such an approach would require physicians to acquire a combination of skills analogous to "shuttle diplomacy and negotiation."

Rights of Children in Criminal Cases

Like the legal system with regard to parental rights, the criminal justice system reflects and reinforces deep differences of opinion regarding the treatment of children accused of criminal acts. The protective view, represented by the separate juvenile justice systems created about a century ago, is now under attack from those who believe that children are entitled to the same civil rights as adults and from others who counter that if children are to have the same rights as adults, they should be held similarly responsible for their actions, or, as the saying goes, "If you're old enough to do the crime, you're old enough to do the time."

In 2001, an American boy who killed a playmate when he was twelve was tried as an adult, convicted of first-degree murder and, at age thirteen, sentenced to life in prison with no parole. Though the sentence has since been overturned, it is worth noting that had he been allowed to plead guilty to the same crime as a juvenile, he would have been sentenced to three years in juvenile detention, a year of house arrest, and ten years on probation. In the same year, the states of Vermont and Wisconsin lowered the age at which children may be tried as adults in criminal cases to ten. The 2003–2004 trials of the two persons charged in the Washington, D.C., area "sniper" case have highlighted unresolved differences of opinion among Americans about the appropriate boundary between childhood and adulthood, in particular, the age at which individuals can be deemed mature enough to control their impulses and judge the consequences of their actions. Those with a protectionist perspective argued that the younger defendant, who was seventeen at the time the crimes were committed, should be treated differently from the second defendant, age forty-one, not only because of his materially and emotionally impoverished early life but also because his youth made him susceptible to domination by a psychopathic adult. The prosecutors, citing the *Gault* decision of 1967 (which extended to juvenile crime suspects the same right to a lawyer granted to adult defendants) to buttress their claims, argued that the two defendants should be treated equally— though they also took pains to have both tried in a state that permitted the death penalty for juveniles as well as for adults. In separate trials, both defendants were found guilty, but only the older defendant has received the death penalty while the younger was sentenced to life imprisonment, though only after prolonged plea bargaining and pending further appeals (*New York Times*, January 5, 2003; August 15, 2003; January 1, 2004; September 25, 2004).

The United States has the distinction of having sentenced more children to death or to life imprisonment between 1990 and 2005 than any other nation, and it may be the only nation to have executed juveniles since 2001.[1] The majority of the American kids put to death by the criminal justice system have been African American or Latino males; most suffered from chronic drug or alcohol abuse or brain damage due to physical abuse; few were represented by an experienced attorney. In 1946, because of an equipment malfunction, a seventeen-year-old convicted of murder and sentenced to die in the electric chair experienced a few seconds of electrocution but lived to tell about it. He said that he felt intense pain and that "my mouth tasted like cold peanut butter. I felt a burning in my head and left leg, and I jumped against the straps. I saw blue and pink and green speckles." A year later, after the Supreme Court was not persuaded by the argument that it was "cruel and unusual" to execute the boy twice, the second attempt was "successful" (Costanzo 1997, 44).

As we were completing this chapter, an important turning point in the global evolution of children's rights was reached when the U.S. Supreme Court ruled, on March 1, 2005, that capital punishment for crimes committed before the age of eighteen was inconsistent with evolving world standards as well as with the U.S. Constitution. With this decision, seventy-two Americans in twelve states were moved off death row, and, in the words of Justice Anthony Kennedy, the United States joined "a world that has turned its face against the juvenile death penalty" (*New York Times*, March 2, 2005). Perhaps it is more accurate to say that it joined the rest of the world part way. The close (5–4) decision by the Supreme Court reflected the continuing dissension among Americans about children's rights. While most other countries have eliminated the death penalty for *all* citizens, the United States has not ruled capital punishment for adults unconstitutional. (Indeed public support for the latter appears to be gaining strength in many parts of the country.) Elimination of the death penalty for child criminals thus reflected the protectionist perspective, with its emphasis on distinctions between adults and children, rather than an extension of universal civil rights to children.

Child Prostitutes: Criminals or Victims? While most kids accused of capital crimes are boys, a disproportionate number of those arrested for prostitution are girls. Though child prostitution is extremely difficult to track and compute precisely, police, social workers, and criminologists agree that it's a worldwide phenomenon, that it is increasing, and that many children are forcibly recruited (see the section on involuntary labor in chapter 10). In 2000, the U.S. Congress enacted legislation ruling that child prostitutes arrested by federal official be treated as "victims of sexual attack" rather than as criminals and charging the government with responsibility for ensuring that suspects receive medical care, mental health therapy, and, if necessary, foster home or group home placements. However, the scarcity of treatment facilities and personnel trained to work with child sex offenders renders enforcement of the law largely hypothetical. And several recent criminal cases illustrate the sharp divide between those who favor the protective approach underlying the 2000 legislation and those who take the "old-enough-to-do-the crime, old-enough-to-do-the-time" position.

In 2002, one New York City police precinct reported that over a third of all persons arrested for prostitution that year were children between the ages of eleven and seventeen. The arrest of a twelve-year-old girl who offered to perform oral sex on an undercover officer precipitated a year of wrangling between family court judges, prosecutors, lawyers, therapists, child welfare authorities, and prison officials. Prosecutors argued that the girl was a hardened criminal who showed no remorse for her behavior and would return to her life on the streets unless she were incarcerated. Lawyers for the defense argued that the girl was too young to have consented to sex and should be set free. In between were some who maintained that she was a victim of sexual exploitation and should be given medical treatment and mental health therapy and others who agreed that she was too immature to be held responsible for her behavior but felt that she should be incarcerated for her own protection.

Like many other municipalities, New York City has no residential programs specializing in the treatment of sex offenders under age sixteen and few foster homes willing to accept them. After several private institutions denied her admission, the judge ordered the girl placed in a "secure" juvenile facility that offered treatment for drug abuse but not for sexual abuse or prostitution; he was finally persuaded to allow her to be placed in a group home for emotionally disturbed youngsters with twice-monthly visits from a specialized counselor—despite the poor record of many of these homes in preventing children in their care from running away, communicating with pimps, or recruiting other kids into prostitution (*New York Times*, September 15, 2004).

Can Juvenile Crime Be Prevented or Treated? In October 2004, a thirteen-member panel convened by the National Institutes of Health to review the available scientific evidence on youth violence and ways to prevent it released a report on their findings. There was general agreement among the panel members that "scare tactics" or "get-tough" programs (including boot camps for juvenile offenders) rarely have the intended effects and that many "exacerbate problems by grouping young people with delinquent tendencies, where the more sophisticated instruct the more naïve." Nor have programs that consist mainly of lectures delivered by adults (e.g., the Drug Abuse Resistance Education [DARE] program) resulted in reductions of the targeted problems. Finally, the panel report states that the growing practice of transferring juveniles to the adult judicial system is for the most part "counterproductive, resulting in greater violence among incarcerated youth."

On the positive side, the panel cited two programs that have been tested using rigorous research methods and found to be effective in reducing recidivism for at least four years after the treatment ended:

1. Functional Family Therapy, a program where youth and their families attend twelve one-hour sessions over three months
2. Multisystem Therapy, a community-based clinical treatment program that targets violent chronic offenders at risk of being removed from their families and provides sixty hours of counseling over four months with therapists available at all hours

Among the characteristics that these and other effective programs have in common, according to the report, are "a focus on developing social competency skills, a long-term approach, and family involvement" (U.S. Department of Health and Human Services 2004). This approach is diametrically opposed to current trends toward translating juvenile offenders into adult criminals and doling out harsh punishments. The preceding discussion suggests, however, that at least in the United States, there are strong ideological and financial barriers to the widespread implementation of programs that prevent and treat rather than punish.

STRATEGY 4: ENHANCING CHILDREN'S PARTICIPATION IN SOCIETY

Kids are undoubtedly weary of being told by adults that they are the "citizens of tomorrow," and the extensive participation of children in civil rights movements in South Africa and the United States and in the Palestinian intifada (see chapter 10) reminds us that many are already political actors, not just future citizens in the making. From his survey of projects ranging from trade unions organized by Philippine and Brazilian street children to environmental programs designed by North American and western European schoolchildren, Roger Hart, director of the Children's Environments Research Group at the City University of New York, concluded that kids are quite capable of designing and managing complex projects if they feel some sense of ownership in them (Hart 1992, 1997). Hart distinguishes between 1) *simulated* participation and 2) *real* participation. The former utilizes—some would say exploits—kids as window dressing to embellish actions initiated by adults—for example, wheeling babies or having young children carry banners (provided by adults) in political demonstrations or inserting unrelated musical performances by cute kids into adult conferences during intervals between the sessions where the real business is conducted. Simulated participation keeps children in their adult-ordained place as "the most photographed and the least listened to members of society" (Hart 1992, 12). Real participation requires that children be real players, at the least informed and consulted about project objectives and activities, at best sharing in its design and management. The role of child participants differs in projects initiated by adults and those initiated by children.

Projects Initiated by Adults

Creative teachers frequently take advantage of community, national, or world events to give their students experience in defining and addressing social problems. For example, when a government official who opposed construction of a playground near a Michigan elementary school with a predominantly low-income African American student body referred to the neighborhood children as "riffraff," a fourth-grade teacher enlisted her students to take action. After brainstorming about what services were needed in their neighborhood, the kids listed activities they could perform and what resources would be needed. With some additional advice from members of an adult neighborhood association and a grant from the Southern Poverty Law Center's Teaching Tolerance program, they implemented a series of community service projects that included making toys for children in homeless shelters, designing bookmarks for the public library's celebration of Reading Month, clearing debris around the school and throughout the neighborhood for Earth Day, and making decorations and writing poems for the residents of a local nursing home. The teacher defined her objective as engaging her students in activities that could "strengthen their character, build self-esteem and promote pride in their neighborhood." The kids defined their community service as proving to hostile adults that they were not "riffraff" (Southern Poverty Law Center 2002, 5).

Fidel Castro's campaign to end illiteracy in Cuba involved a nationwide mobilization of kids during the 1960s. Almost all of the approximately 100,000 teachers were schoolchildren. Forty-seven percent were fifteen to nineteen years of age, 40 percent were between ten and fourteen, and the youngest were eight years old. Among large-scale literacy programs of the 1960s that were evaluated by outside reviewers, including UNESCO-funded projects in eleven other developing countries, only the Cuban campaign came close to reaching its goal of universal literacy (Kozol 1978). Of course, not all large-scale mobilizations of children by adult political leaders have had such benign outcomes. Mao's enlistment of kids to jump-start the Chinese Cultural Revolution and Hitler's Youth Movement encouraged children to spy on their parents, teachers, and adult neighbors and ended in uncontrolled chaos and violence.

Projects Initiated by Kids

Examples of social action initiated by American children can be found in a variety of sources. Among the historical documents collected by Hoose (2001) are accounts of Jessica Govea, the daughter of Mexican American

migrant workers, who began picking cotton and grapes at age four and became a full-time union organizer in her teens, and Kory Johnson, who
founded Children for a Safe Environment at age nine after her sister died
of heart problems, probably caused by contaminated water, and who won
the $100,000 Goldman Environmental Prize ten years later. Among the
"women of the year" featured in *Ms. Magazine* (Bridges et al.2003/2004)
was fourteen-year-old Drew Dakessian, who started a grassroots movement, "GirlCaught," to identify advertisements that portray girls in a demeaning fashion and to persuade them to boycott the products advertised.
Lands' End, the catalog clothing marketer, has been making "Born He-
roes" awards annually since 1999 to U.S. children aged six to twelve who
are "doing great things for the world." (Winners receive a $5,000 donation
to their cause.) In 2003, awards went to a boy (age eleven) who adopted
and found homes for 159 dogs scheduled for euthanasia at a local animal
shelter, to two sisters (ages ten and twelve) who developed a program to
educate kids about cranes and preserving the wetlands where they nest,
and to an eight-year-old advocate for victims of sickle cell anemia whose
activities included speaking at community centers and churches about the
disease and the shortage of blood for transfusions, passing out pamphlets
at malls and grocery stores, and distributing refrigerator magnets of her
own design that urge people to become blood donors.

Arguably the most ambitious and influential child-initiated project is
Free the Children, an international movement against exploitative child
labor founded by a Canadian boy who began to investigate the problem
after reading a newspaper account of the murder of a Pakistani teenager
who had been sold at age five to work in a rug factory. By the time he was
twelve, Craig Kielburger had made presentations at government and labor conferences and raised enough money to make a solo trip to Asia to
observe child labor conditions firsthand. Yet when he approached human
rights organizations for information about child labor, Kielburger found
few people who seemed knowledgeable or concerned about child labor—
and no one even close to him in age. Asked by one interviewer why he
founded Free the Children, Kielburger replied, "I guess it was because I
was tired of being able to speak only to organizations run by adults" (Kielburger 1998, 9). This unsettling experience explains the Free the Children rule that all speakers representing the organization be children, *not*
adults speaking *for* children. Because of the founder's conviction that "the

only way adults and students would take us seriously was if we knew what we were talking about," Free the Children speakers solicit criticism and suggestions from other kids and do research on questions they have not been able to answer satisfactorily. The questions most often raised by children in the audience are, won't your activities make things worse, and what distinguishes Free the Children from other White imperialists?

Free the Children now has chapters in some twenty countries, runs leadership courses for children, raises money to build schools in developing nations, and helps child volunteers plan local projects. For example, students from ten schools in the Albany, New York, area mounted a successful campaign to persuade their school boards not to buy sports apparel made in sweatshops. Though many projects are local, Free the Children's perspective is explicitly international: "Our neighbors were no longer simply the young people down our street in Thornhill. They were the youth in India, in Africa, in Brazil. . . . I thought of us—all of us—as the children of the world" (Kielburger 1998, 25). Free the Children does not oppose children working, only their employment in work that is abusive and exploitative and that prevents them from getting an education.

While Free the Children has worked mainly on behalf of children in poorer nations, Kielburger (1998) believes that it has also filled a gap in the lives of kids in affluent industrialized countries, many of whom long for something more challenging and meaningful in their lives than hanging out in shopping malls and playing video games. "At an age when we were constantly being told by adults what to do, FTC was something we took on voluntarily. It had our names on it. And it was our reputations that were at stake" (32). Kielburger admits that working for Free the Children is not considered cool by the cliques that dominate the peer culture and that the movement's participants are labeled by many of their peers as do-gooders and wimps. But he maintains that the most serious problem now is the same one he has faced since he began the project: the reluctance of most adults to take him—or kids in general—seriously.

STRATEGY 5: CREATING BETTER COMMUNITIES

Some reformers, believing that their societies are beyond repair, look to alternative communities to offer children a better childhood. Though utopian plans are seldom realized in real-life communities and few people choose to live in the ones that exist, they challenge our assumptions about children and childhood. The following examples describe efforts to create a world fit for children in very different environments.

Israeli Kibbutzim

In terms of longevity, size of membership, and influence, the Israeli kibbutz is undoubtedly the world's most successful commune movement. The first permanent community was established in 1910; at the movement's peak, in the mid-twentieth century, there were over 300 kibbutzim, varying in size from less than a hundred members to over a thousand and comprising 7 percent of the Jewish population; at the century's end, there were 267 kibbutzim with a total membership of 120,000 members (Gavron 2000).

A basic tenet of kibbutz ideology is the liberation of women and children. For this purpose, "the parent-child link was deliberately downgraded. The children were not regarded as the exclusive property of their biological parents; they belonged to the whole community," which served as a kind of extended family. Thus, children lived apart from their parents with members of their age cohort—a separation that, it was believed, would allow both children and parents to lead more fulfilling and productive lives. From a few days after birth until they graduate from high school, children are almost entirely in the company of their peers. They sleep in the same room and spend most of their waking hours with the other kids in their age-group, though daily visits with their parents allow the latter to "give their children love, uninhibited by the need to enforce discipline, which was the task of the child care workers and nurses and later also of the teachers" (Gavron 2000; Rabin 1965).

School-age children, now formally identified as a "children's society," move into a building that is a combination of dormitory and elementary school. In order to provide continuity between childhood and adulthood, schoolchildren also spend time on a children's farm where they become acquainted with agricultural life and learn work habits (Rabin 1965). By the time the peer group enters high school, members divide their time about equally between study and productive work in the community. In principle, there are no sex distinctions or segregation in activities or functions. Boys and girls live in the same quarters from infancy through adolescence, sharing the same bathing facilities and sleeping space, though concomitant with this arrangement are "strong taboos with respect to sex play and premarital intercourse" (Rabin 1965, 41).

From the beginning, the separation of children from their parents' living quarters provoked bitter controversy and a flood of research. Rabin (1965) believes that such a system has both positive and negative aspects—on the one hand, promotion of group cohesiveness and solidarity and, on the other, heavy group pressures and discouragement of individual thinking and opinion formation. Empirical research, whether by Israelis or non-Israelis, produced no substantial evidence that children are harmed by living apart from their biological parents when they are embedded in a strong, supportive community. Indeed, on most measures of physical and emotional health, the outcomes tended to be somewhat better for children raised in kibbutzim than for other children, in Israel or elsewhere. Many kibbutzim have also provided temporary homes for disadvantaged and delinquent kids (including some from American urban ghettos), with generally positive results.

Still, community after community closed down its children's dormitories, the last in 1998, a move that was promoted primarily by parents or younger adults who expected to become parents but was strongly opposed by most of the original settlers and by most children (though the latter had no say in the matter because they were not yet full kibbutz members). Interviews with adults revealed an interesting inconsistency in the views of many: "Members who grew up with communal sleeping were adamant that the experience was overwhelmingly positive. While almost unanimously insisting that they wanted their own children at home, they maintained that they themselves had a great childhood and that, in living at home, their children were missing out on something very wonderful that they had experienced" (Gavron 2000, 170). In other words, given a choice between living with their peers and living with their parents, most kibbutz kids opted for the former, but when they became parents, they were willing to withhold from their own children the peer group experience they had valued so highly for themselves!

Communities Created by Afghan Women

Many utopian communities, including the kibbutz, have been designed to enable members to survive under difficult physical or political conditions. It is hard to think of a physical and political environment more dangerous and chaotic than twenty-first-century Afghanistan. On any indicators of children's health and well-being—their chances of surviving birth and early childhood; of having adequate food, water, and shelter; and of attending school or achieving literacy—Afghanistan ranks at or very near the bottom. Half a century of almost constant warfare, both civil conflicts and invasions by foreign military forces, has reduced much of the country to rubble and left the inhabitants with scant resources for rebuilding their society. The mistreatment of ethnic minorities and females of all ages has been particularly brutal.

Throughout this period, members of the Revolutionary Association of the Women of Afghanistan (RAWA), an underground organization founded in 1977 and led by Afghan women, have supplied food, clothing, and medical care in secret; run underground schools and orphanages; carried out political protests; and covertly documented atrocities committed by the Russian occupying forces, militia headed by local warlords, and fundamentalist religious groups. The most extensive study of RAWA to date was carried out by Anne Brodsky (2003), a professor in the Department of Psychology and Women's Studies Program at the University of Maryland. In the RAWA hostels and boarding schools, Brodsky observed "the diverse students, representing various ethnicities, religions, regions, and educational and class backgrounds are still being taught national pride, the importance of helping one another, concern for those Afghans who are less fortunate than they, and the importance of women's equality" (126–27). In exchange for free room, board, and tuition, all students are expected to donate service to RAWA during the summer break; in keeping with an educational model that defines every member of the community as capable of both giving and receiving, older students are tapped to teach younger ones. Effort is made to offer each student at least some instruction in her native language. Despite extreme material poverty (few desks or books and no access to computers, crowded sleeping conditions, few toilets, and no running water), Brodsky was impressed by the extent to which the staff strove to provide children with "safety, food, shelter, clothing, love, friendship, community, and a top-notch education" (184).

In RAWA camps for refugees, women have attempted to create "enclaves that represent the types of community and social structures that they ultimately want to see in Afghanistan as a whole" (Brodsky 2003, 274) while in the short run offering education, food, medical assistance, a chance to earn a living, and other concrete assistance. The Woloswali camp, now fifteen years old and home to 500 families from all parts of the country, is a small village complete with electricity and pumped water, farming and small-business enterprises, an education system, medical services, and a democratic government structure. Beginning with basic literacy classes and training in handicrafts, RAWA activists branched out to establish a school for girls, two orphanages, a medical clinic and ambulance service, social service outreach to new arrivals, and various cultural activities designed to promote community building and empowerment. RAWA is strongly committed to ending the Afghan "tradition" of male violence against females. Brodsky recorded members making repeated visits to households where men were reported to be abusing their wives, daughters, or other female relatives, engaging the offender in lengthy dialogue and making clear that "if he didn't change his behavior they would ask him to leave the camp, while they would keep his family here and take care of them" (129–30).

To residents of prosperous nations where democratically elected governments are taken for granted, the RAWA model, with its insistence on inclusiveness and its willingness to accept slow, methodical, and incremental change, may seem pitifully inadequate. But in a society that offers little freedom and few opportunities to anyone and virtually none to females, RAWA is the only native political movement devoted to empowering girls and women. In contrast to the portrayal of Afghan women in most foreign media accounts as helpless victims, RAWA members, by doing what most Afghans believe women can't or shouldn't do, are promoting resilience and resistance as well as inventing ways to meet "the emotional needs of a displaced people and a displaced gender" (Brodsky 2003, 219).

Alternative Communities in North America

Of the many experimental communities established in the United States, the more long-lasting ones have tended to adhere to traditional age and gender roles that are reminiscent of American life before the demise of the family farm. (Communes established during the 1960s and 1970s by young people seeking to escape the tyranny and dependency associated with the conventional extended or nuclear family often freed adults by ignoring children's basic needs for health, safety, and nurturance and seldom survived more than a few years [Zablocki 1978].) In contrast to the original kibbutz and RAWA models, which rejected traditional religious practices believed to be antithetical to individual development,[2] many American experimental communities were founded by groups that wished to *preserve* them.

Among the most successful and extensively studied are the Amish communities, most in rural areas of Pennsylvania, Ohio, and Indiana, with a total membership of about 150,000. Amish culture, values, and modes of child rearing and education have frequently put them at odds with their neighbors or with government authorities. In the past, children's failure to attend public schools or to continue their formal education after eighth grade led to conflicts with school authorities. Currently, the Amish are battling federal restrictions on child labor. It is customary for Amish children to begin learning a trade by about age eleven or twelve. Formerly this was farming for boys, but recent economic pressures and the decline in available farmland have led most Amish communities to shift to small businesses. (Girls continue to learn sewing and quilting, though many now work in retail shops.) In the Pennsylvania communities, many boys are apprenticed to community-owned sawmills and woodworking shops specializing in custom-made furniture, in violation of federal law barring children under eighteen from dangerous types of employment (Hostetler 1993; Kraybill and Olshan 1994).

From the federal government's perspective, Amish children should have the same health and safety protections as other American children, and it has begun fining Amish workshops that employ them. The Amish, who are seeking exemption from the federal restriction (with the proviso that workers under age eighteen be under adult supervision and remain a "sufficient distance" from the machinery), view early employment as essential for teaching their children Amish values and, not incidentally, keeping them from idleness and the temptations of the outside world. A member who installed kitchens in homes outside the community was disturbed by kids occupied mainly in watching television. In his view, "If we couldn't put our boys to work and they didn't do nothing until they were 18, they'd be absolutely worthless. We want them to be obedient and to learn a trade. If they don't, they'll be out and getting into mischief. Next thing you know, you'll have a bunch of them getting into dope and drinking and partying" (*New York Times*, October 18, 2003).

Since the late 1960s, the proliferation of new religious movements in Europe and North America has produced a new wave of alternative communities that now contain substantial numbers of children. Like the Amish, their founders hope to preserve children's innocence of the consumption-oriented secular world. Ethnographic studies of Hare Krishna, Evangelical Christian, and other new religious communities indicate that the kids often have other ideas. Like their counterparts in mainstream society, they have created distinctive subcultures, combining "contraband music, secret pacts, and shared values" that seem more congruent with the peer cultures discussed in chapters 6 and 7 than with the cultural values of their elders (Palmer and Hardman 1999, 4). The ultimate impact of children's culture on these communities is not yet clear, but Palmer and Hardman believe that the childhoods that are evolving there merit study, not only to extend our understanding of utopian social movements but also to provide fresh perspectives on child rearing and parent rearing in mainstream societies.

THE LAST WORD

In this book we have tried to convey the range of kids' experiences in their various social worlds and from their perspectives. Our analysis of children and childhoods has the inevitable limitations of work by adult researchers written primarily for other adults. It's not likely that many kids will read this book, though we'd be delighted if they did. Yet like the historian John Hope Franklin (1969), who envisioned a future in which the history of the United States in general and of African Americans in particular could be "written and taught by any person, white, black, or otherwise" (15), we can imagine a future in which a researcher's age would no longer preclude her understanding children's worlds from the standpoint of children. The difficulty seems to lie less in children's ability or willingness to speak for themselves than in adults' reluctance or inability to learn from children or even to take them seriously.

We hope that we have made a convincing case for taking children seriously and for involving them more actively in the research process. In keeping with our conception of the sociology of children and childhoods, we'll leave the last word to Craig Kielburger (1998), whose reflections on what he learned from working with fellow children in various parts of the world resonate with some of the major themes of this book:

> In my travels I have found two extremes. In many developing countries, children are often asked to work long hours at hazardous jobs with no opportunity to play or to go to school. They are not allowed to develop physically, intellectually, and emotionally as they should. They support entire families. They fight in wars. They are given too much responsibility at too young an age.
>
> On the other hand, in many industrialized countries everything is done for children. They are segregated most of their lives with members of their own age group and are given little opportunity to assume responsibility, to develop a social conscience, or to learn through interaction with adults. Through media they learn to be consumers, to gain their self-image through the electronic toys they own and the labels they wear. They, too, are exploited. They see violence and suffering on the news every day but are told that they are too young to do anything about it. They are conditioned to become passive bystanders. . . .
>
> We want to help free children from both extremes.
>
> Children are not simply empty vessels to be filled. They are people with ideas, talents, opinions, and dreams. (290–91)

NOTES

1. There is general agreement among human rights organizations gathering data on criminal justice systems throughout the world that at the end of the twentieth century, the juvenile death penalty was legal in the following nations: China, Congo, Iran, Nigeria, Pakistan, Saudi Arabia, and the United States. Some lists also include Yemen and/or Bangladesh. As we saw earlier in this

chapter, the United States and Somalia were the only member nations that had not yet ratified the United Nations Convention on the Rights of the Child, which includes a provision prohibiting capital punishment for those under age eighteen. Most researchers believe that by 2001, all except the United States had disavowed the actual practice of executing juveniles, though reports of recent public executions of teenagers in Iran that surfaced as we were reading the page proofs of this book indicate that rejection of the juvenile death penalty is not yet a worldwide norm. (Amnesty International 2004, www.amnesty.org/ library/themesdeath+penalty, October 20, 2004; Brumberg 2003; Human Rights Watch 2004).

2. The young pioneers who founded the first kibbutz communities defined themselves as ethnically Jewish but at the same time sought to free themselves from the religious beliefs and practices of their countries of origin that they considered oppressive, especially to women and youth. Communities with a predominantly religious membership were a later development. A central tenet of RAWA ideology is strict separation of religion from government and other societal institutions. While some RAWA members are practicing Muslims, all are opposed to forced marriages, forced seclusion of women in the home, male-against-female violence, and other abusive practices condoned or even promulgated by some religious leaders and groups.

REFERENCES

Adler, P. A., and Adler, P. 1998. *Peer Power: Preadolescent Culture and Identity*. New Brunswick, NJ: Rutgers University Press.

Alanen, L. 1992. *Modern Childhood? Exploring the Child Question in Sociology*. Jyvaskyla, Finland: University of Jyvaskyla.

———. 1994. Gender and generation: Feminism and the "child question." In J. Qvortrup, M. Bardy, G. Sgritta, and H. Wintersberger (Eds.), *Childhood Matters: Social Theory, Practice and Politics* (pp. 27–42). Aldershot, UK: Avebury.

Alderson, P. 1994. Researching children's rights to integrity. In B. Mayall (Ed.), *Children's Childhoods: Observed and Experienced* (pp. 45–62). London: Falmer Press.

———. 2000. Children as researchers: The effects of participation rights on research methodology. In P. Christensen and A. James (Eds.), *Research with Children: Perspectives and Practices* (pp. 241–57). London: Falmer Press.

Alwin, D. F. 1991. Changes in family roles and gender differences in family socialization values. *Sociological Studies of Childhood* 4: 201–24.

———. 2001. Parental values, beliefs, and behavior: A review and promulga for research into the new century. In S. L. Hofferth and T. J. Owens (Eds.), *Children at the Millennium: Where Have We Come From, Where Are We Going?* (pp. 97–139). Oxford, UK: Elsevier Science.

Ambert, A-M. 1986. Sociology of sociology: The place of children in North American sociology. *Sociological Studies of Child Development* 1: 11–31.

———. 1992. *The Effect of Children on Parents*. New York: Haworth Press.

———. 1995a. Introduction. *Sociological Studies of Children* 7: ix–xii.

———. 1995b. Toward a theory of peer abuse. *Sociological Studies of Children* 7: 177–205.

———. 1997. *Parents, Children and Adolescents Interactive Relationships and Development in Context*. New York: Haworth Press.

———. 2002. *Divorce: Facts, Causes, and Consequences*. Rev. ed. Ottawa: Vanier Institute of the Family.

———. 2003. *Same-Sex Couples and Same-Sex-Parent Families: Relationships, Parenting, and Issues of Marriage*. Ottawa: Vanier Institute of the Family.

Amato, P. 1993. Children's adjustment to divorce: Theories, hypotheses, and empirical support. *Journal of Marriage and the Family* 55: 23–38.

———. 2000. The consequences of divorce for adults and children. *Journal of Marriage and Family* 62: 1269–87.

———. 2001. Children of divorce in the 1990s: An update of the Amato and Keith (1991) meta-analysis. *Journal of Family Psychology* 15: 355–70.

Amato, P., and Fowler, F. 2002. Parenting practices, child adjustment, and family diversity. *Journal of Marriage and Family* 64: 703–16.

American Sociological Association, Sociology of Children Section. 1998. The Convention on the Rights of the Child. *Childnews*, spring, 7.

Anderson, E. A., Kohler, J. K., and Letiecq, B. L. 2002. Low-income fathers and "Responsible Fatherhood" programs: A qualitative investigation of participants' experiences. *Family Relations* 51: 148–55.

Andersson, E. E. 1992. Effects of day care on cognitive and socio-emotional competence in thirteen-year-old Swedish school children. *Child Development* 63: 20–36.

Aries, P. 1962. *Centuries of Childhood*. New York: Knopf.

Armstrong, S. 2002. *Veiled Threat: The Hidden Power of the Women of Afghanistan*. Toronto: Penguin/Viking.

Avellar, S., and Smock, P. J. 2003. Has the price of motherhood declined over time? A cross-cohort comparison of the motherhood wage penalty. *Journal of Marriage and Family* 65: 597–607.

Backman, R. 1991. Les enfants esclaves. *Nouvel Obervateur* 1381: 4–15.

Baker, D. P., and Jones, D. P. 1993. Creating gender equality: Cross-national gender stratification on math. *Sociology of Education* 66: 91–103.

Balagopalan, S. 2002. Constructing indigenous childhoods: Colonialism, vocational education and the working child. *Childhood* 9: 19–34.

Barnett, W. S. 2004. Does Head Start have lasting effects? The myth of fade-out. In E. Zigler and S. J. Styfco (Eds.), *The Head Start Debates* (pp. 221–50). Baltimore: Paul H. Brookes.

Barnett, W. S., Brown, K., and Shore, R. 2004. The universal vs. targeted debate: Should the United States have preschool for all? *NIEER Preschool Policy Matters* 6: 1–15.

Barnett, W. S., and Hustedt, J. T. 2003. Preschool: The most important grade. *Educational Leadership*, April, 54–57.

Barnett, W. S., Robin, K.B., Hustedt, J. T., and Schulman, K. L. 2003. *The State of Preschool: 2003 State Preschool Yearbook*. New Brunswick, NJ: National Institute for Early Education Research.

Bass, L. E. 2003. Child labor and household survival strategies in West Africa. *Sociological Studies of Children and Youth* 9: 127–48.

Baumgartner, M. P. 1992. War and peace in early childhood. *Virginia Review of Sociology* 1: 1–38.

Bearak, B. 2004. Poor man's burden. *New York Times Magazine*, June 27, 30–35, 50, 56, 59.

Becker, S., Dearden, C., and Aldridge, J. 2001. Children's labour of love? Young carers and care work. In P. Mizen, C. Pole, and A. Bolton (Eds.), *Hidden Hands: International Perspectives on Children's Work and Labour* (pp. 70–87). London and: Routledge/Falmer.

Bell, L. I. 2002/2003. Strategies that close the gap. *Educational Leadership* 60: 32–34.

Bem, S. L. 1993. *The Lenses of Gender*. New Haven, CT: Yale University Press.

Benard, C. 2002. *Veiled Courage: Inside the Afghan Women's Resistance*. New York: Broadway Books.

Bendheim-Thoman Center for Research on Child Wellbeing. 2002. Is marriage a viable objective for fragile families? *Fragile Families Research Brief* 9 (July): 1–3.

———. 2003a. Barriers to marriage among fragile families. *Fragile Families Research Brief* 16 (May): 1–3.

———. 2003b. Union formation and dissolution in fragile families. *Fragile Families Research Brief* 16 (January): 1–3.

Bernard van Leer Foundation. 1996. The rights of children 0–7 years. *Bernard van Leer Foundation Newsletter* 83: 1–5.

Berube, M. 2003. Testing handicaps. *New York Times Magazine*, September 21, 18–19.

Bluebond-Langner, M. 2000. Comments made at opening of the Rutgers Center for Children and Childhood Studies, Camden, NJ, September 15.

Bluebond-Langner, M., DeCicco, A., and Belasco, J. In press. Involving children with life shortening illnesses in the decision to participate in clinical research. In E. Kodish (Ed.), *Learning from Cases: Ethnics and Research with Children*. New York: Oxford University Press.

Blumer, H. 1978. Society as symbolic interaction. In A. Wells (Ed.), *Contemporary Sociological Theories* (pp. 91–98). Santa Monica, CA: Goodyear Publishing.

Bogenschneider, K. 2000. Has family policy come of age? A decade review of the state of U.S. family policy in the 1990s. *Journal of Marriage and Family* 62: 1136–59.

Boli-Bennett, J., and Meyer, J. W. 1978. The ideology of childhood and the state: Rules distinguishing children in national constitutions, 1870–1970. *American Sociological Review* 43: 797–812.

Boo, K. 2003. The marriage cure. *New Yorker*, August 18 and 25, 105–20.

Boocock, S. S. 1975. The social context of childhood. *Proceedings of the American Philosophical Society* 119: 419–29.

———. 1976. The role of the parent: Problems and prospects. In V. C. Vaughan and T. B. Brazelton (Eds.), *The Family—Can It Be Saved?* (pp. 257–66). Chicago: Year Book Medical Publishers.

———. 1980. *Sociology of Education: An Introduction.* Boston: Houghton Mifflin.

———. 1981. The life space of children. In S. Keller (Ed.), *Building for Women* (pp. 93–116). Lexington, MA: Lexington Books.

———. 1998. Long-term outcomes in other nations. In W. S. Barnett and S. S. Boocock (Eds.), *Early Care and Education for Children in Poverty: Promises, Programs, and Long-Term Results* (pp. 45–76). Albany: State University of New York Press.

———. 1999. Social prisms: An international comparison of childrearing manuals. *International Journal of Japanese Sociology* 8: 5–33.

———. 2001. Cultural defects or social constructions? Identifying the educational problems of Buraku children in the early years of schooling. Paper presented at the annual meeting of the Association for Asian Studies, Chicago, March 23.

Books, S. 1998. *Invisible Children in the Society and Its Schools.* Mahwah, NJ: Erlbaum.

Booth, A., Carver, K., and Granger, D. A. 2000. Biosocial perspectives on the family. *Journal of Marriage and Family* 62: 1018–34.

Boothby, N. G., and Knudsen, C. M. 2000. Children of the gun. *Scientific American*, June, 60–65.

Bould, S. 2003. Neighborhoods and inequality: The possibilities for successful transition to adulthood. *Sociological Studies of Children and Youth* 9: 49–66.

Boyden, J. 1990. Childhood and the policy makers: A comparative perspective on the globalization of childhood. In A. James and A. Prout (Eds.), *Constructing and Reconstructing Childhood: Contemporary Issues in the Sociological Study of Childhood* (pp. 184–215). London: Falmer Press.

Bridges, M., Salanio, A., Hahn, C., Cicero, M., Browne, K., Gonzales, S., and Kort, M. 2003/2004. 50 women who made a difference. *Ms*, winter, 53–60.

Brodsky, A. E. 2003. *With All Our Strength: The Revolutionary Association of the Women of Afghanistan.* New York: Routledge.

Bronfenbrenner, U. 1977. Toward an experimental ecology of human development. *American Psychologist* 32: 513–31.

Brubach, H. 1990. In fashion. *New Yorker*, November 5, 126–28.

Brumberg, J. J. 2003. A killing tradition. *Nation*, November 17, 24–26.

Bruner, J. 2000. Tot thought. *New York Review*, March 9, 27–30.

Brunner, C., Bennett, D., and Honey, M. 2000. Girl games and technological desire. In J. Cassell and H. Jenkins (Eds.), *From Barbie to Mortal Kombat: Gender and Computer Games* (pp. 72–88). Cambridge, MA: MIT Press.

Buchanan, A., and Sluckin, A. 1994. Gypsy children in post-communist Eastern Europe. *Children and Society* 8: 333–43.

Bureau of Statistics, Treasury Department. 2003. *Statistical Abstract of the United States.* Washington, DC: U.S. Government Printing Office.

Burr, R. 2002. Global and local approaches to children's rights in Vietnam. *Childhood* 9: 49–61.

Cahill, S. E. 1986. Childhood socialization as a recruitment process: Some lessons from the study of gender development. *Sociological Studies of Child Development* 1: 163–86.

Cairns, E., and Dawes, A. 1996. Children: Ethnic and political violence—A commentary. *Child Development* 67: 129–39.

Calhoun, C. A., and Espenshade, T. J. 1988. Childrearing and wives' forgone earnings. *Population Studies* 41: 5–37.

Cassell, J., and Jenkins, H. 2000. *From Barbie to Mortal Kombat: Gender and Computer Games.* Cambridge, MA: MIT Press.

Ceballo, R., Dahl, T. A., Aretakis, M. T., and Ramirez. C. 2001. Inner-city children's exposure to community violence: How much do parents know? *Journal of Marriage and Family* 63: 927–40.

Cherlin, A. J. 2000. Generation ex-. *Nation*, December 11, 62–68.

Cherlin, A. J., and Furstenberg, F. 1992. *The New American Grandparent.* Cambridge: MA: Harvard University Press.

Chikane, F. 1986. Children in turmoil: The effects of unrest on township children. In S. Burman and P. Reynolds (Eds.), *Growing Up in a Divided Society: The Contexts of Childhood in South Africa* (pp. 333–44). Johannesburg: Raven Press.

Child and Youth Research and Training Programme. 2003. South Africa: Social indicators in the service of social change. *Child Indicator* 4: 2.

Children's Aid Society. 1978. *New York Street Kids*. New York: Dover Publications.

Children's Defense Fund. 2002. *The State of America's Children*. Washington, DC: Children's Defense Fund.

Chin, T., and Phillips, M. 2003. Just play? A framework for analyzing children's time use. *Sociological Studies of Children and Youth* 9: 149–78.

Chisholm, A., and Moorehead, C. 1990. Migrant children in France. In C. Moorehead (Ed.), *Betrayal: A Report on Violence toward Children in Today's World* (pp. 165–83). New York: Doubleday.

Cho, H. 1995. Children in the examination war in South Korea: A cultural analysis. In S. Stephens (Ed.), *Children and the Politics of Culture* (pp. 141–68). Princeton, NJ: Princeton University Press.

Chomsky, N. 1988. *Language and Problems of Knowledge: The Managua Lectures*. Cambridge, MA: MIT Press.

Christensen, P. and Prout, A. 2002. Working with ethical symmetry in social research with children. *Childhood* 9: 477–97.

Chromholm, A. 2002. Which fathers use their rights? Swedish fathers who take parental leave. *Community, Work and Family* 5: 365–70.

Clark, C., and O'Donnell, J. 1999. *Becoming and Unbecoming White*. Westport, CT: Bergin & Garvey.

Clark, R. 2002. *The Fire This Time*. New York: International Action Center.

Clausen, J. A. 1968. *Socialization and Society*. Boston: Little, Brown.

Cohen, A. 2004. The supreme struggle. *Education Life*, January 18, 22–25.

Cole, N. S. 1997. *The ETS Gender Study: How Females and Males Perform in Educational Settings*. Princeton, NJ: Educational Testing Service.

Coleman, J. S. 1987. Families and schools. *Educational Researcher* 16: 32–38.

Coles, R. 1967. *Migrants, Sharecroppers, Mountaineers*. Boston: Atlantic/Little, Brown.

Collins, P. 2000. *Black Feminist Thought: Knowledge, Consciousness, and Empowerment*. Rev. ed. New York: Routledge.

Comings, D. E., Muhleman, D., Johnson, J. P., and MacMurray, J. P. 2002. Parent-daughter transmission of the androgen receptor gene as an explanation of the effect of father absence on age of menarche. *Child Development* 73: 1046–51.

Connolly, P. 1998. *Racism, Gender Identities and Young Children*. London: Routledge.

Coohey, C. 2000. The role of friends, in-laws, and other kin in father-perpetrated child physical abuse. *Child Welfare* 79: 373–43.

Cook, D. T. 2004. *The Commodification of Childhood: The Children's Clothing Industry and the Rise of the Child Consumer*. Durham, NC: Duke University Press.

Coontz, S. 1997. *The Way We Really Are: Coming to Terms with America's Changing Families*. New York: Basic Books.

Corbett, S. 2002. Where do babies come from? *New York Times Magazine*, June 16, 42–47, 74, 82–83.

Corsaro, W. 1988. Children's conception and reaction to adult rules: The under-life of the nursery school In G. Handel (Ed.), *Childhood Socialization* (pp. 193–207). New York: Aldine de Gruyter.

———. 1997. *The Sociology of Childhood*. Thousand Oaks, CA: Pine Forge Press.

———. 2003. *We're Friends, Right? Inside Kids' Culture*. Washington, DC: Joseph Henry Press.

Corsaro, W., and Eder, D. 1990. Children's peer cultures. *Annual Review of Sociology* 16: 197–220.

Corsaro, W., and Molinari, L. 2000. Entering and observing in children's worlds. In P. Christensen and A. James (Eds.), *Research with Children: Perspectives and Practices* (pp. 179–200). London: Falmer Press.

Costanzo, M. 1997. *Just Revenge: Costs and Consequences of the Death Penalty*. New York: St. Martin's Press.

Costello, E. J., Compton, S. N., Keeler, G., and Angold, A. 2003. Relationships between poverty and psychopathology. *Journal of the American Medical Association* 290: 2023–29.

Creighton, M. R. 1994. "Edutaining" children: Consumer and gender socialization in Japanese marketing. *Ethnology* 33: 35–52.

Crittenden, A. 2001. *The Price of Motherhood*. New York: Holt.

Crouch, S. 1996. Race is over. *New York Times Magazine*, September 29, 170–71.

Crowell, N. A., and Leeper, E. M. 1994. *America's Fathers and Public Policy: Report of a Workshop*. Washington, DC: National Academy Press.

Cunningham, H. 1998. Histories of childhood. *American Historical Review* 103: 1195–1208.

Dannison, L. L., and Smith, A. B. 2003. Custodial grandparents community support program: Lessons learned. *Children and Schools* 25: 87–95.

Danziger, S., and Waldfogel, J. 2000. *Securing the Future: Investing in Children from Birth to College*. New York: Russell Sage Foundation.

Dargan, A., and Zeitlin, S. 1990. *City Play*. New Brunswick, NJ: Rutgers University Press.

Davis, J., Watson, N., and Cunningham-Burley, S. 2000. Learning the lives of disabled children. In P. Christensen and A. James (Eds.), *Research with Children: Perspectives and Practices* (pp. 201–24). London: Falmer Press.

Davis, J. E. 2003. Early schooling and academic achievement of African American males. *Urban Education* 38: 515–37.

Davis, K. 1959. The myth of functional analysis as a special method in sociology and anthropology. *American Sociological Review* 24: 757–72.

Davis, P. W. 1994. The changing meanings of spanking. In J. Best (Ed.), *Troubling Children* (pp. 133–53). New York: de Gruyter.

Dawes, A., and Finchilescu, G. 2002. What's changed? The racial orientations of South African adolescents during rapid political change. *Childhood* 9: 147–65.

de Bernieres, L. 1994. *Corelli's Mandolin*. New York: Vintage International.

Demenet, P. 2000. Nobody's children. *Le Monde Diplomatique*, June, 10–11.

Demo, D. H., and Cox, M. J. 2000. Families with young children: A review of research in the 1990s. *Journal of Marriage and Family* 62: 876–95.

Demo, D. H., Allen, K. R., and Fine, M. A. 2000. *Handbook of Family Diversity*. New York: Oxford University Press.

Dencik, L. 1995. Modern childhood in the Nordic countries: "Dual socialization" and its implications. In L. Chisholm (Ed.), *Growing Up in Europe: Contemporary Horizons in Childhood and Youth Studies* (pp. 105–19). Berlin: de Gruyter.

Devine, D. 2002. Children's citizenship and the structuring of adult-child relations in the primary school. *Childhood* 9: 303–320.

de Winter, M. 1997. *Children as Fellow Citizens: Participation and Commitment*. Oxford: Radcliffe Medical Press.

Dickson, P., and Cumming, A. (Eds.). 1996. *Profiles of Language Education in 25 Countries*. Slough, UK: National Foundation for Educational Research.

Dimock, G. 2002. *Priceless Children: American Photographs 1890–1925—Child Labor and the Pictorialist Ideal*. New York: Grey Art Gallery of New York University.

Du Bois-Reymond, M., Ravesloot, J., Te Poel, Y., and Zeijl, E. 2001. New skills to learn in peer groups. *Sociological Studies of Children and Youth* 8: 143–71.

Duffy, E. 2002. The cradle will rock. *New York Review*, December 19, 61–63.

Duncan, G., and Brooks-Gunn, J. 1999. *Consequences of Growing Up Poor*. New York: Russell Sage Foundation.

Durkheim, E. 1961. *Moral Education*. Glencoe, IL: Free Press.

Early Child Care Research Network, National Institute of Child Health and Human Development. 2003. Does amount of time spent in child care predict socioemotional adjustment during the transition to kindergarten? *Child Development* 74: 976–1006.

Economist. 2000. Bright young things: Survey of the young. Insert to *Economist*, December 23, 3–16.

Eder, D. 1995. *School Talk: Gender and Adolescent Culture*. New Brunswick, NJ: Rutgers University Press.

Edwards, C., Gandini, L., and Forman, G. 1993. *The Hundred Languages of Children: The Reggio Emilia Approach to Early Childhood Education*. Norwood, NJ: Ablex.

Elley, W. B. (Ed.). 1994. *The IEA Study of Reading Literacy: Achievement and Instruction in Thirty-Two School Systems*. Oxford: Pergamon Press.

Ennew, J., and Milne, B. 1990. *The Next Generation: Lives of Third World Children*. Philadelphia: New Society Publishers.

Entwisle, D., and Doering, S. 1981. *The First Birth*. Baltimore: Johns Hopkins University Press.

Epstein, H. 1998. Life and death on the social ladder. *New York Review*, July 7, 26–30.

Espenshade, T. J., and Calhoun, C. A. 1986. The dollars and cents of parenthood. *Journal of Policy Analysis and Management* 5: 813–17.

Espinosa, L. M. 2002. High-quality preschool: Why we need it and what it looks like. *NIEER Preschool Policy Matters* 1: 1–10.

Fashola, O. S. 2003. Developing the talents of African American male students during the nonschool hours. *Urban Education* 38: 398–430.

Ferguson, A. A. 2000. *Bad Boys: Public Schools in the Making of Black Masculinity*. Ann Arbor: University of Michigan Press.

Fields, J. 2003. Children's living arrangements and characteristics: March 2002. *Current Population Reports, P20-S47*. Washington, DC: U.S. Census Bureau.

Fine, G. A., and Sandstrom, K. L. 1988. *Knowing Children: Participant Observation with Minors*. Newbury Park, CA: Sage Publications.

Foner, A. 1978. Age stratification and the changing family. In J. Demos and S. S. Boocock (Eds.), *Turning Points: Historical and Sociological Essays on the Family* (pp. 340–65). Chicago: University of Chicago Press.

Forbes, C. 1990. Child exploitation in the Philippines. In C. Moorehead (Ed.), *Betrayal: A Report on Violence toward Children in Today's World* (pp. 230–49). New York: Doubleday.

Foster, D. 1986. The development of racial orientation in children: A review of South African research. In S. Burman and P. Reynolds (Eds.), *Growing Up in a Divided Society: The Contexts of Childhood in South Africa* (pp. 158–83). Johannesburg: Raven Press.

Franklin, J. H. 1969. *The Future of Negro American History*. New York: New School for Social Research.

Frede, E., Lamy, C. E., Seplocha, H., Strasser, J., Jambunathan, S., Juncker, J. A., and Wolock, E. 2004. *A Rising Tide: Classroom Quality and Language*

Skills in the Abbott Preschool Program. New Brunswick, NJ: National Institute for Early Education Research.

Fuentes, A. 2003. Discipline and punish. *Nation*, December 15, 17–20.

Furst, G. 1999. *Sweden: The Equal Way*. Stockholm: Swedish Institute.

Furtenberg, F. F., and Cherlin, A. J. 1991. *Divided Families: What Happens to Children When Parents Part*. Cambridge, MA: Harvard University Press.

Furstenberg, F. F., and Harris, K. M. 1992. The disappearing American father? Divorce and the waning significance of biological parenthood. In S. J. South and S. E. Tolnay (Eds.), *The Changing American Family: Sociological and Demographic Perspectives* (pp. 197–23). Boulder, CO: Westview Press.

Galinsky, E. 1999. *Ask the Children: What America's Children Really Think about Working Parents*. New York: Morrow.

Gans, H. J. 1972. The positive functions of poverty. *American Journal of Sociology* 78: 275–89.

———. 1995. *The War against the Poor*. New York: Basic Books.

Gavron, D. 2000. *The Kibbutz: Awakening from Utopia*. Lanham, MD: Rowman & Littlefield.

Gershoff, E. T. 2002. Corporal punishment by parents and associated child behaviors and experiences: A meta-analytic and theoretical review. *Psychological Bulletin* 128: 539–79.

Gerson, K. 2000. Resolving family dilemmas and conflicts: Beyond utopia. *Contemporary Sociology* 29: 180–87.

Giroux, H. A. 1999. *The Mouse That Roared*. Lanham, MD: Rowman & Littlefield.

Gittins, D. 1998. *The Child in Question*. New York: St. Martin's Press.

Gladwell, M. 1998. Do parents matter? *New Yorker*, August 17, 54–64.

Glauser, B. 1990. Street children: Deconstructing a construct. In A. Prout and A. James (Eds.), *Constructing and Reconstructing Childhood: Contemporary Issues in the Sociological Study of Childhood* (pp. 138–56). London: Falmer Press.

Gobodo-Madizizela, P. 2003. *A Human Being Died That Night: A South African Woman Confronts the Legacy of Apartheid*. Boston: Houghton Mifflin.

Golini, A., and Silvestrini, A. 1997. Family change, fathers, and children in western Europe: A demographic and psychosocial perspective. In S. Dreman (Ed.), *The Family on the Threshold of the 21st Century: Trends and Implications* (pp. 201–25). Mahwah, NJ: Erlbaum.

Goldstein, T. 2003. Contemporary bilingual life at a Canadian high school. *Sociology of Education* 76: 247–64.

Goncu, A. 1999. *Children's Engagement in the World: Sociocultural Perspectives*. Cambridge, MA: Cambridge University Press.

Good, C., Aronson, J., and Inzlicht, M. 2003. Improving adolescents' standardized test performance: An intervention to reduce the effects of stereotype threat. *Applied Developmental Psychology* 24: 645–62.

Goodwin, M. 1990. *He-Said-She-Said*. Bloomington: Indiana University Press.

Grant, J. 1998. *Raising Baby by the Book: The Education of American Mothers*. New Haven, CT: Yale University Press.

Graue, M. W., and Walsh, D. 1998. *Studying Children in Context: Theories, Methods and Ethics*. Thousand Oaks, CA: Sage Publications.

Green, C. S., and Bavelier, D. 2003. Action video game modifies visual selective attention. *Nature* 423: 534–37.

Greven, P. 1991. *Spare the Child*. New York: Knopf.

Grossman, D. 2003. *Death as a Way of Life*. New York: Farrar, Strauss & Giroux.

Groza, V. 1997. Adoption: International. *Encyclopedia of Social Work*, Supplement, 1–4.

Gutierrez, L. G. 2004. Keynote Address, World Congress of Comparative Education, Havana, Cuba, October 26.

Guzman, L., Lippman, L., Moore, K. A., and O'Hare, W. 2003. How children are doing. *Child Trend Research Brief*, July, 1–7.

Hadley, K. G. 2003. Children's word play: Resisting and accommodating Confucian values in a Taiwanese kindergarten. *Sociology of Education* 76: 193–209.

Halle, T. 2002. *Charting Parenthood: A Statistical Portrait of Fathers and Mothers in America*. Washington, DC: Child Trends.

Harris, J. R. 1995. Where is the child's environment? A group socialization theory of development. *Psychological Review* 102: 458–89.

———. 1998. *The Nurture Assumption: Why Children Turn Out the Way They Do*. New York: Free Press.

Hart, J. 2002. Children and nationalism in a Palestinian refugee camp in Jordan. *Childhood* 9: 35–47.

Hart, R. 1992. *Children's Participation: From Tokenism to Citizenship*. Florence: UNICEF International Child Development Center.

———. 1997. *Children's Participation: The Theory and Practice of Involving Young Citizens in Community Development and Environmental Care*. London: Earthscan Publications.

Haynie, D. L. 2003. Contexts of risk? Explaining the link between girls' pubertal development and their delinquency involvement. *Social Forces* 82: 355–97.

Hedges, C. 2002. *War Is a Force That Gives Us Meaning*. New York: Public Affairs.

Hellman, L. 1973. *Pentimento*. New York: Signet Books.

Hendrick, H. 2000. The child as a social actor in historical sources. In P. Christensen and A. James (Eds.), *Research with Children: Perspectives and Practices* (pp. 36–61). London: Falmer Press.

Hengst, H. 1997. Negotiating "us" and "them": Children's constructions of collective identity. *Childhood* 4: 43–62.

Hernandez, D. J. 1986. Childhood in sociodemographic perspective. *Annual Review of Sociology* 12: 159–80.

———. 1993. *America's Children: Resources from Family, Government, and the Economy*. New York: Russell Sage Foundation.

———. 1995. Changing demographics: Past and future demands for early childhood programs. *The Future of Children* 5: 145–60.

Hetherington, E. M. 2002. *For Better or for Worse: Divorce Reconsidered*. New York: Norton.

Hochschild, A. R. 1997. *The Time Bind*. New York: Holt.

Hofferth, S. L., and Sandberg, J. F. 2001. Changes in American children's time, 1981–1997. In S. L. Hofferth and T. J. Owens (Eds.), *Children at the Millennium: Where Have We Come From, Where Are We Going?* (pp. 193–229). Oxford, UK: Elsevier Science.

Hogan, D. P., and Goldscheider, F. 2001. Men's flight from children in the U.S.: A historical perspective. In S. L. Hofferth and T. J. Owens (Eds.), *Children at the Millennium: Where Have We Come From, Where Are We Going?* (pp. 173–191). Oxford, UK: Elsevier Science.

Hoose, P. 2001. *We Were There, Too! Young People in U.S. History*. New York: Farrar, Straus & Giroux.

Horvat, E. M., and Antonio, A. L. 1999. "Hey, those shoes are out of uniform": African-American girls in an elite high school and the importance of habitus. *Anthropology and Education Quarterly* 30: 317–42.

Hostetler, J. A. 1993. *Amish Society*. 4th rev. ed. Baltimore: Johns Hopkins University Press.

Howe, N., and Strauss, W. 2000. *Millennials Rising: The Next Great Generation*. New York: Vintage Books.

Hulbert, A. 2003. *Raising America*. New York: Knopf.

Human Rights Watch. 2004. *Human Rights and Armed Conflict. World Report 2004*. New York: Human Rights Watch.

Humphries, S., Mack, J., and Perks, R. 1989. *A Century of Childhood*. London: Sidgwick & Jackson.

Hutchby, I., and Moran-Ellis, J. 1998. *Children and Social Competence: Arenas of Action*. Bristol, PA: Falmer Press.

Jackson, P. 1968. *Life in Classrooms*. New York: Holt, Rinehart and Winston.

James, A., Jenks, C., and Prout, A. 1998. *Theorizing Childhood.* Cambridge, UK: Polity Press.

Jenkins, H. 2000. "Complete freedom of movement": Video games as gendered play spaces. In J. Cassell and H. Jenkins (Eds.), *From Barbie to Mortal Kombat: Gender and Computer Games* (pp. 262–97). Cambridge, MA: MIT Press.

Jensen, A-M. 1994. The feminization of childhood. In J. Qvortrup, M. Bardy, G. Sgritta, and H. Wintersberger (Eds.), *Childhood Matters: Social Theory, Practice and Politics* (pp. 59–75). Aldershot, UK: Avebury.

Jing, J. 2000. *Feeding China's Little Emperors: Food, Children and Social Change.* Stanford, CA: Stanford University Press.

Jiro, S. 1999. Grownups should listen to kids. *Japan Quarterly* 46: 83–88.

Johnson, D. W., Johnson, R., Dudley, B., Ward, M., and Magnuson, D. 1995. The impact of peer mediation training on the management of school and home conflicts. *American Educational Research Journal* 32: 829–44.

Johnson, H. B. 2001. From the Chicago School to the New Sociology of Children: The sociology of children and childhood in the United States, 1900–1999. In S. L. Hofferth and T. J. Owens (Eds.), *Children at the Millennium: Where Have We Come From, Where Are We Going?* (pp. 53–93). Oxford, UK: Elsevier Science.

Johnson, S. M., and O'Connor, E. 2003. *The Gay Baby Boom: The Psychology of Gay Parenthood.* New York: New York University Press.

Jones, S. 1993. *Assaulting Childhood: Children's Experiences of Migrancy and Hostel Life in South Africa.* Johannesburg: Witwatersrand University Press.

Kafai, Y. B. 2000. Video game designs by girls and boys: Variability and consistency of gender differences. In J. Cassell and H. Jenkins (Eds.), *From Barbie to Mortal Kombat: Gender and Computer Games* (pp. 90–114). Cambridge, MA: MIT Press.

Kagan, J. 1980. The psychological requirements for human development. In A. Skolnick and J. H. Skolnick (Eds.), *Family in Transition* (pp. 427–38). Boston: Little, Brown.

Keeves, J. P. 1995. *The World of School Learning: Selected Findings from 35 Years of IEA Research.* The Hague: IEA.

Kennedy, S., Whiteford, P., and Bradshaw, J. 1996. The economic circumstances of children in ten countries. In J. Brannen and M. O'Brien (Eds.), *Children in Families: Research and Policy* (pp. 145–70). London: Falmer Press.

Khalaf, R. S. 2004. Living between worlds. In M. Halasa and R. S. Khalaf (Eds.), *Transit Beirut* (pp. 58–67). London: Saqi Books.

Kielburger, C. 1998. *Free the Children.* New York: HarperPerennial.

Killen, M. and Sueyoshi, L. 1995. Conflict resolution in Japanese preschool interactions. *Early Education and Development* 6: 313–30.

Kim, D. S. 1977. How they fared in American homes: A follow-up study of adopted Korean children in the United States. *Children Today* 6: 2–6, 36.

Kimm, S., Glynn, N. W., Kriska, A. M., Norton, B. A., Kronsberg, S. S., Daniels, S. R., Crawford, P. B., Sabry, A. I., and Liu, K. 2002. Decline in physical activity in Black girls and White girls during adolescence. *New England Journal of Medicine* 347: 709–16.

King, W. 1995. *Stolen Childhood: Slave Youth in Nineteenth Century America.* Bloomington: Indiana University Press.

Kline, S. 1995. The play of the market: On the internationalization of children's culture. *Theory, Culture and Society* 12: 103–29.

Kowaleski-Jones, L., and Duniform, R. 2004. Children's home environments: Understanding the role of family structure changes. *Journal of Family Issues* 25: 3–28.

Kozol, J. 1978. *Children of the Revolution.* New York: Delta.

Kraybill, D. B., and Olshan, M. A. 1994. *The Amish Struggle with Modernity.* Hanover, NH: University Press of New England.

Kropf, N. P., and Burnette, D. 2003. Grandparents as family caregivers: Lessons for intergenerational education. *Educational Gerontology* 29: 361–72.

La Greca, A. M., Silverman, W. K., and Wasserstein, S. 1995. What do children worry about? Worries and their relation to anxiety. *Child Development* 66: 673–86.

Lamb, S. 2001. *The Secret Lives of Girls.* New York: Free Press.

Land, K. C. 2000. A single index of child well-being. *Child Indicator* 2: 4.

Lansdown, G. 1994. Children's rights. In B. Mayall (Ed.), *Children's Childhoods: Observed and Experienced* (pp. 33–44). London: Falmer Press.

Lareau, A. 2003. *Unequal Childhoods: Class, Race, and Family Life.* Berkeley: University of California Press.

Leavitt, R. L. 1991. Power and resistance in infant-toddler day care centers. *Sociological Studies of Child Development* 4: 91–112.

Lee, S. J. 1996. *Unraveling the "Model Minority" Stereotype.* New York: Teachers College Press.

Lee, S., Colditz, G., Berkman, L., and Kawachi, I. 2003. Caregiving to children and grandchildren and risk of coronary heart disease in women. *American Journal of Public Health* 93: 1939–44.

Lee, V. E., Croninger, R. G., Linn, E., and Chen, X. 1996. The culture of sexual harassment in secondary schools. *American Educational Research Journal* 33: 383–417.

Lee, Y-S., Schneider, S., and Waite, L. 2003. Children and housework: Some unanswered questions. *Sociological Studies of Children and Youth* 9: 105–125.

Lemert, C. 2002. *Social Things: An Introduction to the Sociological Life*. Lanham, MD: Rowman & Littlefield.

Leonard, M. 2004. Children's views on children's right to work: reflections from Belfast. *Childhood* 11: 45–61.

Lerner, R. M., and Spanier, G. B. 1978. *Child Influences on Marital and Family Interaction: A Life-Span Perspective*. New York Academic Press.

Lerner, R. M., Sparks, E. E., and McCubbin, L. D. 2000. Family diversity and family policy. In D. H. Demo, K. R. Allen, and M. A. Fine (Eds.), *Handbook of Family Diversity* (pp. 380–401). New York: Oxford University Press.

Levine, J. 2002. *Harmful to Minors*. Minneapolis: University of Minnesota Press.

Lew, J. In press. *Asian American Achievement Gap: Class, Race, School Context—A Case of Korean Americans*. New York: Teachers College Press.

Lewis, A. 2003. *Race in the Schoolyard: Negotiating the Color Line in Classrooms and Communities*. New Brunswick, NJ: Rutgers University Press.

Lewis, J. 1998. *Walking with the Wind*. New York: Simon & Schuster.

Lewis, M. 2001. *Next*. New York: Norton.

Lino, M. 2002. *Expenditures on Children by Families: 2001 Annual Report*. U.S. Department of Agriculture, Center for Nutrition Policy and Promotion. Miscellaneous Publication No. 1528-2001.

Livingstone, S., and Bovill, M. 2001. *Children and Their Changing Media Environment: A European Comparative Study*. Mahwah, NJ: Erlbaum.

Loissis, P., and Noller, P. 1999. Children's perceptions of their dual-working mothers and fathers. *Contemporary Perspectives on Family Research* 1: 273–86.

Lord, M. G. 1994. *Forever Barbie*. New York: Avon Books.

Lugaila, T., and Overturf, J. 2004. *Children and the Households They Live In: 2000*. Washington, DC: U.S. Bureau of the Census.

Mamdani, M. 2004. *Good Muslim, Bad Muslim*. New York: Pantheon.

Mandell, N. 1991. The least-adult role in studying children. In F. Waksler (Ed.), *Studying the Social Worlds of Children* (pp. 38–59). London: Falmer Press.

Manzo, K. K. 2002. Japanese schoolchildren "cram" to boost achievement. *Education Week*, August 7, 1–5.

Martin, K. A. 1998. Becoming a gendered body: Practices of preschools. *American Sociological Review* 63: 494–511.

Matthews, S. H. 2003. Counterfeit classrooms: School life of inner-city children. *Sociological Studies of Children and Youth* 9: 209–24.

Maundeni, T. 2002. Seen but not heard? Focusing on the needs of children of divorced parents in Gaborone, Botswana, and surrounding areas. *Childhood* 9: 277–302.

Mayall, B. 1994. Children in action at home and school. In B. Mayall (Ed.), *Children's Childhoods: Observed and Experienced* (pp. 114–27). London: Falmer Press.

———. 2000. Conversations with children: Working with generational issues. In P. Christensen and A. James (Eds.), *Research with Children: Perspectives and Practices* (pp. 120–35). London: Falmer Press.

———. 2001. Introduction. In L. Alanen and B. Mayall (Eds.), *Conceptualizing Child-Adult Relations* (pp. 1–10). London: Routledge/Falmer.

McKechnie, J., and Hobbs, S. 2001. Work and education: Are they compatible for children and adolescents? In P. Mizen, C. Pole, and A. Bolton (Eds.), *Hidden Hands: International Perspectives on Children's Work and Labour* (pp. 9–23). London: Routledge/Falmer.

McLachlan, F. 1986. Children in prison. In S. Burman and P. Reynolds (Eds.), *Growing Up in a Divided Society: The Contexts of Childhood in South Africa* (pp. 346–59). Johannesburg: Raven Press.

McLanahan, S., Garfinkel, I., Reichman, N., Teitler, J., Carlson, M., and Audigier, C. N. 2003. *The Fragile Families and Child Wellbeing Study: Baseline National Report*. Princeton, NJ: Princeton University, Bendheim-Thomas Center for Research on Child Wellbeing.

McLemore, S. D. 1994. *Racial and Ethnic Relations in America*. 4th ed. Boston: Allyn and Bacon.

McNeal, J. 1999. *The Kids Market*. Ithaca, NY: Paramount.

Mead, G. H. 1934. *Mind, Self and Society*. Chicago: University of Chicago Press.

Mertens, S. B., Flowers, N., and Mulhall, P. F. 2003. Should middle grades students be left alone after school? *Middle School Journal* 34: 57–61.

Merton, R. K. 1957. *Social Theory and Social Structure*. Rev. ed. Glencoe, IL: Free Press.

Mickelson, R. A. 2000. *Children in the Streets of the Americas*. London: Routledge.

Mitchell, S. 2000. *American Generations: Who They Are, How They Live, What They Think*. Ithaca, NY: New Strategist Publications.

Mizen, P., Pole, C., and Bolton, A. 2001. Why be a school age worker? In P. Mizen, C. Pole, and A. Bolton (Eds.), *Hidden Hands: International Perspectives on Children's Work and Labour* (pp. 38–54). London: Routledge/Falmer.

Moore, K. A., Brown, B. V., and Scarupa, H. J. 2003. The uses (and misuses) of social indicators: Implications for public policy. *Child Trends Research Brief*, February, 1–6.

Moore, K. A., Jekielek, S. M., and Emig, C. 2002. Marriage from a child's perspective: How does family structure affect children, and what can we do about it? *Child Trends Research Brief*, June, 1–8.

Moore, K. A., and Redd, Z. 2002. Children in poverty: Trends, consequences and policy options. *Child Trends Research Brief*, November, 1–8.

Moorehead, C. 1990. *Betrayal: A Report on Violence toward Children in Today's World*. New York: Doubleday.

Morgan, S. P. 2003. Is low fertility a twenty-first-century demographic crisis? *Demography* 40: 589–604.

Morizumi, T. 2002. *Children of the Gulf War*. Hiroshima: Global Association for Banning Depleted Uranium Weapons.

Morrow, V. 1994. Responsible children? Aspects of children's work and employment outside school in contemporary UK. In B. Mayall (Ed.), *Children's Childhoods: Observed and Experienced* (pp. 128–43). London: Falmer Press.

Mullis, I. I. S., Martin, M. O., Gonzalez, E. J., and Chrostowski, S. J. 2004. *TIMSS 2003 International Mathematics Report: Findings from IEA's Trends in International Mathematics and Science Study at the Fourth and Eighth Grades*. Chestnut Hill, MA: Boston College.

Mullis, I. I. S., Martin, M. O., Gonzalez, E. J., and Kennedy, A. M. 2003. *PIRLS 2001 International Report: IEA's Study of Reading Literacy Achievement in Primary School*. Chestnut Hill, MA: Boston College.

Nagler, M. N. 2001. *Is There No Other Way? The Search for a Nonviolent Future*. Berkeley, CA: Berkeley Hills Books.

Nasaw, D. 1985. *Children of the City*. New York: Doubleday.

National Marriage Project. 2002. *The State of Our Unions 2002*. New Brunswick, NJ: Rutgers University Press.

———. 2003. *The State of Our Unions 2003*. New Brunswick, NJ: Rutgers University Press.

Neft, A., and Levine, A. D. 1997. *Where Women Stand: An International Report on the Status of Women in 140 Countries*. New York: Random House.

New, C., and David, M. 1985. *For the Children's Sake*. New York: Penguin Books.

New York Times, July 21, 1995–March 2, 2005.

Nichter, M. 2000. *Fat Talk: What Girls and Their Parents Say about Dieting*. Cambridge, MA: Harvard University Press.

Nishino, H. J., and Larson, R. 2003. Japanese adolescents' free time: "juku," "Bukatsu," and government efforts to create more meaningful leisure. *New Directions for Child and Adolescent Development* 99: 23–35.

Nomaguchi, K. M., and Milkie, M. A. 2003. Costs and rewards of children: The effects of becoming a parent on adults' lives. *Journal of Marriage and Family* 65: 356–74.

Oakley, A. 1994. Women and children first and last: Parallels and differences between children's and women's studies. In B. Mayall (Ed.), *Children's Childhoods: Observed and Experienced* (pp. 13–32). London: Falmer Press.

Obama, B. 2004. *Dreams from My Father: A Story of Race and Inheritance*. 2nd ed. New York: Three Rivers Press.

O'Brien, M. 1995. Allocation of resources in households: Children's perspectives. *Sociological Review* 43: 501–17.

O'Brien, M., Alldred, P., and Jones, D. 1996. Children's construction of family and kinship. In J. Brannen and M. O'Brien (Eds.), *Children in Families: Research and Policy* (pp. 84–100). London: Falmer Press.

O'Connor, C. 1997. Dispositions toward (collective) struggle and educational resilience in the inner city: A case analysis of six African-American high school students. *American Educational Research Journal* 34: 593–629.

O'Connor, S. 2001. *Orphan Trains*. Boston: Houghton Mifflin.

Okely, J. 1997. Non-territorial culture as the rationale for the assimilation of gypsy children. *Childhood* 4: 63–80.

Opie, I., and Opie, P. 1987. *Lore and Language of Schoolchildren*. New York: Oxford University Press.

Orellana, M. F., Dorner, L., and Pulido, L. 2003. Accessing assets: Immigrant youth's work as family translators or "para-phraser." *Social Problems* 50: 505–24.

Orfield, G., and Frankenberg, E. 2004. Where are we now? *Teaching Tolerance* 25: 57–59.

Orme, N. 2002. *Medieval Children*. New Haven, CT: Yale University Press.

Osada, Arata. 1982. *Children of Hiroshima*. New York: HarperColophon.

Paley, V. 1981. *Wally's Stories*. Cambridge, MA: Harvard University Press.

———. 1984. *Boys and Girls: Superheroes in the Doll Corner*. Chicago: University of Chicago Press.

Palmer, S. J., and Hardman, C. E. 1999. *Children in New Religions*. New Brunswick, NJ: Rutgers University Press.

Parse, R., and Heffron, K. 1989. The lore and language of American schoolchildren, as interpreted by Rachel and Kathleen. New Brunswick, NJ: Rutgers College Honors Program.

Passuth, P. M. 1987. Age hierarchies within children's groups. *Sociological Studies of Child Development* 2: 185–203.

Paterniti, M. 2003. The flight of the fluttering swallows. *New York Times Magazine*, April 27, 46–51, 62, 112–13.

Patterson, C. J. 2000. Family relationships of lesbians and gay men. *Journal of Marriage and Family* 62: 1052–69.

Penn, H. 2001. Culture and childhood in pastoralist communities: The example of Outer Mongolia. In L. Alanen and B. Mayall (Eds.), *Conceptualizing Child-Adult Relations* (pp. 86–98). London: Routledge/Falmer.

———. 2002. The World Bank's view of early childhood. *Childhood* 9: 118–32.

Perry, P. 2002. *Shades of White: White Kids and Racial Identities in High School*. Durham, NC: Duke University Press.

Pong, S-L., Dronkers, J., and Hampden-Thompson, G. 2003. Family policies and children's school achievement in single- versus two-parent families. *Journal of Marriage and Family* 65: 681–99.

Postman, N. 1982. *The Disappearance of Childhood*. New York: Delacorte Press.

Poston, D. L., and Falbo, T. 1990. Academic performance and personality traits of Chinese children: "Onlies" versus others. *American Journal of Sociology* 96: 443–51.

Povrzanovic, M. 1997. Children, war and nation: Croatia 1991–94. *Childhood* 4: 81–102.

Preston, S. E. 1996. Children will pay. *New York Times Magazine*, September 29, 96–99.

Prochner, L. 2002. Preschool and playing in India. *Childhood* 9: 435–53.

Prout, A. 2000. Preface. In P. Christensen and A. James (Eds.), *Research with Children: Perspectives and Practices* (pp. xi–xii). London: Falmer Press.

Prout, A., and James, A. 1990. A new paradigm for the sociology of childhood? Provenance, promise and problems. In A. James and A. Prout (Eds.), *Constructing and Reconstructing Childhood* (pp. 7–33). London: Falmer Press.

Pruchno, R. A., and Johnson, K. W. 1996. Research on grandparenting: Review of current studies and future needs. *Generations* 20: 65–71.

Pryor, J., and Rodgers, B. 2001. *Children in Changing Families: Life after Parental Separation*. Oxford, UK: Blackwell Publishers.

Punch, S. 2001. Negotiating autonomy: Childhoods in rural Bolivia. In L. Alanen and B. Mayall (Eds.), *Conceptualizing Child-Adult Relations* (pp. 23–35). London: Routledge/Falmer.

———. 2002. Research with children: The same or different from research with adults? *Childhood* 9: 321–41.

Qvortrup, J. 1987. Introduction to Special Issue on the Sociology of Childhood. *International Journal of Sociology* 17: 3–37.

———. 1990. A voice for children in statistical and social accounting. In A. James and A. Prout (Eds.), *Constructing and Reconstructing Childhood* (pp. 78–98). London: Falmer Press.

――――. 1994. Childhood matters: An introduction. In J. Qvortrup, M. Bardy, G. Sgritta, and H. Wintersberger (Eds.), *Childhood Matters: Social Theory, Practice and Politics* (pp. 1–23). Aldershot, UK: Avebury.

――――. 1995a. Childhood in Europe: A new field of social research. In L. Chisholm (Ed.), *Growing Up in Europe: Contemporary Horizons in Childhood and Youth Studies* (pp. 7–19). Berlin: de Gruyter.

――――. 1995b. From useful to useful: The historical continuity of children's constructive participation. *Sociological Studies of Children* 7: 49–76.

――――. 2000a. A generational approach to a sociology of childhood. Paper presented at the annual meeting of the American Sociological Association, Washington, DC, August.

――――. 2000b. Macroanalysis of childhood. In P. Christensen and A. James (Eds.), *Research with Children: Perspectives and Practices* (pp. 77–97). London: Falmer Press.

Qvortrup, J., Bardy, M., Sgritta, G., and Wintersberger, H. (Eds.). 1994. *Childhood Matters: Social Theory, Practice and Politics*. Aldershot, UK: Avebury.

Rabin, A. I. 1965. *Growing Up in the Kibbutz*. New York: Springer.

Randal, R. and Boustany, N. 1990. Children of war in Lebanon. In C. Moorehead (Ed.), *Betrayal: A Report on Violence toward Children in Today's World* (pp. 59–81). New York: Doubleday.

Redd, Z., Brooks, J., and McGarvey, A. M. 2002. Educating America's youth: What makes a difference. *Child Trends Research Brief*, August, 1–8.

Reddy, D. M., Fleming, R., and Swain, C. 2002. Effect of mandatory parental notification on adolescent girls' use of sexual health care services. *Journal of the American Medical Association* 288: 710–14.

Renold, E. 2002. Presumed innocence: (Hetero)sexual, heterosexist and homophobic harassment among primary school girls and boys. *Childhood* 9: 415–34.

Reynolds, P. 1989. *Children in Crossroads*. Capetown, South Africa: Philip.

――――. 1990. The double strategy of children in South Africa. *Sociological Studies of Child Development* 3: 113–38.

Riley, M. W. 1997. Age integration: Challenge to a new institute. University of North Carolina, Distinguished Lecture Series, April 24.

Roberts, D. F., and Foehr, U. G. 2004. *Kids and Media in America*. Cambridge: Cambridge University Press.

Rodman, H. 1990. The social construction of the latchkey children problem. *Sociological Studies of Child Development* 3: 163–74.

Rosen, D. M. 2005. *Armies of the Young: Child Soldiers in War and Terrorism*. New Brunswick, NJ: Rutgers University Press.

Rossi, A. S., and Rossi, P. H. 1990. *Of Human Bonding: Parent-Child Relations across the Life Course*. New York: Aldine de Gruyter.

Rouanet, M. 1999. *Nous les filles*. Paris: Editions Payot.

Rubin, E. 1998. Our children are killing us. *New Yorker*, March 23, 56–64.

Russell, G. 1986. Primary caretaking and role-sharing fathers. In M. E. Lamb (Ed.), *The Father's Role: Applied Perspectives* (pp. 29–57). New York: Wiley Interscience.

Sayer, L., Bianchi, S. M., and Robinson, J. P. 2004. Are parents investing less in children? Trends in mothers' and fathers' time with children: Time allocation in families. *American Journal of Sociology* 110: 1–43.

Scharf, W., Powell, M., and Thomas, E. 1986. Strollers—Street children of Cape Town. In S. Burman and P. Reynolds (Eds.), *Growing Up in a Divided Society: The Contexts Of Childhood in South Africa* (pp. 262–87). Johannesburg: Raven Press.

Schlosser, E. 2002. *Fast Food Nation*. New York: HarperCollins.

Schmitt, B. D. 2004. Toilet training: Getting it right the first time. *Contemporary Pediatrics* 21: 105.

Schor, J. B. 2004. *Born to Buy: The Commercialized Child and the New Consumer Culture*. New York: Scribner.

Scott, K. A. 1999. First-grade African-American girls' play patterns. Doctoral dissertation, Rutgers University.

———. 2000. The importance of studying first-grade African-American girls' play patterns. *Hofstra Horizons*, spring, 12–15.

———. 2002. You want to be a girl and not my friend? African-American girls' play activities with and without boys. *Childhood* 9: 397–414.

———. 2003. In girls, out girls, and always Black: African-American girls' friendships. *Sociological Studies of Children and Youth* 9: 179–207.

———. 2004. African-American-White girls' friendships. *Feminism and Psychology* 14: 383–88.

Seager, J. 1997. *The State of Women in the World Atlas*. 2nd ed. London: Penguin Reference.

Seccombe, K. 2000. Families in poverty in the 1990s: Trends, causes, consequences, and lessons learned. *Journal of Marriage and Family* 62: 1094–1113.

———. 2002. "Beating the odds" versus "changing the odds": Poverty, resilience, and family policy. *Journal of Marriage and Family* 64: 384–94.

Selman, P., and Glendinning, C. 1996. Teenage pregnancy: Do social policies make a difference. In J. Brannen and M. O'Brien (Eds.), *Children in Families: Research and Policy* (pp. 202–18). London: Falmer Press.

Seltzer, J. A. 1991. Relationships between fathers and children who live apart: The father's role after separation. *Journal of Marriage and Family* 53: 79–101.

———. 2000. Families formed outside of marriage. *Journal of Marriage and Family* 62: 1247–68.

Sen, A. 1990. More than 100 million women are missing. *New York Review* 37: 20.

———. 2003. Missing women revisited. *British Medical Journal* 327: 1297–99.

Senghas, A., Kita, S., and Ozyurek, A. 2004. Children creating core properties of language: Evidence from an emerging sign language in Nicaragua. *Science* 305: 1779–82.

Shaw, J. 1990. Refugee children in Somalia. In C. Moorehead (Ed.), *Betrayal: A Report on Violence toward Children in Today's World* (pp. 208–29). New York: Doubleday.

Sherif, M. 1956. Experiments in group conflict. *Scientific American*, November, 112–16.

Shields, M. K., and Behrman, R. E. 2000. Children and computer technology: Analysis and recommendations. *The Future of Children* 10: 4–30.

Shotaro, T. 1999. Chaos in elementary classrooms. *Japan Quarterly* 46: 78–82.

Shrestha, N. 2000. A personal view of child labor. *Education about Asia* 5: 47–49.

Shultz, J., and Cook-Sather, A. 2001. *In Our Own Words: Students' Perspectives on School*. Lanham, MD: Rowman & Littlefield.

Singham, M. 1998. The canary in the mine: The achievement gap between Black and White students. *Phi Delta Kappan*, September, 9–15.

Skinner, D. A., and Kohler, J. K. 2002. Parental rights in diverse family contexts: Current legal developments. *Family Relations* 51: 293–300.

Skolnick, A. 1978. The myth of the vulnerable child. *Psychology Today*, February, 54–56.

Small, M. F. 2001. *Kids: How Biology and Culture Shape the Way We Raise Our Children*. New York: Doubleday.

Smart, C., Neale, B., and Wade, A. 2001. *The Changing Experience of Childhood: Families and Divorce*. Cambridge, UK: Polity Press.

Smeeding, T. M., and Torrey, B. B. 1988. Poor children in rich countries. *Science* 242: 873–77.

Smith, K. 2000. *Who's Minding the Kids? Child Care Arrangements: Household Economic Studies*. Washington, DC: U.S. Bureau of the Census.

Solberg, A. 1990. Negotiating childhood: Changing constructions of age for Norwegian children. In A. James and A. Prout (Eds.), *Constructing and Reconstructing Childhood* (pp. 118–37). London: Falmer Press.

Song, M. 1996. "Helping out": Children's labour participation in Chinese takeaway businesses in Britain. In J. Brannen and M. O'Brien (Eds.), *Children in Families: Research and Policy* (pp. 101–13). London: Falmer Press.

Southern Poverty Law Center. 2002. Official's slur inspires classroom to take action. *SPLC Report* 32 (December): 5.

Springer, J. 1997. *Listen to Us: The World's Working Children*. Toronto: Groundwood Books/Douglas & McIntyre.

Stafford, M. C. 1995. Children's legal rights in the U.S. *Marriage and Family Review* 21: 121–40.

Steele, C. M. 1997. A threat in the air: How stereotypes shape intellectual identity and performance. *American Psychologist* 52: 613–29.

Steinberg, S. R., and Kincheloe, J. L. 1997. *Kinderculture: The Corporate Construction of Childhood*. Boulder, CO: Westview Press.

Stephens, S. 1995a. Children and the politics of culture in "late capitalism." In S. Stephens (Ed.), *Children and the Politics of Culture* (pp. 3–48). Princeton, NJ: Princeton University Press.

———. 1995b. The "cultural fallout" of Chernobyl radiation in Northern Sami regions. In S. Stephens (Ed.), *Children and the Politics of Culture* (pp. 292–318). Princeton, NJ: Princeton University Press.

———. 1997. Nationalism, nuclear policy and children in Cold War America. *Childhood* 4: 103–23.

Stepp, L. S. 1999. Unsettling new fad alarms parents: Middle school oral sex. *Washington Post*, July 8, A1.

Stevens, M. L. 2001. *Kingdom of Children: Culture and Controversy in the Homeschooling Movement*. Princeton, NJ: Princeton University Press.

Strauss, M. A. 1994. *Beating the Devil Out of Them: Corporal Punishment in American Families*. New York: Lexington Books.

Students at Fayerweather Street School and Rofes, E. E. 1984. *The Kids' Book about Parents*. Boston: Houghton Mifflin.

Subrahmanyam, K., and Greenfield, P. M. 2000. Computer games for girls: What makes them play? In J. Cassell and H. Jenkins (Eds.), *From Barbie to Mortal Kombat: Gender and Computer Games* (pp. 46–71). Cambridge, MA: MIT Press.

Surowiecki, J. 2003. Leave no parent behind. *New Yorker*, August 18 and 25, 48.

Swadener, B. B., and Lubeck, S. 1995. *Children and Families "at Promise": Deconstructing the Discourse of Risk*. Albany: State University of New York Press.

Talbot, M. 1998. Attachment theory: The ultimate experiment. *New York Times Magazine*, May 24, 24–30, 46, 50, 54.

Tapscott, D. 1998. *Growing Up Digital: The Rise of the Net Generation*. New York: McGraw-Hill.

Tate, T. 1990. Trafficking in children for adoption. In C. Moorehead (Ed.), *Betrayal: A Report on Violence toward Children in Today's World* (pp. 142–64). New York: Doubleday.

Teachman, J. D., Tedrow, L. M., and Crowder, K. D. 2000. The changing demography of American families. *Journal of Marriage and Family* 62: 1234–46.

Terry, E., and Manlove, J. 2001. Trends in sexual activity and contraceptive use among teens. *Child Trends Research Brief*, August, 1–6.

Tessler, R., Gamache, G., and Liu, L. 1999. *West Meets East: Americans Adopt Chinese Children*. Westport, CT: Bergin and Garvey.

Tesson, G., and Youniss, J. 1995. Micro-sociology and psychological development: A sociological interpretation of Piaget's theory. *Sociological Studies of Children* 7: 101–26.

Thompson, C. 2004. The making of an Xbox warrior. *New York Times Magazine*, August 22, 33–37.

Thompson, M., and Grace, C. O. 2001. *Best Friends, Worst Enemies: Understanding the Social Lives of Children*. New York: Ballantine Books.

Thorne, B. 1987. Re-visioning women and social change: Where are the children? *Gender and Society* 1: 85–109.

———. 1993. *Gender Play: Girls and Boys in School*. New Brunswick, NJ: Rutgers University Press.

Tierney, J. 2001. Here come the Alpha pups. *New York Times Magazine*, August 5, 38–43.

Tignor, R., Adelman, J., Aron, S. Kotkin, S., Marchand, S., Prakash, G., and Tsin, M. 2002. *Worlds Together/Worlds Apart*. New York: Norton.

Tough, P. 2004. The Harlem Project. *New York Times Magazine*, June 20, 44–49, 66, 72–75.

Tsuneyoshi, R. 2001. *The Japanese Model of Schooling*. New York: Routledge/Falmer.

Turkle, Sherry. 1984. *The Second Self: Computers and the Human Spirit*. New York: Simon & Schuster.

———. 1995. *Life on the Screen: Identity in the Age of the Internet*. New York: Simon & Schuster.

Twenge, J. M., Campbell, W. K., and Foster, C. A. 2003. Parenthood and marital satisfaction: A meta-analytic review. *Journal of Marriage and Family* 65: 574–83.

Tynes, S. R. 1991. The world's children: Economic and social determinants of malnutrition. *Sociological Studies of Child Development* 4: 29–49.

Udry, J. R., Li, R. M., and Smith, J. H. 2003. Health and behavior risks of adolescents with mixed-race identity. *American Journal of Public Health* 93: 1865–70.

UNICEF. 1999. *The State of the World's Children 1999*. New York: United Nations Children's Fund.

———. 2001. *The State of the World's Children 2001.* New York: United Nations Children's Fund.

———. 2004. Children under threat. In *The State of the World's Children 2005* (pp. 1–102). New York: United Nations Children's Fund.

United Nations. 1989. Debt: Killer of third world children. *UN Chronicle*, September, 48.

Ury, W. L. 2002. *Must We Fight?* San Francisco: Jossey-Bass.

U.S. Department of Health and Human Services. 2004. Panel finds that scare tactics for violence prevention are harmful. *NIH News*, October 15, 1–3.

Van Ausdale, D., and Feagin, J. R. 2001. *The First R: How Children Learn Race and Racism.* Lanham, MD: Rowman & Littlefield.

Vandivere, S., Tout, K., Capizzano, J., and Zaslow, M. 2003. Left unsupervised: A look at the most vulnerable children. *Child Trends Research Brief*, April, 1–8.

Visano, L. 1990. The socialization of street children. *Sociological Studies of Child Development* 3: 139–61.

Waite, L. J., and Lillard, L. A. 1991. Children and marital disruption. *American Journal of Sociology* 96: 930–53.

Waksler, F. 1991. *Studying the Social Worlds of Children.* London: Falmer Press.

Wallace, W. L. 1997. *The Future of Ethnicity, Race, and Nationality.* Westport, CT: Praeger.

Waller, W. 1932. *The Sociology of Teaching.* New York: Wiley.

Wallerstein, J. S., Lewis, J., and Blakeslee, S. 2000. *The Unexpected Legacy of Divorce: A 25-Year Landmark Study.* New York: Hyperion.

Walsh, C. E. 2000. The struggle of "imagined communities" in school: Identification, survival, and belonging for Puerto Ricans. In S. Nieto (Ed.), *Puerto Rican Students in U.S. Schools* (pp. 97–114). Mahwah, NJ: Erlbaum.

Walzer, S. 1998. *Thinking about the Baby: Gender and Transitions into Parenthood.* Philadelphia: Temple University Press.

Washington, G. 2002. The cultural context of urban poverty, perceived life options, and the effectiveness of HIV prevention education for inner-city Black males. Doctoral dissertation, Rutgers University.

Weikart, D. P., Olmsted, P. P., and Montie, J. 2003. *A World of Preschool Experience: Observations in 15 Countries.* Ypsilanti, MI: High Scope Press.

Wells, A. 1978. *Contemporary Sociological Theories.* Santa Monica, CA: Goodyear Publishing.

White, E. 2003. School away from school. *New York Times Magazine*, December 7, 34, 41–44.

Whitebeck, L. B., Yoder, K. A. Hoyt, D. R., and Conger, R. D. 1999. Early adolescent sexual activity: A developmental study. *Journal of Marriage and the Family* 61: 934–47.

Woodhead, M., and Faulkner, D. 2000. Subjects, objects or participants? Dilemmas of psychological research with children. In P. Christensen and A. James (Eds.), *Research with Children: Perspectives and Practices* (pp. 9–35). London: Falmer Press.

Wright, E. 2004. *Generation Kill*. New York: Putnam's Sons.

Wright, L. 2004. The kingdom of silence. *New Yorker*, January 5, 48–73.

Yair, G., and Khatab, N. 1995. Changing of the guards: Teacher-student interaction in the intifada. *Sociology of Education* 68: 99–115.

Youth Development Headquarters. 1981. *International Comparison: Japanese Children and their Mothers*. Tokyo: Prime Minister's Office, Youth Development Headquarters.

Zablocki, B. 1978. Other choices: A sociologist explores alternatives to the contemporary American family. *The American Family* 3: 1–8.

Zelizer, V. A. 1985. *Pricing the Priceless Child*. New York: Basic Books.

———. 2002. Kids and commerce. *Childhood* 9: 375–96.

Zinnecker, J. 2001. Children in young and aging societies: The order of generations and models of childhood in comparative perspective. In S. L. Hofferth and T. J. Owens (Eds.), *Children at the Millennium: Where Have We Come From, Where Are We Going* (pp. 11–52). Oxford, UK: Elsevier Science.

Zweigenhaft, R. L., and Domhoff, G. W. 1991. *Blacks in the White Establishment: A Study of Race and Class in America*. New Haven, CT: Yale University Press.

INDEX